TOXIC LITERACIES

TOXIC LITERACIES

EXPOSING THE INJUSTICE
OF BUREAUCRATIC TEXTS

DENNY TAYLOR

HEINEMANN
TRADE

PORTSMOUTH, NH

Heinemann
A division of Reed Elsevier Inc.
361 Hanover Street
Portsmouth, NH 03801-3912
Offices and agents throughout the world

The author and publisher wish to thank those who generously gave permission to reprint borrowed material.

Excerpt from "Our Grandmothers" from *I Shall Not Be Moved* by Maya Angelou. Copyright © 1990 by Maya Angelou. Reprinted by permission of Random House, Inc.

The Nobel Prize Speech by Toni Morrison. Copyright © 1993 by the Nobel Foundation. Reprinted by permission of International Creative Management, Inc.

Library of Congress Cataloging-in-Publication Data

Taylor, Denny, 1947–
    Toxic literacies : controlling the minds and imagination of the American people / Denny Taylor.
        p.   cm.
    ISBN 0-435-08137-3
    1. Socially handicapped children—Education—United States.
    2. Education—Social aspects—United States.   3. Literacy—Social aspects—United States.   I. Title.
    LC4091.T395   1996
    371.9´7´0973—dc20   96-21843
                                                                     CIP

Editor: Toby Gordon
Production: Melissa L. Inglis
Cover design: Linda Knowles
Manufacturing: Louise Richardson

Printed in the United States of America on acid-free paper
99 98 97 96 EB 1 2 3 4 5 6 7 8 9

For

Cindy
Sam
Laurie, Will
and
Kathryn

with love

Might all these things have been different,
if only we had done otherwise?
James Agee

However I am perceived and deceived,
however my ignorance and conceits,
lay aside your fears that I will be undone,

for I shall not be moved.
Maya Angelou

CONTENTS

ACKNOWLEDGMENTS

I AM GRATEFUL TO THE MANY FAMILIES WHO WELCOMED ME INTO their homes. MY gratitude also goes to the members of the community who worked with me and whose anonymity I have protected. Their stories are written between the lines. Together we met with men and women whose lives are marginalized, whose existence is often denied, and whose suffering is often considered inconsequential. There were times when each of us needed a shoulder to cry on and there was always someone close by. We also laughed—at ourselves, at each other, at "the system," at the absurdity of bureaucratic regulations.

I want to thank Cindy for sharing her life with me. We are lifelong friends and I cherish our friendship. My thanks also to Sam, who has become a member of my family. I talk with him each week and look forward to the times I can visit with him. Laurie and Will also have a place in my heart. Every day Laurie struggles to live. Think good thoughts for her and for Will. I also want to thank Kathryn, whose anger often overcomes her heart. She calls herself the outlaw lady. She is feisty and her rhetoric is sharp, but friendships mean a lot to her and I am glad that we are friends.

I also want to express my gratitude to my family for their participation in the literacy project on which *Toxic Literacies* is based. In our house, literacy work is a cottage industry. My husband, David, often came with me at 2 A.M. when I got a crisis call. He cooked at barbecues for participants in the project, kept us in notebooks, and provided funds to support members of the community who were working with me. My daughter, Louise, worked with me during the first two years of the project. She visited families and accompanied members of the community to social agencies. She kept field notes and attended research meetings. Often, when there was a crisis, Louise would be there to help out, to take care of someone's children or accompany someone to the hospital. I cannot even begin to express how much I enjoyed working with her. My son, Benjamin, also worked with me, occasionally in the beginning but more so in later years. On one occasion when Sam was very sick and the local hospital refused to admit him, Benjamin and I drove Sam to a hospital seventy-five miles away. Benjamin organized the filming of conversations with project participants. He then transcribed the audio portion of the tapes. In fact, Benjamin has transcribed audiotapes for me during most of his college years. Most recently he has been taking photos of me for the cover of the book.

For the first two years of the literacy project there was very little money. I received several small grants from local charities, but every national foundation to which I submitted grant proposals denied my request. The reason? The research project seemed to be too much like social work. It is ironic that if I'd begun with the negative assumption that the people with whom I was working were illiterate, I could have received funds to teach them to read and write. But because I began with the understanding that they were literate, I was unable to obtain funding to study either their literacies or the literacies of the institutions with which they came in contact. Fortunately, in the third year of the project, I received funding from the National Council of Teachers of English. The money made a difference, but what was more important was the recognition from NCTE that the work I was doing was worth supporting. I knew it was necessary work, but for a long time no outside agency seemed to care.

Finally, I want to thank Heinemann, and especially Toby Gordon, for always expressing an interest in the work. Toby Gordon is an extraordinary editor. She has an infectious laugh but a serious agenda. She cares about the books she publishes and she is willing to work with authors who don't like signing contracts—the ultimate form of toxic literacy! My copy editor, Alan Huisman, also deserves thanks. The manuscript for *Toxic Literacies* was much too long. After I had cut as much as I thought I possibly could, Alan managed to help me cut another hundred pages. He wrote brief comments in the margins; some were on the social issues raised in the text, others were mini grammar lessons. The former made me think, the latter made me laugh. Either way, I learned a lot from Alan, and I am looking forward to working with him on my future books. There are two other members of the Heinemann team that I want to mention, Cheryl Kimball, who is the head of the trade division, Heather Smith, who is the publicist, and Melissa Inglis, who is the production editor. I thank them for their commitment to the book, and I want to say how much I am enjoying working with them.

1

WHO LIVES
AND WHO DIES

DON'T FEED THE ALLIGATORS

WASHINGTON. THE HOUSE OF REPRESENTATIVES. THE WELFARE DEBATE. THE VERY rich gentleman from Florida is speaking. "Mr. Chairman, I represent Florida, where we have many lakes and natural reserves." The very rich gentleman has a deep resonant voice. The very rich gentleman is honey smooth. I sit back in my chair. I am watching C-Span.

"If you visit these areas, you may see a sign like this"—he holds up a large sign— "that reads, Do not feed the alligators." The very rich gentleman has a reptilian fascination. "We post these signs for several reasons. First, because if left in a natural state, alligators can fend for themselves. They work, gather food, and care for their young." I'm mesmerized. "Second, we post these warnings because unnatural feeding and artificial care creates dependency. When dependency sets in, these otherwise able-bodied alligators can no longer survive on their own."

The men and women who live in the margins of American society are the able-bodied alligators of which the very rich snake charmer speaks. I wonder how far he will go in making the connection.

"Now, I know people are not alligators"—how clever, the very rich gentleman does not take responsibility; his virtue is venomous— "but I submit to you that with our current handout, nonwork welfare system, we have upset the natural order. We have failed to understand the simple warning signs. We have created a system of dependency."

Wait. There has to be more, a historical reference. Something to legitimize the very rich gentleman's assertion that we have upset the natural order. *Of course.*

"The author of our Declaration of Independence, Thomas Jefferson, said it best in three words. 'Dependence begets servitude.' "

What next? The moral breakdown of society? The very rich gentleman speaks with pulpit authority.

"Let us heed these warnings!" His voice rises as he preaches. "Today we have a chance to restore that natural order! To break the cycle of dependency and stop the enslavement of another generation of Americans!"

A few members of the House respond. *"Shame! Shame! Shame!"* *"Hisss, hisssss, hisssss."*

A gentlewoman speaks. "I want to say, do not feed the alligators but please feed the children!"

A gentleman. "Mr. Chairman, I rise in support of the only welfare bill that feeds children, not alligators."

But many members of the House of Representatives appear to support the gentleman from Florida. "Mr. Chairman, the current welfare system is a national embarrassment and outrage. As a nation, we cannot afford to support a program that encourages able-bodied adults to stay at home rather than look for a job!"

Since the beginning of the eighties I have been working with men and women living in poverty. Few of them are able bodied. They suffer from poor nutrition. They live without medical assistance, without dental care, in substandard housing, in abandoned buildings, on the streets, without work, *without work.*

I think about one of the men with whom I worked who died when he was forty-two. The official documentation stated that he died of pneumonia. Unofficially? He died of poverty. From breathing toxic fumes in a silk screen factory. From exhaustion. From neglect.

Listen to what he said just before he died. "I want my kids in a good school. But at the same time the jobs that I get and everything I do"—he gets his breath—"I'm bein' exploited. I am really bein' exploited. Anytime I gotta get up at five o'clock in the morning, catch two buses to get to work by seven-thirty."

He talks of the silk screen factory, of the junkie who owns it. Of getting fired. Of collecting $140 a week unemployment to take care of his family. "I got lost somewhere along the way and I don't have it."

He designs silk-screened T-shirts, does body work on cars, odd jobs, *any job.* He paints portraits, cuts hair, mends shoes. But there are no jobs.

His voice is hoarse. He speaks in a whisper. "I keep us eatin' and a roof over our head. You know, I maintain that, you know. But I don't have what I should have, you know. And sometimes I question whether I should stay here. I do. You are askin' me how I feel. You want to know how I really feel? I am a bona fide artist." His voice is tight. He is crying. "I'm a money maker. Or I'm a producer. *I can produce!*"

There are tears running down his cheeks. "Ain't nobody helpin' me, and I'm losin'. Ain't nobody helpin' me make no money." He wipes the tears off his face with the back of his hand. "You all gotta excuse me, man, because this shit is serious out here." He is quiet. Calm. "I can't keep doin' this. I'm gettin' tired. I'm gettin' old. *This* is makin' me old. Because I don't have the help that I need, and I've been needin' the help sometime. Because I can *do*. But I don't have it, and it's hard findin' people who will really help you without exploitin' you. Without exploitin' you and usin' you. And I am tired of bein' used. I am tired of it." He gets up. It's time to go. "I'm sorry. Book is closed. I'm sorry. *The* book is closed."

It was the last time we spoke. He had no insurance. No Medicaid. For months he coughed up blood. He was unable to sleep and in constant pain. He joked that he was waiting until he was really sick so that he could go to the emergency room, but by the time he got to the hospital it was too late. He died shortly afterward leaving a wife and two young children.

But the book is not closed. In the House another gentleman is speaking. "Mr. Chairman, perhaps not by design, but certainly by experience, the welfare system has become corrupt and immoral. Why would anyone want to spend more on a system that has not only failed but has become corrupt and immoral? It is immoral to take money away from hardworking middle-class Americans and give it to people who refuse to work."

I think of the woman with whom I worked who went to college and obtained an associate degree in computer programming and then could not find a company that would employ her. There were no jobs in the inner city where she lived. She applied for positions an hour away from her home, an hour and a half, almost two hours, on two buses, sometimes three. No jobs.

She used up her money on bus fares. She couldn't afford to look for employment. She stayed home. On the couch. For almost a year. What was the point? We set her up. Get an education and you'll get a job. That's the rhetoric but not the reality.

The gentlewoman in red from Wyoming speaks. "Mr. Chairman, in view of the fact that the alligator analogy was hissed and booed, I thought I should bring up another story that is near and dear to my state. My home state is Wyoming, and recently the federal government introduced wolves into the State of Wyoming, and they put them in pens and they brought elk and venison to them every day." The gentlewoman in red is crisp, matter-of-fact, devoid of emotion. I hold my breath. "This is what I call the wolf welfare program. The federal government introduced them and they have since then provided shelter and they have provided food, they have provided everything that the wolves need for their existence."

The gentlewoman in red trivializes *human* existence. "Guess what?" she says. "They opened the gate to let the wolves out and now the wolves won't go! They are cutting the fence down to make the wolves go out and the wolves will not go!" She continues oblivious of her own depravity. "What happened with the wolves? Just like what happens with human beings— when you take away their incentives, when you take away their freedom, when you take away their dignity, they have to be provided for. The biologists are now giving incentives outside of the gates, trying to get them out! What a great idea!"

Let me introduce you to a real mother behind the gentlewoman from Wyoming's wolf analogy. She is sitting at a kitchen table and she smiles when we arrive. Her hair is not combed and her skin is ashen. She is sitting so at first we do not realize that she is sick from lack of food.

We sit with her and she talks about her children. She tells us that she sits with her little girls on her lap each morning and sings to them so they will enjoy the beginning of each new day.

Her eyes are sunk in her cheeks and there are dark shadows beneath them.

"Are you okay?"

"I'm fine," she says. Again she smiles. She talks of her young son in first grade who is learning to read without difficulty. "He's smart like his father." She talks about her middle son, who does not like school. "They say he is reading on a fifth-grade level. He's in sixth grade, but when he tested, he tested on a ninth-grade level. He should be in the eighth grade getting ready to graduate, but he's in sixth grade." She talks about her eldest son, who used to be an A student, who dropped out of school when he was sixteen. She worries about him.

She is right to worry. He will be incarcerated by the time he is twenty. Most of his adult life will be spent in prison. And his younger brother who is "failing" in school? He will also be jailed.

She speaks with fierce determination. "If it takes all I have, I'm going to help them get out of this situation." When she talks of her children she seems invincible. Her eyes fill with tears but she does not cry. She is strong. Capable.

She says her middle son was beaten by his teacher with the pointer from the chalkboard so she took him to a doctor but the doctor refused to treat him. She took him to a hospital. "They said he had contusions on his right arm and right leg. They told me to put ice packs on the bruises."

She gets up. She holds on to the table. She can't stand. For the first time we see that she is painfully thin. She is malnourished. She shakes with the effort it takes her to stand up.

Holding on to the table, she moves along to the wall, leans back, and closes her eyes.

"What's happened to you? Why have you lost so much weight? What have you been doing?"

She hasn't eaten for two weeks. "What food I got I've given to the kids." She says that there is nothing left in the refrigerator for the children to eat so it looks as if they too will go without food. "It's only three days until the end of the month. But I hate for my kids to go hungry."

We ask her to come to a fast-food place that is down the street. She says that she can no longer eat and that even the thought of food makes her feel sick.

We try to give her money so she can feed her children. She does not want handouts. "We'll make it," she says.

We ask her if she will help us with our research and explain that the money we will give her comes from a small literacy grant. "It's not a handout. You can work for the money." She smiles and agrees.

So, the gentlewoman in red can stick her analogies—unless she is willing to consider the possibility that the wolf is really *she*.

AND STILL MY CONDITION DID NOT IMPROVE

Who's the predator and who's the prey?

I want to reverse the possibilities. To consider other analogies. To introduce you to the men and women with whom I work. To suggest alternate explanations of the political relationships between wealth and poverty. To hold myself accountable. To hold you accountable. And the very rich gentleman. And the gentlewoman in red.

In Tom Stoppard's *Every Good Boy Deserves Favour*, Alexander is a political prisoner in Russia whose "opinions" are considered a sign of insanity. So he is locked up in a mental hospital. In a conversation with Doctor Rozinski—or as Stoppard makes us ask, is it Colonel Rozinski?—Alexander explains the situation, as he sees it:

For the politicals, punishment and medical treatment are intimately related. I was given injections of aminazin, sulfazin, triftazin, haloperidol, and insulin, which caused swellings, cramps, headaches, trembling, fever, and the loss of various abilities including the ability to read, write, sleep, sit, stand, and button my trousers. When all this failed to improve my condition, I was stripped and bound head to foot with lengths of wet canvas. As the canvas dried it became tighter and tighter until I lost consciousness. They did this to me for ten days in a row, and still my condition did not improve.

As I see it, there are many men, women, *and children* living in the margins of American society who are also "politicals." For them punishment and medical treatment are also intimately related. They are imprisoned when they are sick, they are treated with zero tolerance, and sometimes when they are locked up, they are told that it is "for their own good." Even when their condition deteriorates they don't have the liberty to disagree. "They are punishing me because I hurt," one woman said. "Are they going to lock me up indefinitely?"

Some are sent into internal exile by the state. They try to live in anonymity, so they will not be persecuted by those in authority. Even so it is inevitable that sometimes they come into contact with the state, and when this happens there are times when their lives are placed in jeopardy. One man, who was drinking away his misery, went to the hospital because his lungs were congested and he couldn't breathe. The emergency room physician examined him and wrote that there was a possibility he had pleurisy. He was suffering from malnutrition and he was chronically dehydrated, but his blood alcohol was a deadly 510 MG/DL so one of the hospital personnel called the police, and he was taken to jail and placed in "protective custody."

Others who cannot cope with their exiled state are controlled by drugs. One woman, who had spent most of her pregnancy living on the streets, was depressed after the birth of her son, and although she had found a place to live, she could not overcome the sadness of her life. As she tried to take care of her baby, her own childhood kept coming back to her. She imagined herself as a little girl, and for a while she became the memory of herself when she was a child. The authorities said that this was abnormal, that she was manic depressive and a threat to her baby, and so they took her baby away. They gave her drugs that masked her face with a vacant smile. The drugs stopped her talking. They made it difficult for her to speak. They stopped her walking unless she stretched out her arms so she could hold on to objects and guide her feet.

When these men and women get sick they try to take care of themselves. Many doctors turn them away. But when the pain is acute and does not go away, they are forced to accept whatever medical treatment is available to them. Sometimes the treatments that are offered mutilate their bodies even if they cure the disease. One young woman with malignant "cauliflower-like lesions" in her uterus was not given a hysterectomy. Surgery is expensive. Excuses were made and she received a cheaper procedure instead, "external beam irradiation" and "intracavity cesium insertion." She was irradiated for a month with an external beam. Then an implant was inserted into her uterus and she was irradiated internally. Zapped. For three days the radiation implant remained inside her. "The thing that got me," she said, "was they kept telling me that, you know, it wasn't really going to hurt me that badly. The nurses had to stand behind this shield and so what was it doing to the rest of my body?" Now she is crippled. She suffers from "ulcerative and hemorrhagic cystitis" due to the irradiation. When her condition is acute, each time she urinates she bleeds. Her bowels are damaged and her ovaries no longer function. She does not menstruate. Her biological clock stopped when she was twenty-five.

In America these "politicals" are anonymous. Out of work because they are "lazy," unable to get jobs because they are "illiterate," living on welfare because their families are "dysfunctional," they are an irritant to our lives.

We don't want to know that it was Jerry who died. We don't want to know that it was Pauline who got a degree but still lives in poverty. We don't want to know that it was Iesha who went without food so that her children would not go hungry. We don't want to know that it was Laurie whose ovaries were fried.

She is not our responsibility. We pay our taxes for the welfare state. Don't tell us that her biological clock was stopped when she was only twenty-five. It is beyond our imagination that we would damage her insides, especially when we or female members of our families have had hysterectomies for the smallest of cellular abnormalities. Don't suggest that we would leave Kathryn on the streets when she was pregnant, then punish her when the birth of her baby reminded her of her own childhood and the abuse that she suffered when she was a very young child. We know about postpartum depression. It has affected our lives. Our mothers and our sisters have suffered from it. We have suffered from it ourselves. We know how difficult it can be for a mother as she learns to love her new baby.

Don't tell us that we don't understand. We watch news reports on TV. We know what happens to mothers and their children in other countries. We send troops with humanitarian aid. Our husbands and our sons and our fathers and our sisters and our daughters have fought against repressive regimes.

It is inconceivable to us that Sam, who suffers from grand mal epileptic seizures, was sent to jail when his body was totally dehydrated and he was unable to eat. He couldn't have weighed more than a hundred pounds. We would never have sent him to jail.

Don't tell us about the woman who was imprisoned unless you can tell us that she committed a crime. Murdered someone. Committed armed robbery. Don't tell us her name.

Cynthia. Her name is Cynthia, but her friends call her Cindy.

She did not murder anyone, nor did she commit armed robbery. As she will tell you, her only crime was using drugs to help her to forget the abuse she has suffered and the pain she suffers from having been beaten about the head. The bones in her face have been fractured, her jaw is damaged, she experiences constant muscle spasms in her neck, and her head aches each time she wakes. "The drugs helped," Cindy says, "that was my little getaway, like in my own little world. I wouldn't have to tolerate all the bullshit. It made me feel good. It would kind of help me go through all the pain."

The doctor who supplied Cindy with massive doses of prescription drugs is known to the authorities but continues to practice medicine with impunity. Similarly, Cindy's heroin supplier goes free. But not Cindy.

A presentence report written about her by a probation officer after she was arrested for possession of heroin makes it clear that she was incarcerated because her behavior was a shock to the local community:

> In addressing the disposition, one begins first with the seriousness of the offense. Not unlike finding toxic waste in one's community, there is a sense of shock to the local community when there is an arrest for possession of heroin. With the sense of shock, there comes a strong community expectation that there should be zero tolerance for such a hard-core drug surfacing in the local area.

Cindy was sentenced to three and a half to seven years for the possession of one gram of heroin. The *same judge* gave a one-year suspended sentence to a man who beat his wife so badly that she needed seventeen stitches to close the gashes on her face. The man's "punishment" was seven weekends in jail—which the judge deferred until September because he had a summer job in Alaska. For seven weeks on Friday nights at ten o'clock, he reported to the jail to serve the last two hours of the day, then Saturday and Sunday, and at five on Monday morning he left the jail, logging four days for his two-day-and-three-night stay. Fourteen days and twenty-one nights the man received for his act of brutality, but Cindy, who had been similarly battered in the past, remains in jail because she has trouble controlling the prescription medications and other drugs that she takes to ease the pain.

Why is it that the man who obliterated his wife's face only served fourteen days and twenty-one nights, while Cindy has already spent over one thousand days and nights in prison and as I write she is still incarcerated for self-medicating to obliterate the trauma of abuse that she has suffered?

Easy. The man had a job. A felony conviction would interfere with his career. He paid a lawyer to respond to the indictment, and when it appeared that the lawyer would not be able to get the charges lessened, the man paid another lawyer to get the felony reduced to a common misdemeanor. Cindy had no job. She spent just a couple of hours with a public defender who had a work load of about one hundred cases. Rushed, the public defender read some of the documents pertaining to Cindy's case only as she made her way into court.

Too bad that the wife-beating man went free, but Cindy is a junkie. If she is imprisoned, it is because she brought toxic waste into our community.

We have to deal with *our own* toxicity.

Through documented legal procedures Cindy has been discarded by society. Hospital rules and regulations have been used to hide the fact that Sam's life is considered expendable. Medical reports have been used to provide a rationale for the mutilation of Laurie's body and the dismemberment of Kathryn's mind.

Toxic forms of literacy control their lives.

We are not responsible when official documents destroy their lives. It's in the regulations. A rationale for a particular procedure is presented in the doctor's report. The explanation for the prison sentence is in the judge's written ruling. Backing each decision are files filled with paper that contain the facts that support the decision-making process.

Officially maybe, but not in reality. "Facts" are *never* value free. What is written and not written recasts people's lives. Print is used quite literally to decide who lives and who dies. Very often, violent acts are legally sanctioned through paperwork that is required by federal law. None of this is true, of course, if you are privileged by society. If you have status—money to pay for a lawyer, like the man who beat his wife—then the "rules" do not automatically apply. What is written becomes open to interpretation and professional manipulation.

If you have power and privilege in society, literacy can be used to maintain your social status. You can use print to your advantage and to the *dis*advantage of others. Laws, regulations, administrative procedures, affidavits, insurance policies, trusts, reports, memorandums, forms, questionnaires, licenses, credit cards, identification badges, personal codes, and work orders are all forms of literacy used by those in authority to exercise power over those who are denied such liberty.

The most powerful write the laws, institute the regulations, and decide what is written in the reports and memorandums, which are then used by bureaucrats to construct the forms and questionnaires to determine who gets licensed to produce a product that requires an identity code and, ultimately, who gets the order to do the work at $4.25 an hour.

Through official documentation, federal, state, and local agencies have turned poverty into a bureaucratic industry. Mountainous paperwork, multiple cognizance arrangements, labyrinthine accounting procedures, and detailed auditing and negotiation processes provide jobs for bureaucrats and feed the bureaucratic machine. Under contractual agreements with States, consultants use proprietary computer software packages, which do not have any built-in edit checks for compliance with federal regulations and cost principles, to revise allocation systems and to maximize federal administrative and indirect cost reimbursements for public assistance programs such as AFDC, Medicaid, food stamps, and welfare.

In this way, consultants and bureaucrats work together through print, and the public and private sectors are intricately connected. There are an infinite number of hierarchial literacy configurations—patterns of literacy use—that privilege the powerful who control what happens in society through the manipulation of the text.

Professional and personal privilege are similarly connected. Control of print in the one sector privileges the use of print in the other. Money can be protected, investments made, taxes saved, and cash made available twenty-four hours a day to those who have sufficient credit to be given personal access codes.

For "politicals" there is no such opportunity.

Personal access codes are replaced by identification numbers that are called out by case workers who carry files filled with paper that their clients rarely see. Bureaucratic texts are used to control the circumstances in which politicals live their everyday lives. They are forced into literacy configurations of dependency that adversely affect their identity, erode away their personhood, and cripple their ability to survive. They suffer public humiliations and personal violations as official documentation takes away their rights and privileges and leaves them powerless to protest because they have no access to the text.

Cindy has not been allowed to have a copy of the presentence report in which the probation officer stated that she was bringing toxic waste into the community. Other reports have been written about her that she has never seen—including the judge's ruling from her last court hearing, which she has repeatedly requested but never received. She has written to her court-appointed lawyer asking for copies of her files, but her requests have been denied. Cindy has also written asking for her personal journals to be returned after they were read in court, but she has been told that she cannot have them. At the time that the entire United States Senate was pontificating over the propriety of making public the private diaries of a Senator who was under investigation by the Senate Ethics Committee for sexual misconduct and possible criminal violations, Cindy's journals were taken and selectively used against her, and her request for their return was formally refused.

"Those were my private thoughts," she says. "They had no right to read my journals. I didn't know they had them. The first I knew of it was when they read the poem I copied in the rehab that I went to after I was arrested. How could they use that against me? I want them back. Why are they keeping them? Why won't they give them to me?"

While Cindy's files were compiled to support a felony conviction for her drug addiction, Sam's files were constructed to deny him the services for which he would be eligible—if he could comply with the written procedures outlined in the rules and regulations that govern the distribution of welfare and disability funds. For six years he lived on the streets without the benefits for which he was eligible because of the injuries that he had sustained while working that made it difficult for him to get a job. He was exiled on the streets because he did not have the information the welfare agency required in order to process his application for assistance.

Eventually, when Sam was accompanied to the Health and Human Services Office by literacy workers who wanted to assist him with the process, a caseworker for the social agency helped him with the forms. She asked Sam where he had been living, but when he said he had been sleeping in a cupboard, in a hallway, in an abandoned factory, the caseworker told him that the forms would be discarded unless he could give her a street address. Sam looked perplexed. The caseworker persisted. She asked Sam where he had been sleeping before he moved into the abandoned building. Sam told her that earlier in the winter he had been sleeping under the porch of a friend's house, "but if his mother had found me she would have kicked me out for sure."

"What about before that?" the caseworker asked as she wrote down the street address of the house with the porch.

Sam thought for a while, and then he gave her the street address of a house attached to a garage where, at the end of the previous summer, he had hid late at night and slept for a while before leaving early in the morning. Without commenting, the caseworker wrote down the address.

When all of the forms had been filled out, the caseworker gave Sam another form that she told him to take with him and have his doctor fill out. Part of the form had to be filled in by Sam. The caseworker instructed Sam to "answer in ways that are going to help." Then she said, "Every question has to be answered," and she cautioned him, "If you don't know, guess, and put a little question mark beside your answer. If you leave a question blank, your application will be automatically rejected."

Answer every question or face rejection. On a daily basis, men, women, and children are denied the services that they need because of the destructive public policies that are carried out by bureaucratic agencies whose interrogative practices are reminiscent of McCarthy.

You overstate your case. Don't exaggerate.

At the time that Laurie—who has three children—was coping with ulcerative and hemorrhagic cystitis, she was told that in order to receive financial assistance from welfare to support her family, she would have to study for a GED. Laurie tried to attend the mandated GED classes at the local high school, but she had difficulty sitting on a hard wooden chair for the three-hour lesson. "It's embarrassing," she said. "I have to keep getting up to go to the bathroom so I've stopped going."

Laurie was experiencing severe pain in her lower abdomen and was bleeding from her rectum. Lying back in a dilapidated armchair with her knees up close to her chest, she said that she had received a letter and a memo from welfare warning her that her benefits would be cut unless she attended GED classes on a regular basis. In the memo a welfare official wrote, "As you know, you are mandatory [sic] to attend these classes. I am notifying your case technician and this could affect your benefits."

Laurie said that she took the medical records she had managed to collect to the welfare office but her caseworker told her she could be lying because there was nothing in the records to indicate that she was still sick. Laurie had also managed to get a letter from her doctor. The caseworker looked at the date on the letter and again she told Laurie that the doctor had not stated that she was too sick to go the classes. Laurie was concerned that she would lose her benefits, so she went back to the hospital to ask the doctor for a letter stating that she was still sick and that she was unable to sit for long periods of time. She took this second letter to the welfare office, and only then was she temporarily released from her "obligation" to attend GED classes.

After her visits to the welfare office, Laurie's condition deteriorated. The personal indignity she had suffered and the pain she was experiencing overwhelmed her. It was several weeks before she was able to leave her house. "I feel so low," she said.

I cannot overstate Laurie's case. There is no need for me to exaggerate.

Politicals are the nonpeople of society, separated from those in power by the politics of literacy. For them there is no democracy. We can't deny our own pathology. The conditions in which politicals are forced to exist are determined by the circumstances in which those of power and privilege choose to live. In spite of their separateness, their lives are intricately connected in literacy configurations of inequality—complex patterns of abuse that take place through printed procedures—to which no one other than those in authority has access.

Injustice and prejudice are maintained through print and are a permanent part of our national psyche. We enculturate people into poverty. We control their lives through bureaucratic texts, which we then use to deny any responsibility for the conditions in which politicals are forced to live.

We look straight ahead as we pass the woman with three small children who is begging outside the Ritz Carlton in Atlanta, we worry about the cat curled up on the lap of an emaciated man holding up a paper cup on Mason Street in San Francisco, and we move to the edge of the pavement on Fifty-Seventh Street in New York City to avoid getting too close to the unidentifiable pile of old coats and blankets under which we presume someone is sleeping.

Maybe the person under the blankets is sick or even dying. Have you considered that possibility?

What do you expect of us? We give money to local charities that provide hot meals for people living on the street.

And we take a tax break for our charitable donation.

We give our old clothes to the Salvation Army.

Then list the clothes for our accountants, who make sure that we get another tax deduction for our benevolent behavior.

You're too cynical!

It could have been Cindy or Sam underneath the blankets lying in the street. Our lives are no longer separate. We know what happened to Laurie and Kathryn. We know their names. They are more than an identification number allocated by some social agency. Each time a human rights violation is committed against them, we lose something of our own humanity. We have to give them back their dignity. Document their lives, protest their political status, expose the toxicity of bureaucratic literacy. We have to uncover how bureaucratic texts control the lives of men and women living in the margins of American society.

Toxic Literacies is about us. It is about those of us who have the power and privilege to control the text and about those of us who live in poverty and are controlled by it. I began with the underlying assumption that in the reflection of one life are the lives of many. I was convinced that by studying the official texts that control the life of one destitute young woman, I would come to understand something of the ways in which the subtexts of society are embedded in the life situations we all experience. But this was only the beginning. To broaden my understanding of the subtexts of society, I juxtaposed the life of this woman with the lives of other men and women who live in the margins.

Eventually, by examining the written details of these lives, I was able to develop some insights into the functions and uses of official texts. I learned which texts count in the decision-making process, which texts are ignored or discarded, how pathologies are created in bureaucratic records, and how what is written critically affects the minds and imagination of the American people.

In America, who lives and who dies is controlled by the subtexts of society. Official documentation hides the human rights violations that take place in this country. We enculturate members of our communities into poverty. Men, women, and children are incapacitated by legally sanctioned discriminatory practices that occur through the use of bureaucratic texts. There is an official form to deal with every situation. On paper, whatever action is taken can be justified. It's all in the record. Through toxic forms of print we abdicate responsibility—even though we are not always aware of our duplicity.

In *Toxic Literacies* you will meet Cindy and learn how she became a junkie. In writing about Cindy I will take an unpopular position and argue that she is a victim of societal pathologies that have created the conditions of her "deviant" state. Cindy was reinvented so that her "story" fits with the dominant political ideologies of our time. Uncovering the mythology of the official interpretations of her life makes it possible for us to question the veracity of bureaucratic texts. My own take on this is that such official documentation is nothing more than a complex construction, an official invention based on political conventions that impound our thinking and shape our lives.

What happened to Cindy, to Sam, to Kathryn, and to Laurie and her partner Will, supports this proposition, as does what happened to the city manager of the city in which Cindy lived, whose life became a part of the public record when the city council tried to take away his job. Their stories provide us with the opportunity to consider how those with power and privilege in American society take control of official texts and use them to their personal advantage.

On the few occasions that I have talked at conferences about toxic literacies, I've stayed afterward to talk with people. Sometimes I am criticized. A woman is angry. "You have taken away our foundation, made us face harsh realities, but you have offered nothing in return." At times I have had nothing to offer, but I hold on to the possibility that if we can make visible the human rights violations that take place through the use of official documentation, we can interrupt the texts and hold bureaucratic institutions accountable. If we change the way official texts are used, we change the system.

2

Death by Paper

Wednesday, March 14, 1990; the superior court judge is sentencing Cindy, who has pleaded guilty to receiving one gram of heroin through the mail.

"For years we have been talking about rehabilitation as a prime factor in sentencing a defendant." His voice rises. "I have never taken that position. I do not intend to start now."

The silence is audible. The school children who are there to witness the sentencing are on the edges of their seats.

The judge continues. "If a child acts up, you whack the child on the rear," adding almost as an aside, "without hurting them much." Then his voice grows stronger as he qualifies his last statement. "But you let the child know who is boss." The judge looks at the school children. "It isn't any different if you are dealing with a three-year-old child or a thirty-three-year-old woman." Then his eyes fix on Cindy. He tells her to stand.

Cindy is crying.

"You are sentenced to the state prison for not less than three and a half and not more than seven years. Stand committed. Do you understand the sentence?"

"Yes I do, sir," Cindy responds, her voice racked by tears.

As if in response to her grief, the judge looks out across the courtroom, and appearing to speak to nobody in particular, he says, "I don't enjoy doing these things." He turns his head toward the windows. "I have to consider others. Others who are out there." For a moment he seems preoccupied. Abruptly he turns back and looks at Cindy. "I am not trying to push you down. I am trying to help you up." He wishes Cindy good luck.

"Thank you, Your Honor," the public defender says as if speaking for Cindy.

Everyone stands as the judge leaves.

The school children are subdued but they still push each other as they begin to file out of the courtroom.

Cindy is being handcuffed. She turns and looks over her shoulder at her mother. They are both crying. As Cindy is led away her mother says, "I'd like to tell that man that when Cindy was three years old her stepfather would beat her and beat her until she let go of her bladder and then he would beat her some more for peeing on the floor."

WHACKING CINDY

In his summation the superior court judge connected the whacking of Cindy when she was a child of three and her punishment when she was thirty-three—even though he had some knowledge of her life history.

When she was a child she was locked in closets. "In real small closets," Cindy says.

When she was thirty-three, the judge locked her up, and she spent her first night of incarceration in a cold prison cell, on a plastic mattress with no sheets. Her shoes and panty hose were removed, so to keep warm she wound toilet paper around her legs and she tore up her slip and wrapped it around her feet.

When Cindy was a child, alcohol and drugs were used to control her behavior. She says her stepfather gave her alcohol and her mother encouraged her to take pills. "When I was ten my mother handed me a bottle of Darvon and she said, 'Well you're miserable why don't you take all these.' "

In prison the drug she took for manic depression was taken away. Her drug use was manipulated. Painkillers were provided and then the prescriptions were changed. Drugs were used to control her behavior, to reward and punish her. They were given to make her compliant and taken away when she complained.

In sentencing Cindy to three and a half to seven years in prison, the superior court judge recreated and perpetuated the abusive circumstances of her early family life, and he fostered her addiction to prescription medications and illegal drugs. He locked Cindy into a configuration of institutional abuse that was publicly sanctioned through the use of official texts.

Legal rhetoric, official propaganda, and files closed to the public were used to make the case that Cindy was a junkie who brought toxic waste into the community. Through the manipulation of paper, her life was skewed, officially reinvented, bureaucratically reconstructed. Any documentation that did not fit the image of Cindy as a felon was judiciously ignored, prudently set aside, discreetly kept out of the record, so there were no alternative interpretations, no possible explanations to interrupt the text and challenge the "official" version of Cindy's life in which she was portrayed to the public as a menace to society.

The superior court judge—and by extension the legal system—participated in the social construction of Cindy's pathology by condoning her family's brutality and then punishing her for *her* deviant behavior. The judge turned Cindy's drug addiction into something that belonged solely to her and he made it clear that irrespective of what happened around her or to her or however much pain she was in, it was *her* responsibility to stop being an addict.

"I am not trying to push you down. I am trying to help you up," the judge said, denying any connection between the social conditions in which Cindy became a junkie and her own responsibility. From the perspective of the legal system, Cindy owns her addiction. It is her liability and she must be punished for her unlawful activity.

In prison Cindy asks, "What is the sense of living if you are sick and depressed? Why go around being sick and miserable when you can take a pill for the pain? It is abnormal for me not to take anything. I hate it because I feel so shitty. All I do is lie in bed, what kind of life is that? I lie in bed all day. Everybody is telling me how to live. It's the only way I know how to function because without it I don't function. I am not a normal human being."

Cindy teaches us that her drug addiction was—and continues to be—socially constructed. She learned to be a junkie while other children were learning to read. Normality for her is using dope. She has never lived without it. She was enculturated into popping pills.

I am not arguing that Cindy is not accountable for her drug-related activities, but I am arguing that she is not the only one who must take responsibility. We cannot blame Cindy for the role we—and those who supposedly represent us—played in creating the conditions of her drug addiction. We have to acknowledge our own toxicity—for if we continue to deny our responsibility for enculturating Cindy into using drugs, she will remain an addict, a victim of societal pathologies that have created the conditions of her "deviant" state.

HOW CINDY LEARNED TO BE A DRUG ADDICT

For years Cindy has kept journals in which she reflects on her life. She wrote when she was alone—locked in her room in a condo, living on her own in a trailer, listening to music, often high, frequently withdrawing from heroin or cocaine, always lonely, depressed, sometimes suicidal—struggling to understand her life and what she could do to change it, angry with herself, with the men in her life, with her family, and with the agony of living.

Cindy wrote about her childhood, "I was really alone. I felt that the only time I didn't hurt was when I was on drugs. It covered up my hurt and anger. Growing up I had no one. I was trouble. I had hate and anger, no love, comfort, and no mother or father to talk to. I was beaten, yelled at, told to go play, go to your room, just get away."

She describes having a glass milk bottle smashed on her head, being threatened with a knife, and being told that she should have "liar" carved on her back. She writes of being stripped naked, then whipped with a rubber hose. "I just hid away on my drugs," Cindy writes. "They made my problems go away." Talking about school she writes, "I was going to school high. Stoned. Tripping drugs made me feel better. My problems went away for a while when I was high."

In some entries she describes her ambivalence about using drugs. Drugs give her a rush. Sweet dreams. She loves them, they relax her, make her mellow, allow her to hide, and ease the pain as she fades into blackouts from which she emerges disorientated, aching, with migraine headaches, unable to stand up, her muscles in violent spasms, hating the drugs she craves, needing a fix, willing to do anything to feel the rush, relax, mellow out, and once again ease the pain.

When Cindy was in her early twenties, she met a doctor who was willing to supply her with prescription medications. She was given drugs by him for more than ten years. "Doc gave me fifty demerol and I shot and ate them in five days. I have been so sick so I have been doing heroin. I'm still on my tranzilizers, withdrawal pills, painkillers, and my knockout pills. I have just come back—four days ago—I had to see Doc for more pills. I stayed three days. He—the Doc—gave me pills in the hundreds. I also got percodian, fifty of them. I think I'm going to sign off now my mind isn't working today and I'm upset. I want to get straight but it seems impossible."

"Well I don't feel good today. I have such a migraine. I'm going through withdrawal again. I tried to get some heroin but got ripped off. AGAIN. I've been taking pills all day. I'm surprised I am not passed out. I've been up since 5:30 this morning. Oh my God I'm so sick. If I go for more than two days I get sick. What a vicious world we live in. I wish I could stop and don't say you could if you wanted to. No, I'm convinced there is no way out but death. It's too strong—the drugs—I feel every time I've tried suicide I'm a different person. Nothing hurts and I have no cares."

Cindy makes it clear in her writing that she was addicted to both street drugs and prescription medications. She writes of visits to buy heroin and visits to her doctor to get her prescriptions filled. "I am going for more pills. Drown my sorrows more or dig my grave some more I should say. Pills are doing me in but I live for the day. I don't look for the future. I don't have one."

She is overwhelmed by depression. "Drugs overpower you. I've grown up using drugs to survive. I don't know how it is to live without them. I was so depressed last night I wanted to die. If I had a gun I would have blown my head off just to be at peace. Or, if I had enough pills to die I would have. No one can imagine what I've been going through. No one. It's so much pain."

Cindy has tried to commit suicide on thirteen separate occasions. "I went into the bathroom, took the gun out and held it right at me and pulled the trigger. The gun kicked back. It went over my shoulder into the bathroom door. I pulled the trigger again. It hit my chest, missed my lung by a quarter of an inch. I fell to the floor and didn't feel anything more."

"Why does anyone try to commit suicide?" she asks in her journal. "Well I can answer that. Why should anyone live through a life of hell and torment? They say change, well if you are right-handed for twenty years try to write with your left hand. You always go back. I really have tried. I just go back. I'm set in my ways. I go through hell every day wondering am I going to make it through another day."

When Cindy was twenty-one, she gave birth to a daughter of whom she eventually lost custody. Her daughter was made a ward of the state. It was then that Cindy shot herself. Cindy agonizes over the events that took place in her life that so adversely affected the life of her little girl, and there are many references to her child in her journal.

"It's two days since I've written. I'm burnt out on drugs. I did two and a half bags of heroine two days ago. It's hitting me bad now. I'm very sick. I'm stoned now. I never finished writing the other day. I'm hurting so bad all I think of is my daughter. I have eighteen of her pictures on the wall. I'm losing it slowly. I'm back on drugs. This week seven and a half bags of heroine, one and a half of coke, fifteen percodian, seven or nine Fiormial, forty-five tranzilizers, thirty Cloindie, fifteen Elivil, two six-packs, half a fifth of vodka, seven joints and it's Friday the heavy night!"

Cindy told me that she was writing her journal for her daughter. "I want her to know that I love her," she said. "I don't want her to use drugs like me."

Cindy knew that she had to gain control, to try to stop using, to get help. "I need the hospital so much, but I can't bring myself to go. The last three days I can't do anything. I can't get off the couch. All I do is sit down or lie down. I have no strength. I pop pills like crazy to knock me out or dull the pain." Desperately she writes, "I guess I have to get the ultimate high. There is never enough drugs. They are the only way I know to feel good."

She could not stop. She visited her doctor every week and he gave her multiple prescriptions with multiple refills, and her boyfriend sent her bags of heroin through the mail. But there was never enough. The highs got shorter. It took more heroin to feel mellow and more prescription drugs to ease the pain.

CINDY IS BUSTED FOR RECEIVING HEROIN THROUGH THE MAIL

"Well today I got busted for twenty bags of heroin. It was sent through the mail so it's federal. I'm fucked. I don't know what to do. I can't be locked up. It will kill me. I won't be able to handle it. I've thought of killing myself again. That's the only way out. I'm a junkie who for the last five months has been heavily into heroin. The last two months I've been shooting three bags a day maybe more. I'm sick as a mother. I'm going through withdrawal."

Out on bail, facing felony charges and a prison sentence, Cindy returned to the trailer in which she was living. In her journal she wrote, "Heroine is so easy and cheap and a long high. Plus if you use speed balls, coke and heroine together, you get two highs in one, one in a rush on the coke and a down on the dope. I love my drugs. Go morphine, heroine, demerol, coke, xanax, valium. Thanks to my good doctor who gave me everything I wanted. He was a pervert but I got percodian, valiums, diet pills, sleeping pills, shots of morphine anytime. I was on seven different pills—sixty demerol, one hundred valiums, fifty xanax, fifty percodian. I couldn't name all of them. I don't remember too well anymore. I'm fried. My brain doesn't work as well as before just from all the drugs I've done and I wish I never did and I can't stop after doing drugs for eighteen years."

CINDY TRIES TO OVERCOME HER DRUG ADDICTION

Terrified by the thought of being locked up, Cindy tried to find a hospital that would accept her as a detox patient. Fourteen hospitals refused to admit her. The heroin was not the problem. It was the prescription medications. She was taking such large quantities of so many different drugs, no one was sure she would make it through. Besides it would take a long time and she didn't have insurance. Who was going to pay for her hospital stay?

In the records of the hospital that eventually accepted Cindy, a member of the medical staff states that "Cindy presented herself as in need of immediate medical attention. She was appearing very shaky and tearful. After a brief assessment I felt her withdrawal symptoms needed the attention of our medical director. She described a history of migraine headaches. In the last week she has used fifteen bags of heroin, plus PX drugs consisting of Fiorinal, Percodan, Demerol, Codeine, Elavil—the list is endless. She brought a large shopping bag of empty drug containers most used within the last few months, all PX. Her family does not wish to see her."

Included in the notes are observations of Cindy as she detoxed. "Hunched posture, body is twitching, pale, eyelids droopy." "Awake, at the nurse's desk, sobbing uncontrollably." "Withdrawal anxiety level up."

Twenty days after Cindy was admitted to the hospital she discharged herself. She returned to the trailer in which she had been living and continued to detox on her own. Detoxing placed her at odds with her life. She had no foundation on which to build, no memories of living without drugs, no coping strategies that would help her live drug free.

Cindy wrote, "I'm not afraid of dying. It's peace to me. No more suffering. I have no family which is alright, but who buries me? Every minute I think of drugs. Why I don't know. I wish I could fall asleep and wake in six months straight, without withdrawal. It's an awful feeling. Your body aching for drugs, every muscle. You can't think straight. I get migraines. I can't sleep. This is all trying to get off drugs. It's very painful. You don't want to see or talk to anyone."

But Cindy did see people. She started attending meetings of Narcotics Anonymous, Cocaine Anonymous, and Alcoholics Anonymous. Some days she went to an early-morning meeting at the hospital, a midday meeting in a downtown church, and then another meeting at another church in the evening. She began to talk about her life.

"Hi, I'm Cindy and I am a drug addict and an alcoholic."

"Hi Cindy."

Members of the recovering community responded to her. A member of AA sponsored her and she made friends. Her struggle was their struggle. The only difference between them was that she got caught and they were free.

Cindy was encouraged by the support she was getting and she tried to respond by supporting other addicts who were new to the recovery community. At a twelve-step meeting, wearing men's workboots, Levis with a neon green bandanna tied around her waist, a sweater, and a short black Harley Davidson jacket, she told a young woman who was new to the program, "Keep coming kid." And when the young woman kept coming, Cindy would sit next to her and stick up for her when older members of the group made fun of her because she wasn't "hard-core." Once when this young woman was having a particularly hard time, Cindy hitchhiked eight miles to be with her. The young woman said that Cindy would rub her back and say, "Smarten up" and "Don't end up like me."

Cindy struggled to remain drug free. She hoped that if she managed to stay clean and sober for an extended period she would be allowed to remain in the community and continue her recovery. As the months went by, her struggle became less intense. She was beginning to learn how to deal with her life without using street drugs or prescription medications as a way of overcoming her difficulties.

By February 1990, Cindy had lived eight months drug free. Her eyes were bright and her hair shone. Maintaining her sobriety was still very difficult, but she was proud of her efforts and she was encouraged by the friends she had made who supported her struggle to overcome her addiction. She talked more at the NA, CA, and AA meetings that she attended. She encouraged others, listened to their stories, and tried to offer assistance in any way that she could to those who were experiencing difficulties. The more Cindy talked, the more she came to understand the way in which prescription drugs were linked to her heroin addiction.

In the months that preceded her superior court hearing, Cindy tried to document the prescription drugs that her doctor had prescribed. She began by taking her prescription containers and writing down the names of the drugs. Realizing that if the information was to be used at the hearing she would need further documentation, Cindy talked to the public defender, who then sent "Authorization for Release" forms, signed by Cindy, to each of the five pharmacies that had been filling her prescriptions.

Each pharmacy provided computer printouts of the medications that Cindy had received as well as some copies of actual prescriptions. There are prescriptions for Fiorinal w/ Codeine, Percodan, Percocet, Demerol, and Xanax, all written in a small, myopic hand that is difficult to read and would be hard to replicate—especially by a woman whose writing is large and childlike and who writes of "heroine," "percodian," "Fiormial," "tranzilzers," and "Cloindie."

Percodan, Percocet, and Oxycodan are brand names for the analgesic oxycodone, a habit-forming narcotic that increases the effects of other drugs. When taken in overdose it causes drowsiness, restlessness, agitation, nausea, vomiting, weakness, lethargy, stupor, coma, and seizures. Fiorinal w/ Codeine is an opiate, an analgesic, and a narcotic that encourages both psychological and physical dependence when taken in the large doses prescribed for Cindy. Demerol, a strong analgesic synthetic opioid, is similarly habit-forming and can cause psychological and physical dependence. When Demerol (meperidine) is taken with tricyclic antidepressants such as amitriptyline—which Cindy's doctor also regularly prescribed—it increases sedation and depresses the respiratory system. Taking central nervous system depressants like Demerol with sedative hypnotics like Halcion—another drug prescribed for Cindy by her doctor—can cause unconsciousness and death. What follows is a list of individual drugs—on two hundred and forty-four separate prescriptions, amounting to eleven thousand two hundred and thirty eight pills—that were prescribed for Cindy by her doctor between September 1987 and May 1989.

The public defender told Cindy that when the physician who attended her when she was hospitalized to detox questioned the large quantities of medications that she was taking, her doctor had accused Cindy of stealing prescription pads from his office and of forging prescriptions. In a "late note" written after Cindy left the hospital, the physician wrote:

> I had spoken to the secretary of the Medical Society while the patient was still hospitalized here regarding our concern about the large number of prescriptions she had. He had checked with (the doctor) and determined that these prescriptions were obtained fraudulently. Apparently the patient had stolen the prescription pads and was forging his signature.

Cindy knew there was nothing that she could do. "Who was going to believe me, a junkie? I couldn't let it bother me. I had to stay clean. I couldn't risk getting upset. I didn't want to start using again." Cindy gave a small

Table 2–1

Date	Drug	Quantity	Date	Drug	Quantity
3/87	Demerol 50 mg	98	7/2/88	Xanax 1 mg	40 RF 03
24/87	Xanax 1 mg	40	7/2/88	Amitriptyline 150 mg	20 RF 05
26/87	Clonidine .1 mg	20	7/11/88	Amitriptyline 150 mg	15 RF 06
0/23/87	Demerol 100 mg	60	7/11/88	Indomethacin 25 mg	50
1/18/87	Demerol 100 mg	60	7/11/88	Xanax 1 mg	30
1/18/87	Amitriptyline 150 mg	50	7/20/88	Fiorinal/Codeine #3	25
1/18/87	Butalbital Comp	100	7/22/88	Xanax 1 mg	50 RF 05
1/18/87	Xanax 1 mg	100	7/25/88	Demerol 100 mg	10
2/18/87	Butalbital Comp	100 RF 01	7/25/88	Percodan	10
2/18/87	Xanax 1 mg	100 RF 01	7/26/88	Xanax 1 mg	50
6/88	Amitriptyline 150 mg	50 RF 01	7/27/88	Fiorinal/Codeine 30	30
12/88	Demerol 100 mg	100	8/1/88	Xanax 1 mg	50
13/88	Xanax 1 mg	100 RF 02	8/5/88	Metoclopramide 10	25
13/88	Amitriptyline 150 mg	50 RF 02	8/5/88	Percodan	10
13/88	Butalbital Comp	100 RF 02	8/5/88	Fiorinal/Codeine 30	30 RF 01
1/88	Xanax 1 mg	100 RF 03	8/5/88	Xanax 1 mg	50
1/88	Amitriptyline 150 mg	50 RF 03	8/13/88	Amitriptyline 150 mg	15 RF 07
1/88	Butalbital Comp	100 RF 03	8/15/88	Xanax 1mg	50 RF 01
14/88	Xanax 1 mg	60	8/16/88	Percodan	20
22/88	Xanax 1 mg	100 RF 04	8/17/88	Fiorinal/Codeine 30	50
22/88	Butalbital Comp	100 RF 04	8/24/88	Xanax 1 mg	36
15/88	Butalbital Comp	50	8/24/88	Amitriptyline 150 mg	25
25/88	Demerol 100 mg	100	8/29/88	Fiorinal/Codeine #3	25
25/88	Butalbital Comp	50 RF 01	8/29/88	Xanax 1 mg	10
25/88	Xanax 1 mg	50 RF 05	9/1/88	Xanax 1 mg	50
3/88	Demerol 100 mg	50	9/3/88	Fiorinal/Codeine #3	25
7/88	Amitriptyline 150 mg	50 RF 04	9/7/88	Fiorinal/Codeine #3	25
12/88	Xanax 1 mg	50	9/7/88	Xanax 1 mg	40
16/88	Percodan	50	9/17/88	Fiorinal/Codeine #3	25
1/88	Xanax 1 mg	20	9/17/88	Xanax 1 mg	40
3/88	Eskalith Caps 300 mg	100	9/18/88	Amitriptyline 150 mg	25
3/88	Percodan	60	9/22/88	Clonidine .1 mg	30
3/88	Xanax 1 mg	40	9/22/88	Oxycodone/Apap 5	20
15/88	Xanax 1 mg	40 RF 01	9/22/88	Fiorinal/Codeine 30	40
19/88	Oxacillin Sodium 500mg	10	9/22/88	Xanax 1 mg	24
24/88	Dicloxacillin 500 mg	21	9/23/88	Perphenazine 2 mg	50
24/88	Xanax 1 mg	50	9/27/88	Xanax 1 mg	24
24/88	Percodan	20	9/29/88	Perphenazine 4 mg	50
24/88	Percodan	30	9/29/88	Demerol 50 mg	50
27/88	Percodan	30	10/1/88	Fiorinal/Codeine 30	40
2/88	Percodan	30	10/2/88	Clonidine .1 mg	30

Table 2–1 (cont.)

Date	Drug	Quantity	Date	Drug	Quan
10/2/88	Amitriptyline 150 mg	20	1/11/89	Demerol	25
10/12/88	Clonidine .1 mg	100	1/11/89	Percodan	40
10/12/88	Fiorinal/Codeine #3	50	1/23/89	Xanax 1 mg	30 RF
10/12/88	Percodan	30	1/29/89	Xanax 1 mg	30
10/12/88	Perphenazine 8 mg	100	1/29/89	Clonidine .1 mg	20
10/13/88	Amitriptyline 150 mg	20	1/29/89	Amitriptyline 150 mg	25
10/28/88	Amitriptyline 150 mg	15	2/3/89	Fiorinal/Codeine #3	40
10/28/88	Halcion .25 mg	15	2/3/89	Percodan	60
10/28/88	Percodan	40	2/3/89	Xanax 1 mg	50
10/28/22	Perphenazine 8 mg	100 RF 01	2/13/89	Xanax 1 mg	40
10/29/88	Fiorinal/Codeine #3	50	2/13/89	Clonidine .1 mg	100
10/29/88	Clonidine .1 mg	100	2/20/89	Hydroxyzine 25 mg	25
11/19/88	Xanax 1 mg	60	2/20/89	Amitriptyline 150 mg	5 RF C
11/19/88	Amitriptyline 150 mg	15 RF 01	2/20/89	Fiorinal/Codeine #3	18
11/19/88	Halcion .25 mg	10 RF 01	2/24/89	Fiorinal/Codeine #3	22
11/19/88	Clonidine .1 mg	40	2/24/89	Amitriptyline 150 mg	25
11/19/88	Percodan	100	2/24/89	Hydroxyzine 25 mg	50 RF
12/2/88	Xanax 1 mg	60 RF 01	3/5/89	Fiorinal/Codeine #3	40
12/2/88	Xanax 1 mg	30 RF 02	3/5/89	Xanax 1 mg	50
12/2/88	Amitriptyline 150 mg	15 RF 02	3/6/89	Hydroxyzine 25 mg	50 RF
12/2/88	Clonidine .1 mg	40	3/27/89	Amitriptyline 150 mg	15
12/14/88	Xanax 1 mg	60	3/30/89	Fiorinal/Codeine #3	40
12/14/88	Clonidine HCL .1 mg	60	3/30/89	Xanax 1 mg	30
12/14/88	Fiorinal/Codeine 30	50	4/3/89	Xanax 1 mg	50 RF
12/14/88	Amitriptyline 150 mg	20	4/11/89	Fiorinal/Codeine #3	40
12/14/88	Percodan	50	4/12/89	Xanax 1 mg	30
1/6/89	Clonidine HCL .1 mg	60 RF 01	4/19/89	Xanax 1 mg	50 RF
1/6/89	Fiorinal/Codeine 30	50 RF 01	4/27/89	Xanax 1 mg	50 RF
1/6/89	Xanax 1 mg	60	5/2/89	Amitriptyline 150 mg	25
1/6/89	Amitriptyline 150 mg	9	5/3/89	Midrin	30
1/6/89	Halcion .25 mg	10 RF 03	5/3/89	Xanax .25 mg	50
1/11/89	Amitriptyline 150 mg	11	5/5/89	Clonidine HCL .1 mg	25 RF

laugh, recognizing the irony of her situation. "I thought if I use they will send me to jail for sure."

In a letter to the public defender representing Cindy the assistant county attorney wrote, "I am authorized to offer the following terms in exchange for a plea of guilty: 2 to 4 years in the state prison."

One month before the scheduled court hearing, the public defender asked for an evaluation to be made by a drug and alcohol counselor at the local hospital. In his report, dated February 20, 1990, the counselor wrote:

> Cindy seems to have come an enormously long way with her recovery from active use of heroin and other mood-altering chemicals. She apparently has come to a point in her life where she feels it is time to fight a serious problem in a very serious and committed way. Her treatment last summer was quite an intense one. She experienced a very traumatic and extended detoxification procedure and did well and worked hard at her subsequent inpatient treatment. Since that time she has had only one relapse into heroin, and to date has seven months continuous drug-free living, with the exception of a night four months ago, when she had a few drinks.
>
> This attempt at sobriety has been the first serious one she's ever attempted, and she's doing remarkably well given the extremely intense nature of her heroin and polydrug dependency. She attends Narcotics Anonymous and Alcoholics Anonymous meetings on an almost daily basis and has become an active participant therein. In my professional opinion, I see no reason for Cynthia to be involved in any more extensive and comprehensive treatment than what she has done already; at least at this point it seems to be going okay. The difference between Cindy actively addicted and Cindy working recovery is phenomenal. She looks and acts like a totally different person.

Cindy was hopeful. She was overcoming her addiction. By the time the hearing was held she would have been drug free for almost nine months. Her hospital medical records clearly indicated the severity of her addiction to prescription medications, and she felt it would be possible to show the strong link between her use of narcotic prescriptions and her use of street drugs. She convinced herself that when she went to court, the judge would rule in her favor and put her on probation so that she could continue to work on her sobriety. She hoped she might do community service so she could help others recover from their addiction.

The week before the hearing Cindy tried to spend as much time as she could with the friends she had made at the recovery meetings she attended.

They rallied, kept her busy, talked to her on the telephone, and accompanied her to meetings. Her struggle was their struggle and they wanted to see her succeed. It was important to them that the criminal justice system respond to her efforts and recognize that she had done the impossible against all odds. Members of the recovery community watched, some hopeful, others cynical, apprehensive, and distrustful. They waited expectantly. If Cindy was not allowed to recover, what was the point of their own struggle to live drug free?

THE PRESENTENCE REPORT: SEND A MESSAGE OF DETERRENCE TO THE GENERAL SUBCULTURE

On Thursday, March 9, 1990, Cindy met with the public defender and read the presentence investigation probation report. She was devastated. The report stated that she had received the heroin through the mail with the intent to sell, and recommended that she receive a long-term prison sentence for bringing toxic waste into the community. Since the report was not a public document Cindy was not allowed to have a copy.

Cindy read the report when the public defender gave it to her on the Thursday before her superior court hearing and she has never seen it again. However, some seventeen months later she was given the opportunity to read a subsequent report by the same probation officer, in which he refers to the presentence report. Again, she was not allowed to have a copy of the text, but she requested paper and a pencil so she could write down some of the information contained in the report. Cindy copied sections that pertained to the probation officer's presentence investigation report, and those sections are included below.

> The presentence investigation is on file and is used as a point of departure as well as the long nineteen years of substance abuse that culminated in the defendant's heroin addiction. Since the report is on file one will focus on the salient factors of said report. First the offense itself, possession of heroin. According to the police report the police department had received a crime-line report that the defendant was getting 15 bags of heroin through the mail. The caller stated that the defendant was a junkie and was going to sell because the local dealer is in a rehab in the state. Past Express Mail packages of a similar nature. A federal search warrant was obtained and the package opened. Inside were twenty packets believed to be heroin. When

the defendant signed for the package she was subsequently arrested. The defendant's position was that she was receiving such mailing for a month from a rich man and all of the heroin was for her personal consumption.

The biographical section of said presentence report documents the defendant's transient residential history and limited job history. Of note is that the defendant has a daughter who is in placement due to the complications of the defendant's life-style involving drugs and her suicidal attempts including a self-inflicted handgun wound.

The conclusion of the presentence investigation emphasized the seriousness of the offense and the need to send a message of deterrence to the general subculture as well as a message of protective assurance to the community in general. Focusing on the defendant, with a nineteen-year history of substance abuse, there was a clear need for a structured setting for rehabilitation. This section of the evaluation notes the defendant's past effort of self-defined rehabilitation and her poor follow-through.

Overall it was the writer's conclusion that self-defined treatment in an open society was not credible at the juncture. What was needed was a state prison sentence to provide a stabilizing structure to insure a durable follow-up to treatment; the idea was that the structure of both environments would force the defendant to work on some real issues rather than allow her an opportunity to just walk away or define for herself the treatment she will or will not do.

The next day Cindy was trying to spend as much time as possible with her friends. She was anxious and upset, and she didn't want to be alone. Cindy knew that if she isolated she would end up using. She told the young woman whom she had been trying to help that she was worried about the probation officer's report. She said that he had only talked to her for a short time, and that in his report he hadn't taken into consideration anything she had told him about her life and the things that had happened to her or her serious efforts to recover from her addiction.

Cindy was so alarmed by the report that she tried to reach the public defender assigned to her case. She wanted to reread the report, to understand what was being said, and to try to find a way to respond. The public defender was not taking her calls.

At that time I was working on a literacy project in the community, and the young woman who Cindy had supported in the early days of her recovery from drug addiction was working with me. The young woman told Cindy that she thought I might be able to help her. Cindy said she would like to talk with me. The young woman telephoned me and I spent most of that Friday afternoon talking with Cindy.

Cindy talked a lot about her childhood. Her father was an alcoholic, and from the time she was a very small child, as young as two years of age, he would give her beer to get her drunk. When her parents divorced, her mother remarried, and her stepfather would remove her clothes and beat her with a rubber hose. He also tried to sexually molest one of her older sisters.

She lived on her own when she was fifteen, moved back with her family, and then she left permanently when her stepfather broke her jaw. She was just sixteen. Drugs became the only way that she knew to survive, and by the time she was in her late teens she had begun to use heroin. This was also when she began to use prescription drugs. "I was seeing a psychiatrist, that was the first time that I just wanted to kill myself, and he had put me on Valium and some other pills. I just didn't want to live anymore, so I took them all and I was locked up for a few weeks."

When she was twenty-one she became pregnant, and she stopped using drugs for six months of her pregnancy. She was sick after the birth of her baby and was given pills to cope with back pain. After taking the prescription medication, Cindy said, "I had a problem with the pills and then I just got back into drugs." She gave up the custody of her daughter. "I didn't want my daughter to grow up like I did, so I gave her to my sister."

Cindy's daughter lived with her sister for a number of years. When Cindy's sister wanted to adopt the little girl, Cindy would not agree and took back custody. She said, "But I got heavily into drugs and I don't know if I even had her for a year. I was doing a lot of drugs and I didn't see the hurt that I was doing to her, all that I cared about was the drugs and my life was getting worse." Cindy's daughter was made a ward of the state and put into foster care. "I was in hospital. I had shot myself and the last thing I said to my daughter was 'go with these people and when I get out of the hospital I will come and get you.' " Cindy's eyes filled with tears. "And I never got her."

Cindy was always able to get the pills she needed. "I had a quack. This quack, when I was twenty-two I had gotten into the Percodans and all that. When I was twenty-two I found somebody who would give pills. Whatever I wanted. This doctor was giving me Demerol, a hundred milligrams of Demerol and he'd give me about seventy of them. I was also put on Valiums. I was also put on Elavil. I was also in between getting Percodan too. Now this doctor knew how much I was doing. I mean I was going through seventy Demerol in five days. And what I had to do to cover my back was I went to five different pharmacies. No pharmacy knew what was going on with the other."

I asked her if one doctor prescribed all the drugs that she was taking.

"Oh yeah. He prescribed them."

"That many?"

"That many. Of course a lot of times I had to shove them in my back pocket so the ladies at the desk would not know this. I told the doctor, 'You know I am having a rough time,' and he still gave them to me. I went into the hospital a couple of times to try to get dry, to try to get off these pills. It never worked. He just kept on giving them to me."

Cindy also shot prescription drugs. "When I was about twenty-six I started shooting Demerol. That's like liquid Demerol. I could probably do up to three to four hundred milligrams of Demerol. I would crush these things up and I'd inject them all over my body, all over my body. And it would give me abscesses all over my body. They'd swell and I had sores all over my arms and all over my legs. But I still always got my Demerol because I would go back to him once a week. I would always make up something. Towards the end he didn't even charge me to go to his office.

"Finally I tried to kill myself again, which I almost succeeded. I was in a coma. I shot a whole bunch of Demerol. I had taken all the pills that I had. I can't tell you how many bottles or what exactly I was taking. I was miserable, I was in hell, and a lot of times I was by myself. I mean I locked myself up in my boyfriend's trailer for a year while he was in prison. All I did was go to the doctors and I'd sit in that trailer by myself and proceed to get totally messed up. How I survived I have no idea."

At the end of the conversation Cindy said, "I've learned to love myself. I am worth something today. I am a better person today. Before I was just a junkie. I never thought it was possible for me not to use drugs."

I audiorecorded our conversation and I used it that weekend to write a report for Cindy to submit to the public defender. In the report, I emphasized that the ways of coping with abuse Cindy had learned when she was a child she continued to use through her adult life. She learned as a child that alcohol and drugs were the solution to her problems. I also stressed that members of the medical profession had enabled Cindy to become addicted to prescription drugs, and that doctors had helped her maintain her addiction. Taking prescription drugs pushed her back into using heroin. I then focused on the critical steps Cindy had taken toward recovery. She was trying both to help herself and to get help for herself. She had asked for help from people in Narcotics Anonymous, Cocaine Anonymous, and Alcoholics

Anonymous and she was active in the recovery community. I concluded the report with recommendations:

> An alternative to prison would be to provide Cindy with the services that have never been made available to her. Ensure that she attends meetings and that she is given the opportunity to do community service by helping others who are suffering from alcoholism and drug addiction. Help her obtain her GED so that she can work. Provide job training. Give her the opportunity to become a productive member of the community.

I gave the report to Cindy. She then gave it to the public defender with the request that I be asked to testify.

CINDY'S LIFE IS OFFICIALLY REINVENTED BY THE CRIMINAL JUSTICE SYSTEM

On Wednesday, March 14, 1990, Cindy arrives at the superior court in a purple dress and black high heels. She has given up her black leather jacket, workboots, and jeans and instead of wearing her long brown hair straight she wears it curled. Five friends from Cocaine Anonymous have come to the hearing. She hugs them as they arrive, thanks them for coming, and tells them that she loves them. Her mother and her brother are there. Cindy seems glad that her mother has come but in the bathroom she says it also makes her nervous. She tells me that when I testify it is all right to talk about her childhood. Her eyes are edged with carefully applied blue eye shadow, and she opens them wide as she speaks. "Those things happened."

Later, remembering that day, Cindy admits that it was the only time in her life she can remember when friends gathered to support her. As she talks of holidays spent on her own, I imagine that for Cindy this hour before she went into superior court probably felt like a birthday or a wedding.

After one of several conferences with the public defender assigned to her case, Cindy looks worried. "She hasn't read it. Denny's report. She hasn't even opened the envelope." At Cindy's insistence the public defender reads the report just before she goes into the courtroom, and copies of the report are given to the prosecutor and the judge.

The doors of the courtroom open and we file in. Cindy is in front with the public defender. The county attorney, a tall imposing man with graying hair, is sitting with the assistant county attorney, a small red-haired woman wearing a dark "lawyer" suit. As we have been waiting for the hearing to begin, there have been comments made about the assistant county attorney. Her reputation for meanness precedes her.

The door behind the bench opens and the superior court judge enters. A voice tells everyone to stand. There is some awkward shuffling, then silence. For some who have come to support Cindy it might have helped if there had been a book in which a hymn could be found.

Cindy stands up straight, her hands clasped behind her back. In her high heels she is well over six feet tall. The public defender stands beside her. Even in heels she only comes up to Cindy's shoulder. She also wears a "lawyer" suit, but her long brown hair softens her demeanor. She seems no match for either the county attorney or his assistant.

Everyone in the courtroom sits. The judge tells Cindy to stand.

"It is my understanding that you have been charged with possession of a narcotic drug with intent to sell the same, and that the state has agreed to reduce this to knowingly having in your possession and under your control a quantity of a narcotic drug, heroin. You have done this by a waiver of indictment. Are you aware of this?"

"Yes."

The judge continues his questions about her knowledge of the indictment. Later, Cindy tells me that she didn't understand some of them. "I was so nervous."

The judge tells Cindy to sit down.

"The facts in the case, are they pretty much as spelled out in this pretty lengthy probation report?" He does not wait for the question to be answered. "The police version or defendant's version, they seem to be a little bit different. But in any event, on this charge, they would seem to be consistent. At least, the one that she has agreed to plead guilty."

The assistant county attorney—who speaks for the state until it is time for summation, when the county attorney takes over—stands. "This is correct."

The judge continues. "I believe it is the state's position she possessed this amount of heroin for the purpose of selling it. And it is her position that the boyfriend, whoever it was, was mailing her these twenty packets for her personal use?"

The public defender answers, "That's correct Your Honor," then quickly adds, "And that, also, we have in regard to the issue today that it is purely possession, that the issue of sales is not relevant. We had obtained an expert at one time who was willing to come in and testify that a habit of seven to thirteen packets a day was not unusual for a heroin addict. It was the defendant's contention that she was doing a seven packet a day habit. So we want to make clear that the defendant, it was not her intention to sell that heroin. The issue in this case is the possession."

"You can get an expert on most anything, I suppose." The judge moves on, "Let's go over this acknowledgment of rights."

Cindy gives up all her rights.

The judge holds up the indictment. "You know that it is possession of a narcotic drug, heroin. To this, how do you plead?"

"Guilty, Your Honor."

The drug and alcohol counselor who is the program coordinator of the chemical dependency treatment unit at the local hospital and who wrote a letter on Cindy's behalf is called to the stand. The public defender questions him about the likelihood that Cindy can recover from heroin addiction by attending meetings in the local community. She asks him if when he met Cindy she seemed motivated to deal with her drug abuse.

"Most definitely."

The assistant county attorney begins her cross-examination. "Isn't it true that you only spent forty-five minutes with this defendant?"

"Yes."

"Your entire report is an opinion based on what she told you." She turns her statement into a question. "Correct?"

"Yes."

"And you did not seek out other persons or other institutions she might have gone to, to substantiate. Did you?"

"No."

"And you do admit that she in fact had two relapses. Isn't that correct?"

"Yes."

"And one was in fact a relapse back into heroin. Wasn't it?"

"Yes."

Cindy leans over and talks to the public defender. She hasn't used for nine months. The "relapse" the program coordinator mentioned in his letter occurred when she was first detoxing. The public defender nods her head as Cindy whispers to her. She sits up, puts her hand momentarily on Cindy's arm, then listens to the cross-examination.

"And the other one was back into alcohol, which is a drug?"

"Yes."

(Later, Cindy reflects, "When I went to see the program coordinator I answered truthfully when he asked if I had used. I had been clean for a long time. I shouldn't have told him. I've learned that if I tell the truth it can be used against me.")

The assistant county attorney questions the program coordinator about

Cindy's educational background and training, then adds, "So as far as you know, she doesn't have the same ability to come to the opinions you do as to what is a good program and what isn't. Is that correct?"

One of Cindy's friends is called as a witness. The public defender questions her about Cindy's attempts to get into a hospital to detox after she was arrested for possession of heroin. The friend says she accompanied Cindy to "thirteen or fourteen" hospitals and none of them would accept Cindy as a patient.

The public defender then asks if she has seen any changes in Cindy's behavior since she has been drug free.

"She is starting to be able to do what I can do, and probably you can do, and people that don't have drug problems can do every day," Cindy's friend says. "She is starting to be able to deal with day-to-day living and day-to-day problems."

I am called to the stand, and the public defender questions me about my report. I recap the key points, emphasizing the progress that Cindy has made by attending meetings and by participating in the activities of the recovering community. I strongly recommend that Cindy be allowed to continue her recovery in the community, where she can attend meetings and receive the support of other recovering addicts.

In her cross-examination the assistant county attorney focuses on the question of control. "It is fair to say that on Friday, when she desperately needed help, of course, that she couldn't get until Monday, that in fact she was desperate, that she wasn't in control?"

"She was very much in control. You can be in a desperate situation and still be in control. That's not antithetical. She was in control enough to make two phone calls to see counselors, and then persist when mental health said that they couldn't see her. She was in control enough to find a friend to drive her to the mental health institution and insist that a counselor see her. I think that's a woman very much in control and trying to act in her best interests."

"But desperate. Those were your words?"

"They are not antithetical terms. It would be unfair to imply that they are."

When the questioning is over, the judge asks Cindy if she wants to say anything in her own defense. At that moment the door to the courtroom opens and a group of high school students is ushered in by their teacher. They move along looking out of place as they glance at the judge, undo their coats, and take their seats. They are in the seating area to the left of the table where Cindy is sitting with the public defender.

Cindy stands. She is distracted by the entrance of the children. She looks over to where they are sitting and she speaks hesitantly.

"Your Honor, um, I am real nervous." In her hand is a torn piece of notebook paper on which she has written the things she wants to say. "I know doing drugs was wrong. I know it." Her hand is shaking and she sways back and forth. Then she puts the paper on the table and speaks directly to the judge. "Getting busted did help me to recover." She talks to the judge of hitting bottom. "I've hit many rock bottoms. And I am a better person today. Today I feel I can ask for help. Before I didn't. But the most important thing is that I am getting help."

Cindy brings up the probation officer's presentence report, about which she has been worrying. She says, "On Thursday, yes, I was upset. You know, and yes, my instant reaction is going to be, I mean, even you know, okay, I am not going to deal with it. But I did." Then she continues, "I just feel that today I do have a choice. Before I never thought it would be possible for me to stop using drugs. I never thought I could do it. But I've got people behind me. I never trusted anybody. And today, I would like to help people. Say, 'Hey, look, you know, when you are in trouble, you can go, and when you are in trouble you can ask for help.' And that's what I have done. And today, yes, I do have to take it day by day, minute by minute. And that's the most important thing. This has been the hardest thing in my life and right now, today, I can handle it. It's hard and I do need help, and I ask for it. And I think that is the most important thing. And that's about all I can say right now, Your Honor."

In her summation the public defender talks about Cindy's choices. Cindy could have run. She could have gone back out and used drugs again. But she decided to stay and face the charges. "All whom she has had contact with have been very impressed by her success. Many professionals, seven, eight months ago, didn't give her much of a chance. They have been impressed by her success. Last week there was a defendant that got six months in jail for possession of cocaine with intent to sell. The probation department's recommendation in that case was twelve months in jail. As the court knows, the recommendation in the probation report is a fairly lengthy prison sentence." Again she says that Cindy could have run away or gone back to drugs. She repeats that Cindy decided to stay and deal with her problem and for that reason she is a positive force in the community. She asks the court to accept the recommendation that Cindy be given a one-year suspended sentence.

The judge calls on the county attorney. He talks about the needs of the defendant and the needs of society. He says that the recommendation made by the defense "does not in fact do justice to the interests of society." He recommends that "after a one-year period, and upon petition by the defendant, the court will defer the remainder of the minimum sentence if the defendant has completed and meaningfully participated in all the substance abuse programs available at the state prison, has been of good behavior, and will be admitted into a long-term residential drug treatment center on release from state prison. We believe, Your Honor, that in looking at all the facts as outlined in the probation report as well as everything that we have heard here today, there are a number of things that seem to jump out at us that give us some cause for concern." He talks about the defendant's falling back into substance abuse and of the way in which the defendant "feels she is entitled to establish the treatment programs that she needs. Clearly the probation report in its evaluation and analysis lays out a need for structure in the defendant's life." Then, paradoxically, speaking of the report I had written, he states, "Nowhere does it say Cynthia's accepting responsibility for her actions." He returns to the presentence report. "The probation report clearly outlines the horrors of heroin within the community, one of the most addictive of drugs. Society has a right in that case to expect that this court will focus on a deterrence, not just to the defendant in the use of heroin, but deterrence against those who would bring this drug into this community. A deterrence can only be gained in this instance by the imposition of some punitive sanction. While what the defendant has proposed may be rehabilitative, it ignores the deterrent punitive aspect, which society has a right to expect from this court in this particular action."

The judge deliberates. Some of his deliberations you have already heard, but he makes other statements as well. "You know, the defendant can say what she wants. She has. And she may well be right that she was just receiving these twenty packs, whatever they were, of heroin for her own use. I have trouble believing that. Here we are with a class A felony being reduced to a class B felony in the first instance, second offense in the drug field, and asking absolutely no incarceration. Anybody who knows me knows that doesn't sound like me."

He sentences Cindy to three and a half to seven years in prison. "I hope we are in a new beginning. You have for a long time in your life relied on drugs illegally, some legally with prescriptions, whatever the case is."

This is the only time in the court hearing that Cindy's addiction to prescription medications is mentioned.

The doctor's name is *never* mentioned.

None of the documentation from the pharmacies is presented.

Her hospital records are *not* submitted.

Thick files filled with relevant information are *omitted* from the official text.

Cindy is a junkie. All that seems to count is that the probation report states that she is bringing toxic waste into the community.

Cindy is handcuffed and taken to the county jail. The next day she is taken to the state prison for women.

What sticks in Cindy's memory is the way the judge looked at the high school students as he sentenced her. What I remember is the probation officer's presentence report and how much weight was given to a document that was based on a limited interview and contained so much misinformation, a document written for the judge as a function of the sentencing procedure and as such "privileged" information, a document to which a defendant does not have access unless shown it by a lawyer. How could this document carry so much weight when the letter written by the drug and alcohol counselor who knew Cindy and had watched her as she struggled to overcome her drug addiction was dismissed so precipitously?

WHY DON'T YOU PUT ME IN THE ELECTRIC CHAIR AND ZAP ME?

Cindy is angry. She says she has a bad attitude, that the old Cindy is back, that she is ready to fight anyone who fucks with her. She has chronic migraine headaches and severe muscle spasms in her neck and shoulders. Grinding her teeth, Cindy describes prison as being on the streets and not being able to leave. She watches her back, she doesn't trust anyone, she spends most of her time anxiously lying on her bed in her cell.

The psychiatric social worker meets with one of the nurses and a prison sergeant to discuss Cindy's suicide potential. The nurse writes in her progress notes "C.O. staff to perform hourly checks on inmate." On her initial classification profile information form someone types, "Will bear close scrutiny due to past serious suicide attempts."

On March 20, 1990, a week after she is incarcerated, Cindy writes on an inmate request slip. "I would like to request to see the nurse about my mygrains and bad headaches. I cannot get rid of them."

On March 22, Cindy fills in another request. "I need to have asprine for my headache. I need them for the early morning. I'm very sick and this is making me all tense."

March 30. "I need some more asprin. I need to take it every four to six hours. Tylonal does not work. I've had headaches since I was seventeen. That's why I need my medical records from my doctor. I get very sick. I exercise two times daily. It does not make my headache better, but I do it anyway. I was on stronger med on outside. But here I need the apsrin and it just dulls my headaches. I told you this when I came in."

On the telephone Cindy says she is so tense she is grinding her teeth and some of them are breaking off. The pain in her jaw is making her headaches worse. She complains about the hostility she feels from the guards and from other inmates. "This place is making me so nervous."

In a dull voice in another telephone conversation Cindy says, "Everything I worked for is gone. I'm back where I started. Just a junkie." She talks about the constant migraine headaches from which she is suffering. She says that her mother suffers from migraine headaches and that her daughter has also started getting headaches. "I'm losing weight."

April 17, on an inmate slip, "I am out of asprin. My headaches have been real bad all weekend."

April 23. "I ran out of asprin yesterday. May I please have some more Bayer. Today, I exercised and walk outside. I still have a bad headache."

An inmate tongues a Darvocet and gives the pill to Cindy. Someone informs. Cindy is screened for drugs. Her urine test comes back dirty. There are opiates in Cindy's urine. She loses twenty days of good time. Cindy tells a friend who visits her at the prison that one of the guards is walking around singing, "Pop goes the Weasel."

Cindy writes me. "This week has been a bad one I'm very depressed and don't feel good. I try to pick myself up but it only works a little. I'm short tempered and angry. Denny it sucks in here I don't know what to do anymore. Boy I guess they did punish me for doing drugs. I just want to cry. It's been a bad day. Staying in my room doesn't help me anymore either."

The following inmate-request-slip exchanges take place on May 28.

"I would please like to see the dentist. I filled out a request two months ago."

"You have been placed on the dental list."

"I would please like to see the doctor so he can put in writing about taking more asprin. My asprin does not last seven days and for the two days I don't have any I get really bad headaches and this makes these days awful. I cannot do anything. I should not have to go through this much pain. Plus it is difficult in here enough. Thank you for listening."

"Per the state prison women's protocol, twenty-four tablets of aspirin a week is an appropriate amount for your needs. Thank you."

"I would please like some more asprin. I got them last Friday and I have run out. Thank you."

In June I am sick and I don't write to Cindy for several weeks. Not knowing I have been sick, Cindy sends me a letter, "Why don't you write me any more? I thought you cared what was going on. But I guess people do forget about me. I'm far away. Denny junkies don't just get better. It's something you have to work on every day and when there is no help any more you're fucked. Well I got to go."

Cindy has lost contact with her friends in the recovery community. Once she was imprisoned she was no longer a symbol of their own recovery. At first there were letters and cards but after a few weeks the mail stopped coming.

On July 20, Cindy requests, "Can I please have some Bayer. And can you please make an appointment with the psychiatrist so I can get back on my Lithium."

"Sent Bayer. You are on the list for the psychiatrist."

"I really need to go to the dentist. I put in a request three and a half months ago and I see people go in that are new or pretrials that have been in for a month or so. This is not fair at all. It's almost four months now. My teeth hurt and one is fractured and is sharp. This is my third request. Can you please do something. Thank you."

Cindy writes to me on September 20. "Oh I got my six month review it went really good. I'm glad. Every month I get the highest score so that is great. They said keep it up. So I do. I need to get my life together and I have only one more chance to do it. This is do or die. Well I got to go back to school so take care."

In her telephone calls Cindy talks about the difficulties that she is having getting medical treatment. She says it's a catch-22. She is in pain and needs medication but she can't have it because she is a drug addict. She talks about pain management and she says she needs someone to work with her to help her get relief without a relapse into active narcotic addiction. She tells me that she wakes up with migraine headaches and that they get progressively worse throughout the day.

On October 19, Cindy writes another letter to me. "School is going good. I took three of the GED tests and passed all three. I was shocked. Nov 12 is the next test I got to do math which is my worst subject and social studies which I can pass no problem. Man I hope I can make it. Last week was awful it was real bad. But today I'm okay. Life isn't always easy. But I got to pull through this mess and help people who need it. If someone was there for me I wouldn't be here."

On October 25, Cindy explodes. "I cannot stand the pain in my neck and head. I'm in bed all the time. You know something is wrong. I'm not making this up. Why should I be in so much pain just because I'm in prison. I'm not asking for narcotic demnerol or anything like this. I go to school then I'm in bed. You ask the guard on second shift. I've really tried everything that you asked me to. This is cruelty to make someone stay in such pain. Why don't you put me in the electric chair and zap me?"

The response is passive: "I plan to review your current treatment with the physician."

On November 14 the nurse writes in her progress notes, "Dentist requests stress management/relaxation as there is +1 mobility of all teeth which was not present one month ago and is due to grinding teeth."

A referral is sent to social services.

"I would like to see you. My tooth has cracked. I cannot eat on that side. It's too sensitive. Can you try to see me when you can."

"We are coordinating your medical care with your dental care."

"Can you see me and look at my tooth. It is very loose."

"Can I please have some Bayer."

"Request denied. You are on Anaprox. Please work with your counselor on addressing stress management techniques and issues related to drug use."

A December 17 entry in Cindy's progress notes documents the first time she has seen the prison psychiatrist since she has been in prison. He states, "33 y.o. WF, here x 9 months, doing $3^1/_2$ to 7 for possession of heroin." The entry is difficult to read, but some phrases are decipherable. "Reports 17 months of sobriety at this point"; "long hs of seeing psychiatrists"; "$3^1/_2$ years ago shot herself in the chest"; "she notes hs of manic depression at the age of seventeen" "she became tearful when talking about her 11 y.o. daughter."

Under "Assessment" the psychiatrist concludes: "The Elavil may be helping with her mood and possibly with her other pain symptoms (e.g. back and headaches). In other words if we stopped her Elavil we may see ↑ amount of complaints."

On February 6, Cindy confides that she has been trying to get the warden to recommend a community-based program for her when she has completed a year. She sounds agitated. "The warden said 'You haven't done anything spectacular since you've been in here.'" Cindy is talking quickly, her voice is raised, "Why should I go into a long-term in-program. I helped myself before I came in here." She takes a breath, then rushes jaggedly through her words. "I was talking to a couple of guards and they said, 'You've been a model inmate.' It's so hard to get out of here. People go well over their minimum."

Later in the same conversation her voice smooths and lightens as she tells me she has a new job. "I help the hairdresser and I make all the appointments." The upbeat moment quickly fades. Cindy talks about her daughter, who is in an institution. "I not only ruined my life I ruined hers. I'm just going to have to do everything I can to make it better. It will be four years since I talked to her. She's like a child without anybody. She's been ripped up and thrown away."

In a dull voice Cindy forces herself to speak. "I've gotta go. I'll call you. Thanks for listening to me."

THE PUNISHMENT IS THE CRIME

At the end of February Cindy calls. She asks me if her court hearing a year ago was on March 14 or 15. I tell her 14. She tells me again that she wants to be released from prison so that she can be readmitted to the day program at the drug and alcohol rehabilitation center at the city hospital. The prison is recommending that she be sent to a long-term drug treatment center for one year.

Cindy says she won't go. She thinks the treatment center the prison is recommending is for hard-core addicts when they first detox. "I haven't used in nineteen months," she says. "Why should I go there now?" Then sounding frightened she adds, "I've been abused all my life. Going there would just be more abuse. I can't stand it."

She tells me that she was in a drug rehab once where she had to scrub the floor with a toothbrush. "They take away all your rights. They break down your personality so they can build it up again. This place has broken me down. I feel there is nothing left of me. I want to be in control of my own life. I was doing good until they locked me up in here."

Again she tells me that she won't go. She says, "I'd rather stay in prison."

In endless telephone calls we discuss the possibilities of Cindy's being released from prison. In one conversation she says she is going to retain a lawyer. She says, "It will take more than a public defender to get me out of here."

There is talk of sending Cindy to the prison drug rehab. She says if she goes there she will not be allowed to take any medication, including Elavil, which is an antidepressant, noneuphoric, nonaddictive drug. She says that she is scared that her mood swings would be uncontrollable without the moderating effects of an antidepressant. Cindy is upset. "I need my Elavil. I'm a different person without it. I get suicidal. I'm a threat to myself. I might try to kill myself without it." She repeats, "I'm a different person without it."

There are new developments every day. Cindy is on a roller coaster of official possibilities. She says there is increasing talk about taking her off medication so that she can be put in the prison drug rehab. Other drug rehabilitation facilities are mentioned and, of course, there is always the possibility that she will have to remain in prison for the full seven years. Cindy tells me that if she cops an attitude they will keep her in prison. She says that she is being watched. "I'm trying to stay calm. But it is hard, you know, I just don't know what is going to happen to me."

Cindy is told that the probation officer who interviewed her before she went to prison might do another interview. We talk about the report written by the probation officer in which Cindy was portrayed as a threat to society. We discuss the possibilities of getting a copy of the report. Cindy sounds doubtful. "I was told before the hearing that I was not allowed to have a copy."

"How can they write things about you that you are not allowed to read?" I ask her. We both know it is a rhetorical question.

Cindy laughs. "Who knows what they've written about me!" It's a light moment and we joke about Cindy's "official" situation.

CINDY HIRES A PRIVATE LAWYER

Early in March Cindy talks about getting a private lawyer. During her incarceration Cindy has worked hard to reestablish her relationship with her mother, who has just been given custody of her daughter. Cindy writes letters to her daughter and occasionally talks with her when she telephones her mother. Cindy's mother is encouraged by their conversations and offers $500 to help pay for a private lawyer to represent Cindy at the upcoming hearing. Cindy also has a small amount of money set aside, so she decides to hire a lawyer to represent her.

Cindy telephones me to tell me that she has just talked to a lawyer. She says that she thinks he will do a good job. She gives me his name and telephone number and asks me to call him. When I do, he asks for a copy of the report that I wrote before Cindy's first hearing.

In notes dated March 13, Cindy's lawyer outlines the community-based plan that Cindy has put together to continue her recovery from drug addiction if she is released from prison. Then on the next page he writes:

probation report suggests heroin is unknown in [the city she lives in]; not true

no psych workup as basis for the report

<1 gram cocaine wouldn't get that sentence

He requests Cindy's prison records and when they are not forthcoming he subpoenas them.

In the notes that he makes prior to the April 12 hearing, he refers again to the original presentence probation report:

"credibility issue" re: personal use p.6

—convicted of possession

—no evid. of intent to sell

—amount possessed consistent with her stated level of use

—*no evidence*

He also meets the man with whom she will be living if she is released from prison. I ask if Cindy's release is contingent on her living with someone. The lawyer answers carefully. He says that in his opinion the court would be less inclined to release her if she were going to be living on her own. He adds that it is Cindy who has made the arrangements to live with her friend.

I ask Cindy if she had a relationship with the man before she was incarcerated. She says no. She tells me he is a good person, that he has visited her in prison. Dismissing my questions she tells me, "They would never let me out if I was on my own."

CINDY SENDS A "NASTY GRAM"

The petition for sentence reduction hearing is scheduled for April 12, 1991.

Cindy is upbeat. Energized. We talk on the telephone and laugh about the food she is going to eat when we have lunch together on the outside.

Then I do not hear from her for several days.

Finally she calls. "I couldn't talk," she says. "I am so angry. The social worker and the warden have sent a report to the superior court. It is supposed to be a record of what I've done since I've been in prison." Cindy is crying. I wait. "I'll read it to you." I can hear Cindy breathing. It is a while be-fore she begins to read.

"'Major disciplinary report for being under the influence of drugs not prescribed by medical staff. Fifteen days punitive and one hundred and twenty days loss of good time.'"

Cindy's voice is stronger. "I didn't lose a hundred and twenty days. I lost *twenty* days and it was just after I came in here. I was still angry. I haven't had any write-ups in eleven months." She is talking quickly, angrily, bitterly. She sounds frustrated, exasperated, and perplexed. "Why would she do this to me? She knows how hard I have been trying."

There are other problems with the report. "None of my work assign-ments are on it. None of the GED classes." Cindy tells me that the report states, under "Education and Vocational Training," that there is no informa-tion in the file. Most of the mental health and substance abuse programs that she has attended are not listed.

"This is what she has written about me. 'Cynthia has attended individual and group counseling. She has attended one AA meeting weekly out of three available.' She doesn't say anything about the other meetings I attended. It's hard to talk at the AA meetings. What can you say when there is a guard lis-tening to every word?" Cindy talks about some of the other meetings that she attended and says she went to them because it was easier to talk at them. She continues reading. "'She had dirty urine in April 1990 and constantly seeks medication for neck and back spasms. Mind-altering drugs lead to relapse. I feel a long term in-house treatment program would be in her best interest and facilitate her recovery.' I told you. I'm never going to get out of here."

Then she reads the warden's recommendation. "She's written that she 'recommends no action be taken at this time. Cynthia is in need of residen-tial drug and alcohol treatment. She will be programmed for the prison re-habilitation center, a one-year treatment program at the state prison. If she successfully completes this program I would then recommend a suspen-sion.'"

"How long do you think you would have to wait to get into the prison rehab?" I ask.

"Forever."

A copy of the report has probably already been sent to the county at-torney and his assistant, and the judge will also read it. This new report is the same kind of toxic document as the probation officer's presentence re-port. It could influence the outcome of the hearing. Cindy is sure the assis-tant county attorney will use the report in her oral argument to support the state's position that Cindy should remain in prison for at least another year.

Cindy sounds exhausted. She asks me to phone her lawyer to tell him that the report is inaccurate. I tell her I will call him as soon as we get off the phone.

Her lawyer listens and asks me to help him compile a list of all the programs Cindy has attended while she has been in prison.

Meanwhile, Cindy decides to respond to the fabricated information contained in the prison report. She writes a letter to the social worker, then calls me and asks if she can read it to me. I ask her if I can make a record of it.

"Sure. I'll call back in a few minutes."

I switch on my computer and get ready to type. The phone rings.

"Okay?"

"Yes, go ahead."

"This is what I wrote," she says. I am sitting at my computer with headphones on so I can type. "Ready?"

"Yes."

I type as Cindy reads.

"'I am writing you because that is the only way that I can talk to you right now. I feel you have not given me enough credit for this whole year that I have been here. In your report you said nothing about how good I have done. You also did not report that for seven months I went and completed Domestic Violence, and for five months completed Adult Children of Alcoholics, and for one year have been in AA, and one year have been in a Drug and Alcohol group. So on Monday I went to Domestic Violence, Tuesday, Drug and Alcohol group, Thursday, AA, and Friday, Indian spiritual meeting.'"

I am rushing to keep up.

"Have you got that?"

"Just about."

"I'll go slower."

Cindy reads more slowly. Every so often she waits for me to catch up. Her reading catches the rhythm of my typing and she paces herself to it.

"'I have no idea why you wrote that report the way you did, because it sounds like I haven't done a damn thing this year. The judge is going to take one look at that report and make me do another year. Now is that right? So how many more years in prison do I need to be cured? So you took it upon yourself to say this girl needs more time, she's not doing a thing to help herself, she's just a junkie who is just conning medical for more drugs, there's nothing medically wrong with her so just maybe give her some more time to do.

" 'Now this is exactly what the judge is going to read in your report, you should have talked to the dentist and the physical therapist and not just wrote down a report. I have a lot of people behind me and I know I can make it out there and I know I will. I never wanted anything so much in my life and I know it isn't going to be easy but I have the tools to work my program, and family and friends who are going to help me.

" 'You know I have no write-ups or bad spots except that one major. I have gotten a perfect score of sixty for eleven months, I must be doing something right! If I am so unstable as you say then why do I have such a good record? Plus I have been going to school for a year and I have passed four tests, only have my math text left before I get my GED. So I think I have done pretty good for myself.'

"What do you think?"

I'm quiet. Cindy has written a letter advocating for herself. It's an important moment. I hesitate. I am not sure what to say. "I think it is a fine letter."

"But?" Cindy asks, hearing the hesitation in my voice.

"I think you need to be prepared for some fallout if you send it."

"I don't care. I'm going to send it. I have to send it."

Cindy receives a response from the social worker on an inmate request slip. The social worker calls the letter "a nasty gram."

"Does she say anything about the inaccuracies in the report?" I ask.

"No."

I tell Cindy that her lawyer and I are putting together a list of the programs she has attended and that he will make sure the information reaches the superior court. But we both know that the inaccuracies in the prison report will still be included in her official record.

THE SUPERIOR COURT HEARING

Two P.M., April 12, 1991. Cindy is standing in the courtroom. Her long hair is curled and barrettes pull it back off her face. She has on a purple skirt and a pink-and-white sweater. She has gained about twenty pounds, but at six feet she is still not overweight. Her lawyer is standing beside her. Tall and thin, he is quiet and understated in an unremarkable dark blue suit. The assistant county attorney with her short red hair is more definitely dressed, but she is equally unremarkable in her navy blue suit. The county attorney is not present at the hearing.

Cindy's mother and sister are there, and so is a longtime friend who has visited Cindy regularly in prison. I meet the man Cindy will live with—if she is released from prison. He is dressed in light gray slacks and a beige shirt. He looks as uncomfortable with his clothes as with the place. According to Cindy he rides a Harley and usually wears a biker's black leather jacket.

The judge enters the courtroom. We are told to stand.

"Good afternoon."

The assistant county attorney responds, "Good afternoon, Your Honor."

The judge sits. We sit.

"All right," the judge begins, shuffling through some papers. "We're here on a motion. Petition or motion? I guess petition for sentence reduction to which the state objects." He pauses, "Let me clarify one thing for my own edification or whatever. This was a waiver of indictment."

"No, Your Honor." Again it is the assistant county attorney who responds.

"Wait a minute." The judge is incoherent. "Just—just—was it? I shouldn't say it was. I say—should say was it?"

In my notes I write, "This is confusing!"

The assistant says, "She was indicted, and I believe there may have been a waiver to a class B or a change to class B."

"Well, that's what I'm saying. She pleaded guilty to a waiver of indictment on the 14th of March. That's what I've got in front of me. And I would assume, therefore, it was a negotiated plea."

"No, Your Honor," replies the assistant. "It was a naked plea."

"Who typed up this order?" The judge holds up some papers. "This sentencing order? Did I do that?" He turns to the lawyer representing Cindy. "Do you know?"

Speaking quietly, respectfully, with no outward response to the judge's confusion, Cindy's lawyer replies, "Judge, I'm sorry. I didn't represent the defendant at the time so I don't know."

"*I* don't know," the judge continues, sounding irritated. "What I'm saying is did the state disagree with this order that I issued?" He leans forward and speaks to the assistant county attorney. "Do you know? Do you remember?"

The assistant tries to clear the matter up. "I believe what happened, Your Honor, is at the time it was a naked plea. We listened to what the witnesses had to say for the defendant, then made a recommendation. I believe this was our recommendation after hearing witnesses, but it was not agreed to by defendant. I believe defendant was going either for house or no-time disposition."

"My point in raising this is, this looks like it was a recommendation from the state unless I came up with it myself. But I couldn't imagine my doing it."

"It was a recommendation from the state, Your Honor," the assistant replies. "But it was on a naked plea."

The judge still seems confused. "That's okay, but the recommendation. And that's what I did. I followed your recommendation," the judge looks down at the document he is holding in his hand, "which was that she may petition in one year for deferment of the remainder of the minimum if she completes a meaningful participation in all substance abuse programs at the prison and of good behavior, admitted into a long-term residential treatment center on release from state's prison." The judge looks up. "Okay. Well, I just wanted to—I can't remember the details that far back so that's why I—" In midsentence he stops speaking.

There is an uncomfortable silence in the courtroom.

"Your Honor." It is Cindy's lawyer. "I can't speak for the state's position, but it is my understanding that the presentence investigation recommended this sentence."

The judge says, "Could be."

The presentence investigation recommendation is the probation officer's report, of which Cindy has never been allowed a copy. I look at her, wondering if she realizes which document they are talking about, but Cindy is staring at her hands, which are on the table in front of her.

The assistant county attorney begins by objecting. "This defendant has not met any of the requirements stated in the sentencing order."

Cindy looks up.

"She has not been of good behavior due to the fact that on April 23 of 1990 her drug screening test came back positive. It was a major disciplinary for which she was found guilty and for which I believe she lost some good-time credit. One hundred and twenty days."

This time it is Cindy who looks at me.

The assistant continues with her list of Cindy's official deficiencies and then states, "We would ask this motion be denied at this point." She sits down.

Cindy's lawyer stands. "Judge, all the factual issues that the assistant county attorney has raised would be the subject of the hearing, including the circumstances surrounding the major disciplinary and including the allegations that Cynthia hasn't complied with what the state prison has required of her." He makes his case, carefully, deliberately, and persuasively.

The judge responds, still sounding confused. "We're here under my order that allowed her to come back in here. Now—"

The assistant county attorney interrupts, "But your honor, if I may . . ."
Cindy's lawyer interjects as well.

Finally the judge states, "Well let's go forward with the first part of it anyway, and that is whether or not she's complied with being of good behavior for certain."

Cindy's lawyer states, "Your Honor, I would submit a package of documents to the court." He says that copies have been given to the assistant county attorney. Then he describes the documents.

Sounding perplexed, the judge says, "Well, a lot of these are original. Do you—are these from the file? Do these have to be returned to the state prison's file?"

"They will not, Your Honor. I believe the originals, the certification of the originals accompanied the materials that were provided to me. The state prison made no request that we return them. Certainly I'd be happy to do that if the court thinks it's appropriate."

"Well, these are original aren't they? Most of them." He holds up a prison document and waves it in the air. "*That's* an original."

"Those documents were received by us prior to the issuance of the subpoena. The terms that we received, according to the subpoena, are those that immediately follow the certification here. These were provided in connection with this hearing before the subpoena."

The judge says, "Okay."

The document negotiations come to an end, and the lawyer, still outwardly calm, calls Cindy to the stand.

The lawyer asks some introductory questions and then asks Cindy where she was living prior to the time that she was arrested and went to prison.

"Where was I living? In the city." Cindy's voice is steady and she looks straight at her lawyer as she speaks.

"You were arrested in 1989 and at the time of your arrest you had in your possession some twenty bags of heroin?"

"Yes."

"Where did those come from?"

"Um—through the mail."

"And at the time that you picked them up, you knew that they were heroin?"

"Yes."

"And at the time that you picked them up and were arrested, would you say that you had a significant drug problem?"

"Yes, I did."

"Tell the court, if you would, what those bags were, how big they were, and what they contained."

"They're—they were just little tiny bags about maybe an inch, and there's just a little tiny line of drug in those little packages, but it all weighed up to one gram because after I got arrested they had to weigh it and—um—make sure it was heroin. But in all those twenty, it was just a gram."

"How much is a gram in lay terms?"

"About a teaspoonful. About a teaspoonful of sugar."

"At that time, how many bags of heroin were you doing a day?"

"Sometimes seven to twelve. Some days I'd do ten to fifteen or fourteen. I mean it would all depend on how it was."

"So that twenty bags represented a couple of days worth of consumption for you?"

"Yes."

"Were you selling drugs then?"

"No, I was not."

"Were those bags for your personal use?"

"Yes."

"How long have you had a drug problem, Cindy?"

"Objection!" The assistant stands up. "Your Honor, we've heard all this at the original sentencing hearing." The assistant requests that the questioning be limited to the period of time that Cindy has spent in prison.

Cindy's lawyer responds that he is simply offering a foundational background.

"All right. Go ahead."

Her lawyer asks Cindy about the time she spent in recovery after her arrest and before she went to prison.

"So that by the time you were sentenced you had been drug free for eight months?"

"Right."

He asks Cindy about alcohol. She says there were two occasions when she had a drink but that she was not drunk.

The lawyer asks her about the major write-up in prison.

"I guess I was very nervous while I was in there. I had been to medical and a girl that I know had a Darvocet. My roommate had seen me take that Darvocet and that night—she had a major write-up—so she figured if she told on me that it would lessen her time. But I only took one Darvocet. I know it was wrong and I know that I shouldn't. But I did not get locked up."

"Objection!" The assistant is standing again. "Your Honor, hearsay."

The judge is quick. "Overruled."

Cindy finishes. "And I had lost twenty days good time."

The lawyer focuses on her punishment. "You were sentenced essentially to fifteen days suspended sentence, so that if you misbehaved in the one hundred and twenty days, you would get fifteen days in the lock-up."

"Right. Yes."

"I take it that you never did that fifteen days in the lock-up?"

"No. I did not."

"The loss of good time was twenty days?"

"Right."

"It wasn't one hundred and twenty days?"

"No, it was not."

Next, the lawyer asks Cindy about the programs in which she has participated since she has been in prison. "Would you tell the court, please, what those programs were and how you took advantage of them."

"I've completed every single program in the prison except parenting. I have gone through a drug and alcohol program for a year on Tuesday nights. I've gone to an AA meeting every Thursday night. I went to domestic violence for seven months. Recently on Friday I've gone to an Indian spiritual renewal meeting where just a few of us sit around and talk."

The lawyer asks Cindy about the volunteer work she has done taking photographs of inmates and assisting the hairdresser who cuts their hair. Then he asks Cindy about her physical condition.

Cindy tells him about her headaches and the problems she has with TMJ. She says "My neck is messed up. My jaw's been broken twice and it's very messed up. I'm going to have to have a lot of dental work."

"How did it happen, Cindy, that your jaw was broken?"

"Well, my stepfather—"

"Objection! Relevancy!" The assistant is on her feet. "Again, Your Honor. This is going way beyond the scope of this hearing. We don't need to know her entire personal history to determine if she's met the requirements of the court order."

There is a sidebar conversation, and the judge tells Cindy's lawyer to go ahead.

"How was it that your jaw was broken, Cindy?"

"My stepfather broke it."

"How old were you then?"

"Sixteen."

The lawyer leads into the medications Cindy has been taking while in prison.

Cindy tells the court, "If I thought that a strong aspirin was going to, you know, lead me to drugs, I would not do it. I've been drug free for almost two years."

Her lawyer asks her about the prison drug and alcohol rehabilitation center.

"It is in the men's state prison and you still have the guards all around you. It would be just like prison."

The lawyer asks Cindy what programs she would attend if she is allowed to return to the community. Then deliberately, and in a quiet voice, he asks, "Do you feel that if you're allowed to live in the community and pursue the programs that you've described, you're going to be increasing the risk to yourself—that you're going to lapse back into addiction?"

"What?" To Cindy the possibility is unthinkable.

"What are the chances of your sliding back, Cindy, if you're released?"

"I will not slide back, because I never want to be in the hell again that I was in."

"Cindy, is there anything else that you want to tell the court this afternoon?"

"I just feel that I would not be a threat to society. When I was out there I was a threat to myself. I really feel I have come a very long way and that I've proven myself. I really feel that I can make it out there, and um I just think that I'm a good person."

It's the assistant county attorney's turn. She goes back to the documentation gathered before Cindy was incarcerated.

"I have a letter here dated February 22, 1990, which was admitted by your counsel during the sentencing hearing." Cindy looks nervous as the assistant holds up the letter. "It states that during the time that this person was talking to you that you did in fact relapse into heroin use."

"I most certainly did not."

The assistant reads from the letter. "'Her treatment of last summer was quite an intense one.' Um. 'Since that time, she has had only one relapse into heroin.' "

"But I—"

Cindy's lawyer interrupts to tell the judge that the letter was part of the package presented to the court.

The assistant county attorney pursues the question. "So you disagree with something that was made an exhibit into the court?"

"One relapse from where? From what?"

"According to this letter, from sometime between the summer of 1989 and February of 1990."

"As of the end of August I had not touched any."

"So summer of '89?"

"Um, yes, at the beginning. The end of May maybe."

The assistant county attorney questions Cindy about discharging herself from the hospital after twenty-two days of detoxification, and about her refusal to enter a Methadone clinic.

"And then at the time that you talked with a probation officer you were seeing a counselor. He left the agency so you stopped going to counseling because you couldn't open up to a new person."

"No." Cindy stumbles over her words. "I just stopped going to him." She is looking down at her hands. "I had been going to a lot of meetings. He left, and I—" Her voice is shaking. "It hurt that he left, yes." She looks up, "Back then it was very hard for me to talk to people so I just went to my meetings."

When the assistant county attorney finishes her cross-examination, Cindy's lawyer redirects, clarifying the methadone clinic situation.

The assistant recross-examines. "Your Honor, the state would ask if the court has a copy of the department of correction's—they call it a synopsis—which is sent down by the warden, concerning the recommendation of the warden?"

"I do."

"The state would also ask the court to review the probation report."

"Thank you."

Cindy's lawyer calls me to the stand to summarize my report that was used at Cindy's sentencing hearing, which is also a part of the documentation package. Then the assistant county attorney cross-examines me. "You were in here last March saying that Cindy shouldn't go to jail at all. Weren't you?"

"I said that I thought and I still believe that her recovery from drug addiction could be monitored through the programs described today."

"So your opinion as to what she needs hasn't changed over the last year?"

"I think my opinion has strengthened from watching her resolve."

"But you admit that prison has been good for her."

"I'm not sure that I have to admit that prison was good for her."

"She did the programs didn't she?" asks the assistant county attorney, taking precisely the opposite position to the one that she had taken with Cindy.

"Yes she attended programs."

"She has resolved to do well, hasn't she?"

"I can't say whether she has done better in prison than she would have done in the community. I am not sure that she has."

"But a year ago it was your opinion that prison would be detrimental to her. Isn't that correct?"

"I'm not sure I said that."

Cindy's lawyer objects.

"Overruled."

"You have to answer."

I feel trapped. If I say Cindy has not done well in prison, it will imply that she hasn't fulfilled all the requirements for her release. If I say she has done well, the response could be that she would be better off staying in prison so that she could enter the prison drug and rehabilitation facility.

"You have to answer the question."

"Repeat the question."

"The testimony you gave last year was such that you were informing the court that you thought jail would be detrimental to Cynthia."

"The emphasis of my testimony last year was that I believed and I still believe that it is in Cindy's best interests and in the interests of the community that she should be allowed to rehabilitate within the community."

"Based on the fact that jail would be detrimental to her."

"Based on the fact that I think her rehabilitation would be more long-term and have a lot more impact upon her life if she had the opportunity to reconstruct her life within the community—in ways that she would not be able to in prison."

"So you don't think that prison would be good for her?"

"I'm not sure that it's good or bad—I'm sorry. Good or bad doesn't make sense to me. I mean I can't imagine prison being good as opposed to bad. It's whether or not it's applicable to the person who is before the court."

Finally, the judge tells me to step down. I sit down feeling that I haven't helped Cindy and hoping that I haven't made her situation worse.

The assistant county attorney speaks to the judge. "Your Honor, first of all it is for the defendant to argue whether or not they have met the requirements of the court's order and have the court rule whether or not the requirements have been met. The state believes we must first address whether or not she's met the three requirements of the March 1990 order."

"Well, it's ludicrous!" The judge is speaking. "You know they haven't met one of them and they have no intention of doing that."

In his summation Cindy's lawyer includes every detail. He points out the inconsistencies in the prison report. He states that Cindy's been a model inmate for eleven months. He speaks of long-term drug rehabilitation in the prison facility and of Cindy's contacts in the community. He concludes, "I can argue until I'm as blue as my suit, Judge, but if you're not convinced from her testimony that she's ready to do this then I don't think you will be convinced, but I hope you have been."

The assistant county attorney stands. "Your Honor, the state objects to this motion." She lists the problems with Cindy's petition. "Her past shows her not doing anything this court would like her to do. She was supposed to be of good behavior for one year. She came up dirty." She reminds the judge that Cindy chose to go to an Indian spiritual meeting rather than an AA meeting. She ends her list with a statement of Cindy's medical needs. "Cindy needs some very intensive and in-depth rehabilitation counseling in a long-term program." I wonder whether the assistant county attorney is qualified to speak of Cindy's "medical needs." Then she speaks directly of the presentence report prepared by the probation department. "The probation report, Your Honor, states that at the time of the interview she was seeing a counselor. It goes on to state that she had no motivation to seek treatment until she was arrested. Well, Your Honor, we have a woman here who thinks that she is doctor as well as patient. This court did not invite her back. Since she has not met the requirements of this court back in March of 1990, her request for deferment should be denied, and she should have to finish her state prison sentence."

"All right." The judge gathers his papers. "I want to review a lot of these materials which were given me, as well as the file itself, and back to my notes of the sentencing hearing. All right." He is standing. He grabs a handful of pencils. "Thank you all."

Quickly, we all stand.

Cindy's lawyer says, "Thank you."

For a moment no one speaks.

Cindy's lawyer looks over to where the assistant county attorney is arranging papers on the table in front of her. "Is he coming back?" he asks.

"Not today," she replies, pushing papers into her briefcase.

The lawyer turns and speaks to Cindy. She has been expecting a decision and is looking confused. She nods as he speaks to her.

It's over.

CINDY WAITS IN PRISON

Cindy goes back to prison to await the judge's decision. We speak on the telephone about the hearing. We go over and over again the questions that were asked and the positions that were taken. We talk about the presentencing recommendations made in the probation report and of how this document has been used to make decisions about what happens to her life.

Cindy brings up the one hundred and twenty days. "I knew that would come up." She says her lawyer did a good job. Then her voice goes flat. "But he told me he still doesn't think I have much of a chance of getting out of here."

We are both quiet.

"Once you're in the system they won't let you go," Cindy says. "They *won't* let you go."

A few days later Cindy telephones to tell me that she has spoken with her lawyer. "He told me the judge has taken the matter under advisement and he will not make a decision until the probation officer presents his recommendations in a second report."

"That could take months," I say, then wish I hadn't. "I'm sorry, I'm not being helpful."

"I'm fucked." Cindy is in tears. "If they put me in here for another year, I won't do it. They can go and get fucked. Nothing is going to help. The decision was made before I left the courthouse."

Grasping at straws, I tell Cindy not to underestimate the ability of her lawyer. "He's still working on your release."

"I know," Cindy says. "I sent him some more money two days ago, but I owe him so much. I got another bill. He's charging me interest. I owe him almost two thousand dollars. I'm never going to be able to pay him."

I ask if her mother would help with the bill.

"No," Cindy says. "I can't ask her for any more money."

Cindy spends the month of May waiting for the probation officer to come to the prison to interview her. He doesn't come. The social worker no longer speaks to her. "She is still pissed with me," Cindy says. "It's because I wrote her that letter, the nasty gram."

It is June. Cindy continues to wait.

Late in the month, she learns that the probation officer has talked to the prison social worker.

"I'm fucked," she says. She is convinced that whatever the social worker has told the probation officer, it will only make her situation worse. We talk about the prison report. We talk about writing letters—to the probation officer, to the judge, Cindy writing, me writing. We discuss whether such letters would make matters worse.

Cindy says, "It can't get any worse."

I tell her I don't think I should write. We both know that my support of Cindy has irritated the assistant county attorney and that while I have maintained a working relationship with the lawyer representing her, I am persona non grata at the women's state prison and at the superior court.

"I just hope I haven't aggravated the situation." I say what I have said many times before.

"I wouldn't have got through the year without you. You listen to me. You don't treat me like a piece of shit. You make me feel good about myself."

Cindy and I have become friends, and there are times when I too feel disenfranchised. In some ways I am imprisoned with her, trapped in the documents that control her life, snared by questions about literacy and social justice, and violated by the corruption of those who control the text.

When our conversations become too intense, we joke about my compulsive work habits. Cindy tells me I need to take a day off.

I laugh and say, "We're all addicted to something."

"Yeah," she says. "You're an addict, just like me." We laugh.

"I've gotta go," I say.

"I'll call you tomorrow."

"Okay."

Cindy continues to worry about the second probation report. She knows it will weigh heavily with the judge. She decides to write a letter, not in anger or in haste, to make sure that the probation officer knows how hard she has been working to rehabilitate herself while she has been in prison. On June 24, 1991, she phones to read her letter to me. "Do you want to put it in your computer?"

Cindy reads and I type. She speaks slowly and clearly. " 'This letter comes in reference to myself, Cindy, and the decision that you will soon be making concerning my future. I am hopeful that you will soon come to a conclusion as to whether I shall stay in the prison system or if I may continue my rehabilitation through an outpatient program.

" 'It is my understanding that you spoke with [the prison social worker] concerning myself, Friday June 21. I realize the importance of speaking with all concerned parties before reaching a decision as to where I go from here because this decision is a very crucial factor in my life. I would like to make you aware of the relationship between my counselor and myself. This I believe is only fair.

" 'She was my counselor from March 1990 until December 1990. I decided to stop seeing her at that point because of a personality conflict between us, I believe that was detrimental to my recovery process. However, knowing the importance of my counseling in my life I immediately started counseling with [another prison counselor]. This has turned out to be one of the best things that could have happened during my incarceration. As I am sure you are aware, [the first counselor] wrote my recommendation for my court appearance in April of 1991. However, I believe that she neglected some very important information. Thankfully you are now aware of the various groups that I have enjoyed attending and satisfactorily completed. I would also like to remind you of my continuing effort to obtain my GED. There are approximately 104 women in this prison and unfortunately we have only two social workers. My question is how could they possibly know my growth when they have no time to stop and say hi while passing in the corridor.

" 'I have come a long way throughout this last fifteen months. I like the person that I have become. My request is that you would give me an opportunity to prove myself. I have many positive things that could happen for me if I was given a chance in an outpatient program. I have some wonderful people who are standing behind me a hundred percent of the way. These people will be there for me through thick and thin. I couldn't ask for any better support. Thank you for taking the time to read this letter. I am sure that your careful consideration in this matter will be the best for me. I am looking forward to seeing you soon.' "

"I think you've written a fine letter," I tell Cindy. "I don't think it will do any harm if you send it."

"It took so long. This is the third letter that I've written to him."

"Send it."

Two weeks later the probation officer interviews her. Cindy talks to him about the social worker's report, and she says that he was very nice to her. Nevertheless, Cindy says she knows that it doesn't matter what he said to her when he met with her at the prison—all that matters is what he will write for the judge.

"I'm worried about what he will write," she frets. "He seemed so nice, but that doesn't mean anything. If he writes a report like he did last time, I'll never get out of here."

On July 9, Cindy telephones and asks me if I will phone the probation department to see if the report has been written. "I can't wait much fuckin' longer."

I call. A clerk says the probation officer is not available. I ask about the report.

She sounds distant but not disinterested. "I don't know if a decision has been made yet. I don't believe so."

Cindy calls me late in the afternoon of the same day. I read her the notes I made of my conversation with the probation office clerk.

"What does she mean? What decision?"

"I guess about what kind of recommendation to make to the judge."

It is almost four months since Cindy's petition for her sentence to be reduced.

THE COURT ORDER IS ISSUED

On Wednesday, September 11, 1991, Cindy is summoned back to the superior court to hear the judge's decision. Before the hearing she will be allowed to read the probation report which contained the references to the original presentence report. Afraid that she will be too nervous to understand what she is reading, she plans to copy the sections that appear important. At the superior courthouse she asks for some paper and a pencil, and although questions are raised, they are provided. She is allowed to take them with her into the holding tank in which she is closeted with the text.

Cindy looks for inaccuracies, replicates sections verbatim, searches for references to the prison report that represented her so inaccurately, and hastily writes down the probation officer's recommendations, which he endorses by referring to the prison report:

> In review, one has an original offense which was serious in nature. Multiple packets of heroin were confiscated and there remains a credibility issue as to whether they were for personal consumption or whether they were for other purposes. Prior to her commitment to the state prison the defendant had an extensive substance history that traced back to age thirteen. It also appeared that the defendant did not seek treatment until the arrest for possession of heroin. Even this effort was self-defined with the defendant walking out of the treatment settings whenever she felt like it. In the end she felt if she could just attend Narcotics Anonymous daily and go to some counseling she could address her problem of abuse.

> The second area of note is that this is also the recommendation of the women's state prison. Both her counselor and the warden recommend the prison drug rehab. Credibility must be given to these sources as they see relapses of people not ready for the open community.

> The prison rehab is a transitional concept with a halfway house. It is a therapeutic setting with a greater freedom granted the inmate. It is a critical stage of working one's way back to the opportunity of community treat-

ment. Nineteen years of addiction is not balanced out with one and a half years of prison. The most common finding by the commission of corrections is that people are being returned to the prison at a high rate because the foundation of substance treatment has not been durable.

Finally, the probation department will be the department to take responsibility for the defendant. This is of note as if there is regression by the defendant in the open community it will be the probation officer who is called on to act. The agency that takes responsibility for the offender in the open community should have confidence that a durable program of treatment has been completed. Successful completion of the prison drug rehab would be a prerequisite to such confidence.

Her time is up. Cindy folds the yellow sheets on which she has been writing and is taken from the room. She does not expect the judge to rule in her favor. In his report the probation officer supported the position of the social worker and the warden at the women's state prison.

Cindy's mother and two of her sisters are in the courtroom. Also present is the man with whom she is going to live if she is released.

I sit with Cindy's family.

Court has become routine. We wait for the judge, we are subdued, our expectations are low, we try not to anticipate. We breathe shallow breaths, stand automatically as the judge enters, and look down as if in prayer.

Perhaps those who pray *are* praying.

The lawyer representing Cindy stands. "By way of updating the court," he tells the judge that Cindy has completed her GED. He talks about her work program and then says that "there have been no disciplinary actions since April 1990."

He says the probationary report is "generally accurate."

The assistant county attorney objects.

There is a to and fro, after which the judge overrules.

The lawyer persists. "We have some concern." He focuses on the section of the report that states that Cindy received the heroin with intent to sell.

"I know what she pleaded to." The judge sounds irritated. "I've been around a long time."

Cindy's lawyer questions whether or not there was any evidence to support the assumption that Cindy was possibly selling. He then turns his attention to another section of the report. " 'Nineteen and a half years of substance abuse is not balanced by one and a half years of prison.' "

He looks up, pauses. "I'm troubled by the implication that she should spend longer in prison because of the years of her substance abuse."

He names the people who are ready to support Cindy, her mother, the man with whom she is going to live, who is in the court ready to testify on her behalf. "She has never had the kind of support systems that she has at this time. The evidence that we present suggests that now is the best time for her to be released."

The assistant county attorney raises the state's concern about Cindy's ability to make decisions about what kind of rehabilitation program she needs. She refers to the length of time Cindy has been an addict and the length of time she has been in prison.

"To cut her loose now is to give her only half of what she needs." The assistant talks about the issues of medication.

The judge tells the assistant county attorney that medication is not the basis on which he is going to make his decision. "There is no cure for drug addiction or alcoholism." He talks about the presentencing report. "Where would we have been if I had not done what I did?" he asks. Then he looks straight at Cindy. "I'm taking a very serious gamble. I've gone over your background many, many times and I'm trying to weigh one thing against another. I characterize your life as disastrous. I have a fear that if you remain in prison any longer you may take one step forward and two back." We wait. "I'm going to grant your motion."

Speaking directly at Cindy, he tells her that if she violates her probation he will return her to prison for the maximum sentence. "Returned to prison for the purpose of being released."

Cindy's court appearance ends when the judge stops speaking. Against the recommendations of the probation officer, the social worker, and warden at the women's state prison, the judge orders Cindy's release from prison.

In a telephone conversation following Cindy's release I talk with the lawyer who Cindy had retained to represent her. We talk about her return to the community. I tell him I will see Cindy on a regular basis and I thank him for helping her. He dismisses my thanks. "I did my homework, that's all."

Afterward I think about what he said. He was right. He did do his homework. I remember my conversations with Cindy when she talked about trying to pay for a private lawyer because—as she put it—with a public defender she'd be dead.

Curious about the differences between public defenders and private lawyers I telephone the public defenders' office at the state capital, and I ask how many cases a public defender might have at any one time. At first, the lawyer with whom I speak is evasive. Then he tells me that it is not uncommon for a public defender to be working on one hundred cases, and at times as many as one hundred and fifty cases. But he explains that the numbers are deceptive. Many lawyers have large case loads. What distinguishes public defenders from private for-profit lawyers is the amount of activity on individual cases. Usually, public defenders carry a much heavier load of *active* cases.

Rushed. At the first court hearing, the public defender who represented Cindy read documents only when she was going into court. My first meeting with her was when she put me on the stand to testify. Cindy didn't testify. The public defender never asked her about the twenty bags of heroin. It was not made clear that the amount of heroin that Cindy received through the mail was the equivalent of one packet of artificial sweetener, that Cindy sometimes used fifteen bags a day, and that at most, at *most*, the heroin she received through the mail would last her only two days. Cindy was not questioned about how she became an addict, nor about the abuse she suffered as a child. She was not asked about her medical needs. The public defender allowed the probation officer's presentencing report to shape the course of events. It was his decision—as the clerk put it—that Cindy should be incarcerated for three and a half to seven years.

At the second hearing, the lawyer representing Cindy quickly established that the twenty bags of heroin weighed no more than a gram of artificial sweetener, was only enough to maintain Cindy's habit for a couple of days. Before going to court, he had time to sift through the documentation, to talk with potential witnesses, to obtain letters and affidavits, to build his case methodically. In court, he was able to provide alternate interpretations of Cindy's heroin addiction. He questioned the official story—possession with intent to sell—put forth in the probationary report and upheld by the state. He deliberately interjected into the bureaucratic version of Cindy's life critical information that the probation officer and the medical social worker at the prison chose to exclude. Thus, Cindy's lawyer was able to *interrupt the official text.*

For a brief time Cindy's political status changed. Hiring a lawyer to represent her brought her into the "mainstream" of American society. Her defense was a financial transaction—her money for his legal representation. His time and the time of the paralegal secretary who worked for him were booked to her case and Cindy was billed for the services that she received. At first she paid money off the bills as they were sent to her, but as the money that she owed mounted up and interest charges were added she stopped paying. The small amount of money that she had would not pay even the interest.

For years the bills still came, with the added interest amounting to more than the money for the time that the lawyer spent on the case. Cindy was destitute; she couldn't pay the money she owed. Finally, one day when I was copying documents at the lawyer's office, we talked about the bills that Cindy was still receiving; the lawyer said he would talk to accounting. Recently when I visited Cindy with the manuscript of this book, I asked her if she was still getting bills. "No," she said, smiling. "They finally stopped."

CINDY RETURNS TO THE COMMUNITY—OR DOES SHE?

Wednesday, September 18. Cindy telephones me in the evening after she is released from the women's state prison. We talk for a while about the hearing. Even though we had joked that the judge was going to suspend her sentence—"why else would he bring you back to the superior court?"—it was still a surprise. She sounds happy but scared. "I feel weird. I'm really confused and I keep hyperventilating. It's going to be hard for me, Denny. I hate it when I get these feelings. It's not that I am going to use. It's just that I am scared. I feel good about living in a small town. I really want this to work because i don't want to go back to prison."

A small town? I'm confused. I thought Cindy was going to live in the city. The man she's going to be living with went to AA and NA meetings in the city—that's where she met him. I assumed that he lived there. Cindy tells me that he's moved to a much smaller town. I ask her how she is going to get to meetings.

"He's going to come back here after work and he'll drive me."

"How are you going to get to morning meetings?"

"Someone will have to drive me." After a hesitation she adds, "I'll be okay if I can get to a meeting with him in the evening."

Cindy has not spent much time with this man up to now, just the few hours a week that he spent visiting her in prison. I worry about her beginning a new relationship at the same time as she adjusts to her newfound freedom. I worry even more when I realize it will not be easy for her to reestablish herself as a member of the recovery community in the city.

I say nothing. All I can do is be supportive. We talk on the phone on Thursday and again on Friday. I ask Cindy if she would like to have lunch. She reminds me that she doesn't have a car.

"I could come and pick you up."

"Okay."

"We could go to the steakhouse. I've eaten there before. They used to have good food."

She gives me directions to the apartment complex where she is living, and as she speaks I realize Cindy is living several miles out of the town on a lonely country road. She is isolated. She cannot walk into the town. Without a car, she will have to stay in the apartment when her friend goes to work.

I arrive at his apartment a few minutes after 12:30. Cindy is sitting on the grass watching for me. She is wearing a pink blouse and a navy cardigan. She runs over to the car and opens the passenger-side door.

"Hi! Just a minute."

She drops her purse on the seat and goes back to lock the apartment door. When she gets in the car she laughs and says she forgot to ask me what kind of car I'd be driving. "I've been watching all the cars that go by wondering which one was yours!"

We talk on the way to the restaurant. I wonder if this is too soon to go out to lunch. "Do you need more time to yourself?"

"I'm fine," Cindy says, "because I know you. I get nervous around people I don't know. I've been busy going through all of my belongings." She laughs, "None of my jeans fit. I got so fat while I was in prison."

At the restaurant we sit in the smoking section and Cindy lights a cigarette. The waitress comes up and asks us if we want cocktails. She says the special drink of the day is a shrimp bloody Mary.

We laugh. I ask for water and Cindy asks for a ginger ale. Over lunch is just the talk of friends. We discuss our families, our medical problems, Clarence Thomas, and abortion.

Cindy is calm and smiling. She says she was nervous when I first picked her up but she feels all right now. Her eyes are shining and she looks healthy. She talks about the prison and the probation officer's report. She tells me about the AA meeting she attended the previous evening, and expresses regret that it was not in the city. After she mentions heroin, she raises her hand quickly and covers her mouth. She leans forward and whispers the word so that no one else will hear. She talks about her addiction and of how determined she is to overcome it. "I think about it a lot," she says. "But I am not going to use."

Cindy tells me that she wants to keep a journal, so as we are leaving the restaurant I ask her if she would like to go and buy a notebook. She tells me that she has one that she was writing in before she was incarcerated, but that she would like to buy a toilet plunger. This makes us laugh, and we leave the restaurant giggling like schoolgirls.

There is a hardware store up the street. As we walk Cindy tells me she has to be careful because she knows people who have been sent back to jail for what she calls "little things." "I can't do anything wrong," she says as we reach the store and open the big door. Inside all we see is a wide staircase and mail boxes on the wall. We quickly realize this is the entrance to the apartments above the old hardware store.

"Breaking and entering," I whisper as we retreat laughing into the street.

We find the door to the hardware store and go in to look for toilet plungers. They are hanging in a row, attached to the ceiling by a plastic rope. Cindy inspects them and chooses one. She takes it off the rope and holds it up to have a closer look. I start to laugh.

"Possession of an illegal weapon," I say.

Cindy laughs and holds it like a club. Then, she pays for the plunger and we leave the store.

As we walk across the street to my car we talk about meeting for coffee or lunch the following week. On the drive back to the apartment we discuss the possibilities of Cindy's helping me with my literacy research. She tells me that she wants to work with children who are facing problems similar to her daughter's. The conversation becomes serious. It is clear from what she says that Cindy is still tormented by what happened to her daughter. She tells me again that she has not only messed up her own life but the life of her little girl as well.

But by the time we reach the apartment complex we are joking again. Cindy says she is going to have to climb in through the bedroom window.

"Why?"

"I locked myself out." She laughs. "I don't have a key."

"He didn't give you a key?"

"No."

It's not funny but I start laughing too.

"Breaking and entering!" Cindy says as she tries to look serious.

"I'd better stay in case someone thinks you really are trying to rob the place."

The window that Cindy is trying to climb through is quite high up and she has to go through the bushes to get to it. She tries to raise the screen and when it looks as if she isn't going to be able to, she grumbles, "I should have left the door unlocked." The screen begins to move and she is able to push it up.

Cindy tries to lift herself up, first by jumping and then by taking her weight on her hands and finding footholds for her feet against the side of the building.

Cindy is too big for me to lift and so I stand and watch. "It's a good job the probation officer can't see you now!" I tell her.

Cindy drops to the ground. "I need something to stand on." She goes over to where some car tires are stacked at the edge of the parking lot, rolls one over to the window, puts it on end against the building, and climbs on top of it.

"Have you done this before?" I ask, joking.

"Yes," she says, as she lifts her right leg through the window. "But only when I've been locked out."

"I wish I had a camera."

Cindy turns, poses for my imaginary camera, then she gets her body through the window and pulls in her left leg. Seconds later she comes out of the apartment door to say good-bye.

I leave feeling good about her. As I drive away she looks happy, and I wonder what her life would have been like if her childhood had been different. What would have happened to her if the court had allowed her to remain in the city to recover from her drug addiction—would she have made it? Will she make it now? I know it is possible for Cindy to live drug free, but I am uneasy. She is isolated, alone all day, and totally reliant on her friend to drive her to meetings.

On Thursday, September 26, I again drive over to meet Cindy. She invites me into the tiny, two-room apartment. She speaks quietly as she shows me around. She points at her friend's belongings and expresses concern that he has a gun. She says she is worried that living in a place where there are firearms is a violation of her probation. She says she has asked her friend to get rid of it and that he has agreed.

From the way that Cindy speaks and behaves it is clear that she is living in some other person's space. She may have been released from prison, but she still does not have a place that she can call home.

Cindy gives me the yellow notepaper on which she copied sections of the probation report at the courthouse before being released by the judge. "Here, you'll need these for your research." At the time they do not seem important. I stuff them in my pocket. Cindy tells me that she is lonely and that she feels depressed. She has gotten up early a couple of times and her friend has given her a lift to her sponsor's house in the city before he goes to work. "Then I have to stay there all day. I get to a morning meeting, though, so that's good."

We drive into a nearby pizza place for coffee. Cindy asks if I will go with her to cash a check. I take her to a branch of my bank where the teller asks if I will countersign Cindy's check, which is from the state prison. As I sign it, I joke that if it bounces the prison director might end up in his own prison.

Outside the bank Cindy says, "I can walk from here."

"Where are you going?"

"Just up the road."

Immediately I know where she is going. I panic. No longer a researcher, I am only her friend. "You can't go back there."

"Why? I'm not going to get any drugs."

"No!"

"I need to see a doctor. My Elavil is running out. What am I supposed to do? I want to find out what is wrong with me."

"It's an old pattern. All he'll do is give you pills. You can't go back to him. Your lawyer would have a fit. So would the probation officer."

"But why can't I go? I'm not after drugs. I just need to get some more Elavil. I'm depressed. I need something for depression otherwise I might go back out."

"No."

Cindy is angry. She is six inches taller and she glares down at me. For a moment neither of us moves.

"How are you going to get home?"

Cindy says her friend is going to pick her up. I tell her I'll wait until he arrives. Suddenly she smiles. "You're lucky I didn't hit you." I grin back, but we are both close to tears.

"I'll get you an appointment with a doctor that I've seen in the city," I tell her. "I think he's okay."

"Will you talk with him first? Explain the situation?"

We sit in my car and wait for her friend.

"You won't say anything to him will you?"

"No. Of course not."

It's a while before he arrives. I go over with Cindy to say hello. I ask about his day.

"They're always hard," he says.

A few minutes later I am in my car on my way home. In the rearview mirror I watch Cindy and her friend drive off in the opposite direction. I hope she doesn't persuade him to turn around and go back to the doctor's office.

When I get home I telephone Cindy. "Are you all right?"

"Yes, I'm okay," she says, "and you were right, but I went to him for such a long time and he knows me. Will you make an appointment with this other doctor?"

The next morning I telephone the doctor. I tell him about Cindy and he says that it is important for her to have consistent care. I tell him that if he will take her as a patient, she will see him on a regular basis.

Cindy left her leather jacket in my car and so later I return it to her. She tells me that she is having "a good day."

We talk about yesterday.

"I just wanted to say fuck you."

"But you didn't."

"It was hard. In the past I would have told you that nobody tells me what to do."

"You did okay." Smiling I continue, "But I am not sure what I would have done if you had decided to go and see him anyway." I laugh. "Trip you up maybe?"

Cindy gives me a hug. "Sometimes I need a kick in the pants."

I tell her about my conversation with the doctor in the city. "I've explained that you have difficulty taking prescription drugs, and we talked about you taking Elavil and he said that was not a drug that caused patients to become addicted."

"Will you come with me when I go?"

"Sure."

I arrange to pick her up the following week.

CINDY IS REFUSED SERVICES BY WELFARE AGENCIES AND MEDICAL INSTITUTIONS

At the beginning of the next week Cindy tries to sign up for welfare so that she can have some money of her own, but because she is living with her friend, she is not eligible. She tries to apply for Medicaid but she does not qualify. Then she telephones the mental health facility in the city and finds out that the regulations have changed. There is now a $25 minimum fee.

Cindy calls me. She tells me that she doesn't want her friend's money. "He's earning minimum wage." Her voice is flat. "He doesn't have any money to give me. He's still paying off his bike. How can I ask him for money?"

I telephone the mental health office myself. The person who answers the telephone is friendly but unhelpful. The only clients who are not charged are those who are certified by the federal government. "What do you mean by *certified*?" I ask.

"Clients have to be chronically mentally ill before they can be certified, and then a counselor will see them without charge."

I relay the message. "You'd have to be suffering from schizophrenia or something."

"What am I going to do? Mental health won't see me so I can't work things out with a therapist, I'm not eligible for Medicaid so I can't find out why I get these terrible migraine headaches, and I can't get welfare to pay for a therapist or a doctor because I am living with someone who is making money—if you can call it money."

I telephone the lawyer who represented Cindy.

"The courts don't care, Denny. She said she could recover from drug addiction in the community and so now that's what she has got to do."

I ask him whether I should telephone the probation department and tell them that she can't get assistance.

He says no, sounding irritated with me. He makes me feel naive, as if I should know better, as if Cindy is using me.

"She can't do this on her own," I tell him.

"The probation department is only responsible for making sure that she remains drug free."

"How can she do that if no one will help her?"

"She has to take responsibility."

"So do we."

Later in the week I pick up Cindy and together we drive into the city so that she can see the doctor with whom I have made an appointment.

"Do you have insurance?" the receptionist asks.

"No."

"Medicaid?"

I interject. "I'm going to pay for this visit."

Cindy is given a clipboard with new-patient forms. She writes quickly, occasionally asks me how to spell a word, and takes the forms back to receptionist when she is done.

We wait.

After about fifteen minutes a nurse calls Cindy's name.

Cindy looks at me nervously. "Come with me?"

"Sure."

Cindy follows the nurse along a corridor into one of the examining rooms and I follow Cindy.

Again we wait. After a while the doctor knocks and enters. He is of average height, middle-aged, and slightly out of shape. Cindy answers his questions without hiding that she has just been released from prison and without downplaying the seriousness of her addiction.

He looks in her eyes, down her throat, and in her ears. Then he examines her head and her neck. He says that extensive tests will need to be conducted before he can treat her for the conditions from which she says she suffers. He mentions CAT scans and other tests. "It will cost at least five hundred dollars."

Cindy says she doesn't have any money to pay for the tests. The doctor asks her about Medicaid. Cindy tells him she isn't eligible.

The visit is over. He opens the door and starts to leave the examining room. Angry at the way in which he has treated Cindy, I tell him that I am going to pay for this office visit. The doctor turns. He looks at Cindy. "In my experience," he says, "there are two types of people. Those who are not eligible for services who go out and get a job, and those who are not eligible and who do nothing but complain about it." Cindy is still sitting on the examining table. She looks angry, embarrassed, and ashamed. "If I was you I'd go out and get a job," the doctor tells Cindy from the corridor. He has already left the room.

CINDY IS UNABLE TO REESTABLISH HER CONNECTION WITH MEMBERS OF THE RECOVERING COMMUNITY

Isolated, Cindy is totally reliant on her friend. She does have a small amount of money left, and so she is able to pay for some of the food that she eats, but she cannot go to any daytime AA meetings, and she has to wait until her friend comes home from work to go to AA in the evening. In the late afternoon she begins cooking his evening meal and when he has eaten supper she travels with him on his motorbike to different meetings around the state. She tries to persuade him to take her to recovery meetings in the city so she can see the friends she made before she was sent to prison, but he does not like attending meetings in the same place on a regular basis. He likes traveling, visiting new towns, listening to new speakers and attending different meetings—Big Book, twelve step, AA, NA, and CA.

On the telephone Cindy sounds depressed. She gets upset. "I hate crying. You must get fed up with listening to me. All I do is complain." Living in such a remote place she has to rely totally on other people. "I hate it here. Hate it. I might just as well be back in prison. I can't go anywhere unless I ask someone to take me."

One morning Cindy telephones to tell me that the day before she went to the city. She got up early and got dropped off at her sponsor's house before her friend went to work. "I waited until the drop-in center opened at ten o'-clock and then I spent the day there." Cindy is upbeat. "I saw lots of people that I know." Working at the drop-in center for recovering drug addicts is a part of the recovery program that she agreed to follow when she was released from prison.

"Are you going to volunteer?" I ask.

"I want to but they won't put me on the schedule until I can get in there on a regular basis."

Cindy says maybe she can get her friend to move to the city. "That way I can get to meetings at the hospital, help out at the drop-in center, and work with you on your literacy project."

Often when I talk with Cindy on the telephone she cries. She tells me she needs to see a psychiatrist, she needs to talk to someone she can trust about the thoughts that kept filling her head. She says she is having flashbacks, that she keeps thinking about events she would rather forget. "When I start thinking, I feel like such a bad person." Cindy's voice is low and she speaks slowly as she tries to explain. "I need to talk with a counselor, someone who'll agree not to call the probation department and tell them I'm thinking about using drugs. The thoughts are so strong but it's not as if I'm going to use."

CINDY MOVES

At the end of October, Cindy tells me that she and her friend are moving to the city. She sounds happy. "I can't wait to get out of this place." The apartment she's found is near the hospital and she will be able to go to a meeting every morning.

On November 1, Cindy moves into a dilapidated turn-of-the-century house in an old part of the city. Her apartment is on the second floor. There are no lights on the stairs, and when I knock there is no answer. I am on my way down the stairs when Cindy opens the door. She smiles and invites me in.

The apartment door opens into a big kitchen with cupboards and counters on two sides. Half-unpacked boxes fill the kitchen floor. Cindy waves her hand at the boxes and tells me she is still unpacking. She walks slowly through an open doorway into the living room. She sits down on the couch and I sit in an easy chair.

"I haven't spoken to anyone," she says. "I'm not feeling well. All I do is sleep." There are more unpacked boxes on the floor in the living room. "I was going to unpack these today but I'm so tired all I've done is lie down on the couch." She says that she has had a migraine headache for days, that she wakes up in the morning with her head pounding and that it gets worse during the day. She is having difficulty focusing her eyes, and she can't read anything.

"Why don't you go to the walk-in clinic at the hospital?" I suggest encouragingly. "They can't turn you away."

Cindy raises her eyebrows and pulls a face as if I've lost touch with reality. I encourage her to apply for Medicaid, even though she was told that she is not eligible. Our conversation turns to mental health, and once again Cindy tells me that she needs to talk with someone "who is neutral." Her eyes are dull. She gets up and goes in the bedroom to get some aspirin. When she comes back she is crying.

"I don't want to think about the things that keep coming in my head." She looks at me. Wet mascara is running down her face. "I'm so lonely. I feel all alone. I can't get anything done. I don't have any energy. All I do is sleep."

A week later I am operated on for thyroid cancer, and then I am unable to drive for a month because of an old back injury that takes advantage of my lack of exercise when I am recuperating.

Just before Thanksgiving Cindy tells me on the telephone that she feels as if she is still in prison. She is spending more and more time just sleeping. All she wants to do is forget what is happening to her. She talks about needing medical treatment because she is in constant pain. She says her headaches are causing muscle spasms in her back and neck. "Mental health won't see me. So that puts me in violation of my probation agreement. I'm supposed to see a psychiatrist on a regular basis."

I suggest that she talk to her probation officer. Cindy's response reminds me of what the lawyer said.

"They don't want to know!" She speaks as if she doesn't believe my stupidity. "And I can't tell them! I don't want to go back to prison!"

I telephone mental health. Again I am told that "chronically mentally ill" are the only ones who are provided with free services—their visits are paid for with federal subsidies. The person I talk with says Cindy can come in and talk to a psychologist on an emergency basis but that if she wants to go on a regular basis she has to pay.

On November 25, Cindy phones. "I went down to the city to see if they would pay for a place for me to live. Welfare won't help me. I took off. I had such a bad attitude I was ready to use."

"I think you'd have to move out first and then go to the welfare office. If you don't have a place to live they are supposed to help you find emergency shelter—but there are no guarantees."

"Forget that." Cindy changes the subject. "I've been seeing a psychologist. I've got five emergency visits." She accentuates the e in emergency, as it seems to be the word of the moment. I laugh, sharing the joke. Cindy speaks seriously. "In a couple of weeks I'm going to try and get a part-time job. I've been so damn lazy and I've got to stop it."

A few days later Cindy tells me that the psychologist at mental health wanted her to sign a release so that he can talk to her probation officer. Cindy refused. "How can I talk to him if he can tell my probation officer everything I say?" Cindy stops going to mental health.

CINDY CONTINUES TO WORK ON HER RECOVERY FROM HEROIN ADDICTION

By December, I am back on my feet and I visit Cindy. Even though she is chronically depressed, she continues to struggle to reestablish her life in the community. When she was in prison, she often talked about helping me with the literacy project on which I was working, and her participation in the project is one of the requirements of the community program that we developed when she was released from prison. I ask Cindy if she would like to help Laurie, whom you met briefly in the introduction to this book. "She is studying for her GED. You could help her."

Cindy knows Laurie because Laurie's boyfriend is in recovery, but she doesn't know that Laurie has had cancer and is still sick. "She had massive doses of radiation for cervical cancer," I explain. The radiation caused serious damage to Laurie's bowels and bladder. "She rarely leaves her house. She is in almost constant pain because of the effects that the radiation had on her body."

Laurie is struggling like Cindy. Working for a GED is one of the stipulations that she has to fulfill if welfare is going to continue providing her with financial support. But Laurie is finding it hard to attend classes because she is physically unable to sit for extended periods of time and she is embarrassed because she needs to make frequent visits to the bathroom.

"I don't know if I can help her." Cindy sounds doubtful.

I tell Cindy how nervous Laurie was when she first worked with me. "She's going to be just as nervous as you."

"But I've never taught anybody before."

"I know, but you have studied for the GED. You can show her how you did that."

Cindy works with Laurie. She helps her with the workbook exercises that are a part of a GED correspondence course that Laurie is taking. When Cindy visits Laurie, they work together on a workbook exercise that focuses on parenting. Laurie has to write about ways to provide stimulation for a very young child. Laurie tells Cindy that she used to give her children pots and pans to play with when they were very young. Cindy encourages Laurie to write about that, so Laurie writes and Cindy helps her by spelling out the words that Laurie is writing.

"You could have him in the kitchen with you when you are cooking?" Laurie asks, waiting for approval from Cindy.

"Put that then," Cindy responds. "Yeah, because that would stimulate his sense of smell." Again Cindy spells words as Laurie writes. Then, sounding worried, Cindy says, "I have no idea how to spell kitchen. Shit."

Laurie laughs. Cindy laughs with her.

"It's gotta be—" Cindy is thumbing through the pages looking in the workbook for the word. "Okay this is it." She points to the workbook word. The two women laugh. Laurie starts to copy the word. Cindy spells it as Laurie writes, "K-i-t-c-h-e-n."

Cindy reads the next exercise. Laurie joins in. Together they read and Laurie writes. Cindy tells Laurie that the answers are usually somewhere in the workbook, that you just have to read what is written to find out what you are supposed to write. Smoking each other's cigarettes, they work together for almost two hours, and then Cindy leaves. "I have to get ready for a meeting," she tells Laurie. She looks at the clock. "I'm late. Do you want me to come back?"

"Sure," Laurie says. "I hate doing this stuff on my own."

"Okay. I'll be back next week."

The next week Laurie is sick. She is bleeding from radiation cystitis and is unable to work with Cindy. It is almost a month before she feels better, and by the time Laurie is well enough to work with Cindy, Cindy is no longer able to work with her.

CINDY IS PRESCRIBED LARGE DOSES OF PRESCRIPTION DRUGS BY THE DOCTOR WHO SUPPLIED HER WITH DRUGS BEFORE SHE WAS SENT TO PRISON

Cindy is taking pills. Unable to find a doctor who will treat her without insurance or Medicaid, Cindy gets pills from the doctor who supplied her with prescription drugs before she was incarcerated. She says she can handle it, that she has been clean for almost three years. I tell her that I am worried about her.

"I'll be okay, Denny," she reassures me. "I'll be okay."

"One painkiller and you'll be hooked."

"I won't take any painkillers."

In January 1992, the drop-in center for recovering drug addicts closes. Cindy spends more and more time on her own. The man with whom she is living is angry with her for taking pills and their relationship is deteriorating. Cindy rationalizes the friction between them—he is fed up with her always being sick. Her friend calls me and tells me he can no longer help her. He is worried about his own sobriety. He says he can't be around Cindy if she continues taking pills.

In a very short time, Cindy is using the medications that the doctor is supplying her with as if she were using street drugs. Much later I learn that at the time of which I am writing she was taking sixty Flexeril a day. Did she know that Flexeril is a synthetic narcotic that contains opioids?

"No," she says. "I just knew that if I took enough it would relax me like heroin, but I didn't know it was the same kind of drug as heroin."

CINDY IS HURT WHEN SHE JUMPS OUT OF A MOVING CAR

Following a fight with the man with whom she has been living, Cindy opens the door of a car in which she is a passenger and tries to get out while the car is moving. Her head hits the road and she sustains a concussion. She is taken to the emergency room, treated, and released.

I know nothing about the accident. I am traveling, attending spring conferences, talking about literacy, out of touch—like most academics—with the people whose lives I am supposed to care about. When I return I telephone Cindy but no one picks up the phone. I keep calling. Several days pass. No answer.

I call a friend in the city who goes to AA. He tells me that Cindy was in an accident, that she has left the man with whom she's been living, and that she has moved in with the man with whom she lived before she was sent to jail.

I get a call from the man Cindy lived with when she was released from prison. "She's using. I had to cut her loose." He sounds upset and angry. "She's taken a turn for the worse. She's certainly using something. She jumped out of a van at thirty miles an hour. She was all beaten up and she ended up in the hospital." He talks about the hospital. "They're cutting her loose and I'm saying, the girl is sick, give her a bed." Cindy is seeing the doctor who supplies her with drugs. She left some prescription containers behind in the apartment when she left. He reads the names of the drugs on each container, spells the name, gives the date when the drug was prescribed, and then names the doctor, spitting out his name in disgust or exasperation. "Cephalexin, Amitriptylene." He stops. "I came in unexpected the other day. She had a pile of pills on the bed. There were at least six different kinds. Naprosyn. Anaprox. Fioicet. Butalbital. She's been higher than a kite and everybody at the hospital knew but nobody would do anything to help her."

Anxious, I continue to try to find Cindy. Eventually I get the telephone number of the man with whom she is now living. I hardly recognize her voice. She speaks slowly, slurring her words.

"I've missed you. I knew you were at a conference so I didn't call."

"What's happened to you?"

"I've been sick. I've seen a neurologist. I've been having tests. This is terrible. I'm in such pain. I keep falling down. I can't get out of bed in the morning. It's too hard."

"How many painkillers are you taking?"

"None. None at all. I'm staying away from them. I've been to the hospital three times this week. I pleaded with them to admit me, and they said it's not bad enough. My neck hurts so much. I'm in so much pain. I can't handle it. This has nothing to do with drugs. I haven't been taking them. It's physical. I've been bleeding from my rectum. One doctor gave me painkillers and I said, I don't want those things. I can't take them."

There is a loud noise. Cindy has dropped the telephone. She picks it up and continues speaking. "I'm real confused. I think it's from the concussion. I was knocked unconscious. It's affecting my thinking. I hate it. I feel like a jerk. I hate going out in case I fall down."

Again Cindy drops the phone.

"Can I do anything?" We both know that there is nothing I can do. If I try to get her into a rehab she'll be sent back to jail.

"There's nothing anyone can do. I have to see my probation officer every week now."

Cindy tells me that the man she was living with before the accident telephoned the probation department. "He really screwed me. I talked with him on the phone and I asked him, 'Why did you do this to me?' It doesn't make any sense. The only thing I can think is that he read my journal." Cindy is crying. "He had no right reading all my private thoughts. They aren't very pretty."

I ask Cindy if I can go with her to mental health.

"No. I wanted to talk to a counselor but mental health wanted to talk to my probation officer. He must have said something because when I saw my probation officer he said, 'Well if you have nothing to hide what will it matter?'"

Cindy's probation officer has told her she can't live with the man who took her in after the accident, the man with whom she lived before she went to prison. She is sobbing. It is difficult to understand what she is saying.

"I have nobody. Nobody." Again she drops the phone. "I have to get out of here. I have two weeks to get out of here. It's like being in prison. I feel I'm back in prison. It's been six months and nothing's different. I'm just as miserable. Not one good thing has happened."

I call Cindy again the following evening. She tells me she has been back to the hospital. "They think I might have a slipped disk. I can't walk. I can't get off the toilet. I'm fucked." Her probation officer is insisting that she move out of the trailer even though the man she's staying with is trying to help her. "He's cooked, cleaned, and taken care of me. He's even helped me off the toilet. But my probation officer won't listen. He just wants me out of here." Cindy has trouble speaking. "I can see why people go back to drugs and drinking. That life is better. You don't have problems. You cover them up."

I ask her if I can telephone her mother.

"If I phoned my mother and said, Ma, I need help, she'd say, what can I do. I can't give you money. I can't give you a place to live. So what good are mothers? If half us kids were treated right we wouldn't do drugs. If I phoned my mother she'd say forget it."

I am overwhelmed by the hopelessness of Cindy's situation. Staying drug free no longer makes sense to her. She reasons that drugs are the only possibility. "I tell you, it's a hell of a lot easier on booze and drugs. That's why people go back out. It's easy. I can't work right now so what am I supposed to do? Where am I supposed to live? What am I supposed to eat?"

She pauses. I say nothing. There is nothing I can say.

"So the chances of me going back to prison are fifty-fifty."

I try to be constructive. I tell Cindy about the boarding houses that I know in the city. "I'll try to help you get a room."

"That's a cell with a television and a toilet," she says.

CINDY IS UNABLE TO CONTROL HER DRUG ADDICTION

Cindy finds a two-room apartment, and some friends from AA help her move. She says it is the first time she can remember having a place of her own. She is going to garage sales to find furniture. I do not ask her about money. An old friend of Cindy's tells me that the man who sent Cindy heroin through the mail is sending her money.

I visit her. Our conversations seem to take place in slow motion, so badly does she slur her words.

"It's hard for me to talk." Her voice is thick with emotion. "I'm struggling to say how I feel because I know it's important." Now she is on her own, she can get welfare and Medicaid. "I had to wait until it is too late." She speaks bitterly. "I'm not a bad person. I'm in pain. I need help. I'm seeing a physiotherapist. She says it is going to take a long time because my muscles are so tight."

I keep calling, keep talking, keep trying to help Cindy stay in touch. Sometimes we talk of silly things, nail polish, diets. We find things that make us laugh. We joke, trying to hold on to our friendship as Cindy disappears inside herself. I am traumatized by what is happening to her. I want to intervene, take her to a hospital, find a rehab that will treat her. I want to help her. *Help her? Send her back to prison?* I will not participate in her imprisonment. She is sick. She needs medical treatment. Our prisons are not hospitals. What good will it do if she is returned to jail?

On the telephone Cindy tells me she is going to physiotherapy three times a week and that she has a new therapist. She sounds hopeful. She talks about Medicaid. She tells me again that being able to pay for medical treatment is making a difference. "I have a chance. I think I might make it."

Two days later I get a call from the therapist who is working with Cindy's daughter. Cindy's mother is concerned that Cindy might be heading toward another suicide attempt. I tell the therapist that the last time I spoke with Cindy she sounded a little better but that I will telephone her as soon as we get off the phone.

I call. The line is busy. I call again, and again. I can't reach her. I call and call. Eventually Cindy picks up the phone. She is crying.

"I am so depressed. I can't stand the pain in my neck and legs. I keep falling down and I've sprained my ankle." Her doctor gave her three Darvocet. "That's all I've taken," she says defensively.

I ask if I can take her to the hospital.

"No. I'll be okay."

"Are you going to meetings?"

"Yes. Two today. I've only missed one meeting in three weeks. I need to go twice a day."

We talk some more, until she stops crying. Her speech is slow and her words are slurred, but I can understand what she is saying. "I'm not going to give up now. I've worked hard."

I mention that her mother is worried about her. Cindy immediately starts to cry again. She sounds angry. "She called me last week, and she said I sounded high." Cindy is shouting. "She didn't ask me how I am doing. She just kept asking me if I am using drugs." Cindy hung up when her mother would not stop accusing her of using drugs. She hasn't spoken with her mother since. "I'm so lonely. I hate being all on my own."

I ask Cindy if she is going to an evening meeting.

"I'm going to go, but I don't like going anymore. Some of my friends have stopped talking to me." She mentions a woman who she has known for years. "The other night when I was talking at a meeting, she told me to stop talking. She said I was using and that I should sit and listen." Cindy is almost incoherent. "It's hard for me to speak. I struggle to say how I feel because I know it is important. I have to keep talking and she told me to be quiet."

I am as lost as Cindy. I want someone to tell me what to do.

The following morning, May 21, I visit Cindy. Her apartment is in an ugly brown apartment complex on a main road in the city. I climb up to the third floor and knock on her door. I can hear her inside dragging her feet across the floor.

Cindy opens the door and smiles at me. She raises her eyebrows and shrugs her shoulders as if to say, You can see how I am, don't be angry with me. She is haggard. Her skin is parched and pulled tight across her cheekbones. Her hollow eyes have black shadows and she looks as if she's been punched in the face. She is wearing black jeans and a black tank top, which hang loosely on her emaciated body. She has lost a lot of weight. She is six feet tall and probably weighs less than one hundred and twenty pounds. I follow Cindy into the living room and sit down opposite her.

We talk about her new apartment. In spite of her difficulties it is neat and orderly. I ask her if I can take her out to lunch. "We could go to Friendly's."

"I don't think so." Then, sounding reluctant, she changes her mind. "Oh, okay."

Cindy gets up slowly and goes into the bedroom. She comes back with socks and workboots. I watch her as she pulls the socks on and puts her feet into the heavy boots.

We walk slowly out of the apartment. Cindy makes her way down the stairs holding onto the rail. Outside she puts on dark glasses and together we cross the road to my car.

In Friendly's the hostess is visibly shaken when Cindy takes off her dark glasses. She tries to cover up her reaction to Cindy's war-torn face by asking if we want smoking or nonsmoking. Cindy manages to smile. "Smoking." She tries to joke about her eyes as she slides into the booth. "I thought it was mascara, so I tried to wash the marks off," Cindy tells me. "I rubbed with a wash cloth and nothing happened."

"What are you going to eat?"

"Oh, I'll just have a strawberry milkshake."

"You need to eat."

"I'm not hungry."

"How about a hamburger?"

Cindy pulls a face.

The waitress comes and takes our order. Cindy orders a strawberry milkshake. I order a vanilla shake and a cup of coffee. Cindy lights a cigarette. "I just eat cans of soup and Spagettios." She talks slowly. "Sorry. I'm just in a bad mood."

She tells me that she is back on lithium.

"Who prescribed it?" It is the first time I have asked her a direct question about who's supplying her with medication.

Cindy names the doctor who has drugged her for years. She knows I don't think she should see him. "I asked him for it." She speaks defensively. Again she tells me that he is not prescribing narcotics. "He'd lose his license."

"Probably not," I say. We drop the subject.

Cindy talks about the physiotherapist who she is seeing about her back and neck. She also talks about the counselor at mental health who has agreed to see her because Medicaid will pay for emergency visits. "I told her I don't like her." I sense how angry Cindy is and how angry she could be. "She's giving me the same bullshit as the other one. She wants to talk to my probation officer. How can I tell her anything if she is going to report what I say?" Cindy looks trapped. "I need to talk, but I can't talk to her."

She tells me that the therapist spent an entire hour making her take tests. "She'd say three words and I'd have to repeat them. Then I had to count backwards." Cindy stubs out her cigarette and gets another one out of the pack. "What does that tell her?" She lights the cigarette. "What has that got to do with my problems? I don't fuckin' know."

Again we change the subject. I ask Cindy if the Darvocet showed up in the urine test that she was given by the probation department.

"No, they did the urine test before I took the Darvocet." The waitress refills my coffee cup. "When you're finished let's go. I'm real tired. I need to lie down."

As I quickly drink my coffee, Cindy talks about her mother.

"She's worried about you," I tell her.

Cindy is scornful. "The first thing she said to me when she phoned was, Are you using drugs? I don't want anything to do with her. When I was in prison I tried to have a new relationship with her. Start again. Forget what happened. But it didn't change. She visited me five times in eighteen months and every time she came to the prison she asked me if I was using." Cindy stands up.

I drive Cindy back to her apartment. We arrange to meet at the beginning of the following week. "I'd like that," she says as she opens the car door. "Thanks for the milkshake."

"Anytime."

She smiles.

I watch Cindy cross the street. She is slumped over and she does not look up when cars pass her. There is no doubt in my mind that she is taking massive doses of prescription drugs, and I have difficulty imagining that the probation officer does not know that she is using. He'd have to be stupid not to know.

When Cindy was released from prison the lawyer who was representing her asked me what I would do if I thought she was using again. I answered that I would tell him, but now, guessing that she is hooked on prescription drugs, there is nothing I can say or do. If I try to help her get into a drug rehabilitation facility she will be sent back to prison for violation of parole. Cindy is trapped in a no-win situation, and I am trapped too. Be her friend is all I can do.

CINDY'S APARTMENT IS SEARCHED AND SHE IS ARRESTED FOR VIOLATION OF HER PAROLE

On May 28, the girlfriend who visited Cindy in prison telephones me to tell me that Cindy has been arrested. "She came to see me yesterday. She looked worse than I have ever seen her. When she left she said she was going to see her probation officer." She is worried about Cindy's detoxing without adequate medical supervision. She reminds me that thirteen hospitals refused to admit Cindy the last time because of the large quantity of prescription drugs she was using.

I telephone the police station. The officer who answers the phone says that Cindy is not there. I telephone Cindy's apartment. A man answers. He identifies himself as a police officer, and I tell him my name. He says Cindy is at the jail. I ask if he can tell me what happened. Speaking to someone in the room, he says, "Do you know a Denny Taylor?" I can hear muffled voices. Then he tells me he cannot give out any further information.

I telephone the jail. Cindy is there. She is "being processed." I leave my number and ask the person with whom I am speaking to tell Cindy that she can call me collect. I do not mention that Cindy needs medical supervision if she is in detox. I am worried that I will exacerbate her difficulties.

I telephone Cindy's lawyer. He is in court but he returns my call during the lunch recess. I tell him that Cindy has been arrested and recap the events leading up to her arrest—the automobile accident, her breakup with the man she'd been living with, her difficulties trying to get medical treatment, her return to the doctor who supplied her with prescription drugs before she went to prison.

The lawyer tells me that whatever the situation, it was her responsibility to stay clean.

"What was she supposed to do?" I ask, more irritated than I should be. "She couldn't get to meetings, I was hospitalized, the drop-in center closed, not one social service agency would help her, and mental health would not treat her except on an emergency basis, and even then the only way the psychologist would see her was if she signed a release so he could talk to her probation officer."

The lawyer is patient but firm. "The court doesn't want to know, Denny. It was up to her. She was supposed to phone me every week. She didn't. I know there have been times when you had difficulty keeping in touch with her." He asks me if she is using heroin.

"I don't know," I answer. "I never asked her. Right now I'm more concerned about her detoxing without adequate medical supervision from all the prescription drugs she's been taking."

The lawyer tells me he will find out what's happening. He doesn't think there will be a hearing in front of the superior court judge who sentenced and released her. "It will be a probationary hearing, and if she has violated her parole she will be returned to the women's state prison."

Feeling guilty that I sounded off, I thank him for talking with me. I know most lawyers wouldn't take the time to discuss the situation with me.

Later that day the man with whom Cindy was living in the trailer tells me Cindy telephoned to ask him to get the parakeet and that she told him the police found syringes in her apartment. He laughs. "Cindy needs to wake up and smell the coffee." Still laughing. "She'll never learn."

Cindy's girlfriend calls. She has been to Cindy's apartment to get her parakeet. She tells me that she did not want to look around but that there were some empty prescription bottles and some prescription receipts.

I ask who wrote the prescriptions.

"Guess."

I name the doctor.

"All but one."

She reads the names of each drug, the number of refills, and the date when the drug was prescribed. "Flexeril. Librium. Buspar. Lithium. Relafin. Amitriptyline."

"What's the date?"

"9-19-91."

I am quiet. Was this an old prescription that Cindy had refilled, or did she go back to the doctor who supplied her with drugs as soon as she left the prison? Was it already too late the day I stopped her from going to see him? Later, I ask Cindy about the prescription. She tells me that she talked to him on the telephone and that for several months he called prescriptions for antidepressants into the pharmacy. "It was November before I went to see him. Then he would say, What do you want? and I would tell him. I don't think he even knew what drugs I was taking. He never looked back to see what prescriptions he had given me."

I know very little about the drugs Cindy has been using, and I am concerned about what will happen to her when she detoxes. I telephone a local pharmacist and read her the list of drugs, and I ask her if any of the drugs are considered narcotics. The pharmacist tells me that Flexeril and Librium are both opiates and that while amitriptyline (Elavil) is a nonnarcotic substance, when taken with Flexeril it can "potentiate addiction."

"If a person is in recovery from addiction, could these drugs lead to the recurrence of the active use of an illegal drug such as heroin?"

"I would say so," the pharmacist says. She also says she wonders why a physician would prescribe some of these drugs as they have competing functions.

I relay the information about the medications to the lawyer who I hope is still representing Cindy. I also tell him that her girlfriend has spoken with Cindy's mother, who is concerned that Cindy might try to kill herself. I remind him that Cindy has a long history of attempted suicides.

The lawyer says he will telephone the jail. He suggests that I telephone the jail as well and ask who they notify in case of emergency. The guard who speaks with me when I call sounds tired, but he is pleasant. Cindy is being held for seventy-two hours for parole violation and there is no bail status. I start to tell him, "Cindy's mother is worried—" He finishes it for me. "She might be suicidal. Cindy's been here before. I'll make a note of it."

A few hours later Cindy's lawyer telephones me. Heroin was found in Cindy's apartment. His voice conveys the seriousness of the situation. In addition to the parole violation, Cindy is facing new charges of heroin possession. He says that since it is her second offense it will be regarded as a first-degree felony. He talks about how difficult it is going to be to go back into court and face the judge. "We're going to have to eat humble pie. She could be facing seven to fifteen years."

There is to be a bail hearing. The man who had supplied Cindy with heroin through the mail is willing to testify that he left the heroin in Cindy's apartment. He is willing to travel from another state to testify that the heroin belonged to him.

CINDY IS HELD IN JAIL

Cindy calls me collect. She sounds sick, but she is not speaking in the slow monotonous monotone, nor is she slurring her words. She tells me that she is detoxing from all the prescription drugs.

"I lost control. It's my own goddamn fault for being stupid. I did want to get into a rehab, but there was no way that I could. It's going to kill my daughter. I did this to her." Cindy is crying, "I can't make it. I can't do it. I wanted to go into a rehab. I was talking about it at meetings but I was afraid they'd put me back in prison." She is talking rapidly. "I didn't know what to do. It started slowly. I don't know what happened. At the end I was taking twenty Flexeril a day. When I left my house I had a little bottle with some of every pill that I needed so I could get through the day. When we went to Friendly's I wanted you to take me home because I needed more pills and I didn't want to take them in front of you."

In another conversation Cindy tells me she sometimes took sixty Flexeril in one day. She talks about the friend who used to supply her with heroin. "He's willing to come up here and say that it was his heroin. They are not going to put me back in jail for taking prescription pills." She talks about the doctor who prescribed them. "What was I supposed to do? I needed help and no doctor would treat me."

I had been researching the drugs that she was taking and I asked her what Parafon 40 was used for. "It's a muscle relaxant. When I couldn't get Darvocet he gave me shit. It's a generic. He also gave me codeine which is a painkiller. I was probably taking—" she paused. "He gave me Flexeril, Darvocet, Librium, lithium." Her voice trails off. For a moment we are both quiet. "By then I was so hooked I was going every week, getting more prescriptions. I had a hundred Flexeril saved up. I was hooked. I was taking three at a time and I was scared I would run out. He stopped giving me Darvocet because he said he'd get in trouble. And then he started giving them to me again. Altogether I must have had over four hundred pills in my apartment." Again

Cindy is quiet. When she speaks again her voice is steady. "I wanted to help myself so bad but I didn't know what to do. It just got worse and worse and there was nothing I could do to stop it."

On Saturday, May 30, Cindy asks if I will go to the bail hearing. She is expecting to be released. She tells me that the lawyer who represented her at the last hearing is going to represent her. "But I don't know for how long. I still owe him money." She also tells me that the man who supplied her with heroin before she was first incarcerated is coming up to testify. "He's going to tell them that those were his works. They were his. This way I might get off. They can't charge me on anything. Those drugs were prescribed." She says, "I just kept taking more and more and asking for more and more and he kept giving them to me."

On Sunday, Cindy tells me on the telephone that the probation department has the results of a urinalysis. "My urine test came back dirty. It was the Darvocet." In my notes I write that Darvocet contains opiates. "I've been classified," Cindy sounds scared. "I'm in maximum security. I have to stay in my cell."

On Monday, Cindy is told that the hearing will take place on Wednesday, June 3.

Tuesday the lawyer calls and tells me he has the probation report. I ask if it would help if I tried to get more information about the prescription drugs that Cindy has been taking and put the documentation together for the court. He says that he doesn't think it will make much difference, but he tells me to do it anyway.

There are several more calls that day. The last call is from the lawyer. The man who said he left the heroin in Cindy's apartment is going to turn himself in at 9:30 the following morning. "I'll eat my hat if he does," he jokes. Then, laughing, "I'll need a good hollandaise sauce." He asks me to come to the bail hearing. "It's important that the judge is made aware that she still has support."

On Wednesday I stop writing at eleven o'clock and put on a suit. At 12:15 a paralegal from the lawyer's office calls and says the hearing has been canceled. Fifteen minutes later Cindy calls and says that the man did not show up. "I'm in a lot of trouble. I can stand trial and then I might get fifteen years or I can go back to the women's prison for two to five."

"What are you going to do?"

"I don't know. I canceled the hearing. I'm so confused." Cindy is crying. "I talked to my mother. All she's done is give me a friggin' lecture. I told her that I needed her and she told me she had to friggin' work."

Cindy's girlfriend calls me. She says she has received a letter addressed to her about Cindy's legal bills. "This letter should be addressed to Cindy, not to me." The girlfriend's husband is concerned that in some way they are responsible for Cindy's bills. I try to reassure her. "I've stuck by her all these years," she tells me. "She's lied to me. I deserve better. I don't know if I can continue to be friends with her."

Cindy is worried that the lawyer will no longer represent her because she cannot pay his bills. "If I go to trial it will cost $10,000. But I have some good news." The man who brought heroin into her apartment has agreed to send a signed statement to the lawyer.

"Did he say why he didn't show?"

"He said he was scared. He just couldn't do it." Cindy sounds hopeful. "But he phoned my lawyer and he said he'd fax a statement." Cindy's voice trails off.

On June 4, the lawyer speaks on the telephone with the man. A paralegal takes notes.

"I understand that you were visiting at Cindy's and left something there and that caused Cindy to be arrested."

"Uh-huh. What would happen if I showed up and admitted it?"

"What would you be admitting to?"

"It's conjecture. I'd rather not say. Can you tell me what someone would face?"

"I represent Cindy. My understanding is that heroin was found in Cindy's apartment and that it was yours."

"Yeah."

"Would you give a statement?"

"Over the phone?"

"Well, we could start by using the phone. I could prepare a statement from our conversation and then I could send it to you."

"Then what would happen?"

"With a parole violation, Cindy faces forty-five to sixty days. A hearing hasn't been scheduled yet, but she has a bail hearing tomorrow. Without your cooperation Cindy probably won't be released."

The lawyer waits, then continues.

"Her chances at being released or going to state prison depend on you telling the truth. If you won't come up, then maybe you would sign and send me a statement under oath.

"Uh-huh. Her hearing is tomorrow?"

"Yes, it is."

"Could I be arrested where I live on the basis of a statement?"

"My guess is that a state arrest warrant could be issued on the basis of a statement. Whether the county attorney would seek to extradite you, I don't know and I won't guess. I won't make you a promise that I can't keep—or that the county attorney would go along with. I can't tell you what would happen. I can tell you that Cindy got stuck and she's not just facing state prison for the balance of a couple of years, but adding possession of heroin second offense will assign state prison time for her. She is very confused and upset about what she is facing. If for the probation violation, you take responsibility, then they can't charge her for the possession of heroin.

"She could walk?"

"Very possibly."

The man says he needs time to think.

He phones back on June 5, at 9:50 A.M. The lawyer has a draft statement ready but there is still some information that he needs. "There's one other thing I wanted to ask you about. There were syringes found in the ceiling. You told me you are not sure which room. Did you put them in anything?"

"I don't remember."

"Would it be typical for you to put them together?"

"Yeah. Obviously you know all about this and you are trying to elicit answers from me. Couldn't you word it as you know what happened and I could sign it?"

"That's what I am going to try to do."

The questioning continues, this time about the bags in which the heroin was contained.

"My only other question is about the number of bags. You told me you had two bags that were marked 'beef.' Are you sure you had two bags or could there have been more?"

"It could have been more."

"Well, could they all have had heroin?"

"You mean, could they have had other substances?"

"Well, one that was left was about a half bag, because you said you used about half. You said you used an entire bag earlier and that you don't know how much else there was, that there might have been more than two bags. Would they also have had heroin in them or could they have been empty?"

"I'm not sure."

"The bags you said had beef on them. Do they come that way or do you mark them?"

"They come that way."

"Do they come with heroin in them?"

"Uh-huh."

"So they come from your supplier that way?"

"Yes."

"Might there have been empty bags?"

"I don't remember."

"All right. Thanks."

After several telephone conversations with Cindy's lawyer, the man who supplied Cindy with heroin through the mail does sign an affidavit and has it notarized. In the affidavit he accepts responsibility for the heroin and the hypodermic needles that the officers from the sheriff's department found in Cindy's apartment:

> On Sunday, May 24, 1992, I drove to visit Cindy. I did not tell Cindy that I was coming to visit. I arrived at about 10:00 A.M. I had with me several sets of hypodermic needles, and several bags of heroin in glassine envelopes, with stripes on them and the word "beef" on them, made of something that feels like wax paper. I am not sure if all of the envelopes had heroin in them or if they were empty.
>
> After I arrived, I went into the bathroom in her apartment. I dissolved one of the doses of heroin in water in a spoon which I took from her kitchen, with cotton, cooked it with my lighter, and injected it using one of the hypodermic needles I brought. I didn't tell Cindy what I was doing and I did not tell her that I had any of these items with me.

He ends the notarized affidavit by stating that he hid his "works" and that he forgot them when Cindy told him to leave the apartment because he was high.

CINDY'S JOURNALS ARE USED AT THE BAIL HEARING AND SHE IS DENIED BAIL

Cindy's mother sits alone in the waiting room of the superior court house. "I don't know what to believe anymore," she says. She talks about her conversations with Cindy on the telephone. "She sounded like a slowed-down gramophone record." She shakes her head. "One time her daughter answered the phone and Cindy just kept saying 'I love you' over and over again."

Cindy's mother says that her granddaughter didn't know what to do so she just kept saying "I love you too" every time Cindy said "I love you." "In a month the adoption papers will be signed. It will give her some security."

It is the first time that I've heard that Cindy's daughter is going to be adopted by her grandmother. I ask if Cindy knows that her daughter is going to be adopted.

"No," her mother says, shaking her head. She talks about the therapist who is working with her granddaughter. "I wish I'd had help with my own children," she says sadly. "I've learned so much in the last year."

Cindy's sister arrives and sits with her mother. They talk about the man who supplied Cindy with heroin and then about the doctor who supplied her with prescription drugs. "I wrote to the AMA," Cindy's mother says, "but nothing came of it."

The assistant county attorney walks through the waiting area, followed by Cindy's girlfriend. The girlfriend joins Cindy's mother and sister. The conversation returns to the man who supplied Cindy with heroin and the doctor who supplied her with prescription drugs. Cindy's behavior is also discussed. Cindy's girlfriend is angry with her and confides in Cindy's mother.

Cindy's lawyer arrives. He comes over to where Cindy's mother is sitting and says hello to everyone. He has a piece of paper in his hand. He holds it up and says that the man who says it was his heroin has faxed him a written confession.

"Is it notarized?" I ask.

"Yes. But the county attorney isn't interested. He says he has enough to go ahead. But the information will be important if there is a trial." I raise my eyebrows, silently anticipating what follows. "If there is a trial I will probably be called as a witness." He says this will present an ethical dilemma and that he will have to withdraw as Cindy's lawyer. He quickly adds that of course he will testify on her behalf.

A court official comes over and tells the lawyer that the hearing is about to begin. As the lawyer starts to walk away, Cindy's mother asks him if he thinks there is any chance that Cindy will be sent to a long-term rehab. The lawyer shakes his head. "Not a chance."

Cindy's mother says she has written to the judge to ask for Cindy to be sent to a rehab. "Jail isn't going to help her." In the letter, which is a part of the court record, she writes of Cindy's relationship with the doctor who supplied her with medication:

> The last time she went to him, years ago, she told us, during one of her periods of trying to be straight, that she performed sexual favors for him in return for prescriptions. She now has several prescriptions from him in her possession.

She then asks for Cindy to be sent to a drug and alcohol rehabilitation facility and she requests that she not be allowed out on bail. She writes:

> Cindy has said many times, if she had to go back to prison, she would kill herself. I think if she gets out on bail, this will be the first thing she'll do. Either that or run away.

She finishes by writing about the way Cindy was able to "con" me and she refers to me as "the proverbial ostrich in the sand."

We follow the lawyer into a courtroom. It is small, cramped, and less imposing than the courtroom in which Cindy's other hearings were held. We sit right behind the county attorney and his assistant. To our right, Cindy is sitting with her lawyer.

Cindy looks around as we come in but she doesn't seem to make eye contact with anyone. She looks ill. Her face is haggard. The dark shadows under her eyes are still there. She looks as if she is still detoxing from the prescription medications that she was taking. Even so she has made an effort. She is wearing a dark blue flowered dress with black hose and black high heels.

Cindy's lawyer is talking to her. She nods as he speaks and every so often she glances over to where the county attorney and his assistant are sitting. On the table in front of them are sixteen bottles of pills and two large plastic bags filled with more pill containers. Beside the bottles in front of the assistant county attorney are three of Cindy's journals.

The judge enters. He looks at Cindy with disdain. His disapproval of her can be felt throughout the courtroom.

The preliminaries are quickly over and the assistant county attorney stands to address the court. Then she picks up one of Cindy's journals and opens it and begins to read. "The hot chills and cold sweats can only be saved by my little white grains. . . ." Cindy is visibly shaken. She leans across and whispers to her lawyer. He nods. The assistant reads another entry. "I'm going down. . . ."

Cindy looks angry. Her eyes flash, and again she whispers to the lawyer. He puts his hand on her arm.

When the assistant has finished, Cindy's lawyer stands and questions the use of the journals. He states that there was no clear indication of when the entries were written.

Later Cindy tells me that one of the entries read in court was a poem that she copied into her journal when she was in a drug rehab before she first went to prison for receiving heroin through the mail. "I used to open up one of my journals and write. They aren't in any order or anything. It's not right that they took them. Those are my private thoughts."

I am also disturbed by their use—especially when no other documents are presented. The prescription containers lined up on the table in front of the assistant county attorney have a dramatic effect but no questions are asked about the doctor who supplied Cindy with such large quantities of so many different prescription drugs. The affidavit of the man who said the heroin found in Cindy's apartment belonged to him is not presented in the courtroom. If this information is inappropriate to the bail hearing, then so are the journals.

But whatever the argument, the *only* documents produced in the courtroom are extracts of Cindy's journals, which became a part of the official court record.

The judge leans forward. His arms are folded on the bench. "I don't want to prejudge this case, but I must be one of the most disappointed people in the courtroom." He shares his disappointment. Then he says, "I just don't feel comfortable letting her out. I'm not going to set bail for her own safety."

The assistant county attorney asks for the hearing to be set as soon as possible. "As she sits there warehoused we are not helping the defendant."

Cindy's lawyer stands and asks the judge to release him from the case. He talks of conflict of interest, of his conversations with the man who said that the heroin found in Cindy's apartment belonged to him. He says that he anticipates that he will be asked to testify on Cindy's behalf at her trial.

The judge instructs him about preparing "new counsel." The lawyer tells the judge that Cindy will need a court-appointed lawyer. She is unable to pay. He adds that Cindy was not happy with the public defender who represented her before she was incarcerated.

The judge says he will make a note of Cindy's request, adding that he is not playing games. He stands, we stand, Cindy tries to speak to her girlfriend but is told that she cannot and is quickly led away.

CINDY IS WAREHOUSED

On June 30, Cindy telephones me from the county jail. "I've been indicted for possession, so now it's a class A felony. The pretrial is on July 15 and there's going to be a trial by jury in October. I haven't even seen a lawyer yet. They're going to select the jury the first of October. October 12 is the beginning of the trial week."

July 8, one week before the pretrial, Cindy still has not seen a lawyer. She talks of fighting the charges and says that if she gets a good lawyer she thinks everything will be okay.

"They've taken me off my meds. I was taking two hundred milligrams of Elavil. I'm going crazy. They've had me locked up front where they can see me all the time. This week has been a nightmare. They've got me taking mineral oil because I'm so constipated. I'm worse than ever."

"Why do I have to go back to prison because I wanted the pain to go away?" she asks, knowing that I can't answer her question. "I had no place to go." Then angrily she names the doctor and says, "I never want to see him again."

Six days later Cindy still does not have a lawyer. "Will you phone the court and find out who is going to represent me?"

I telephone the superior court. The person I speak with is officious. She says that Cindy is not the only person to be arraigned and that as she has done something wrong she has nothing to complain about.

On July 14, the day before the pretrial is scheduled to take place, I telephone the superior court and ask again if a lawyer has been appointed to Cindy's case. This time the person with whom I speak is civil. She gives me the name of the lawyer and the law firm for whom she works.

I telephone the court-appointed lawyer, who is businesslike. "I was not assigned to the hypodermic until today so I didn't know about the hearing tomorrow."

I try to ignore her pejorative label for Cindy. I tell her what happened when Cindy was released from jail. I stress that Cindy tried to get medical treatment and psychological counseling and that she had been unable to obtain these services. I also tell her about Cindy's use of prescription drugs and of the multiple prescriptions given to her by the doctor who had supplied her with large quantities of opiate-based drugs before she first went to prison. The lawyer thanks me, tells me that the meeting the following day is not open to the public, and abruptly hangs up the phone.

The next day Cindy phones and says she has met with her lawyer. She talks about a negotiated plea. The court-appointed lawyer has told Cindy that the man will never testify that the heroin was his. "She told me he would take the Fifth."

"So what is she telling you to do?"

"She said I'm facing nine and a half to fifteen years." Cindy sounds worried. "She said the jury would convict me. She wants me to plead guilty, but I don't want to do that. I don't think it is fair. I tried you know. I tried."

Cindy waits in jail. Another month goes by. She speaks to her lawyer on several occasions but there is no preparation for trial. On September 23, Cindy calls and asks me if I will phone her lawyer. "She's got me all confused."

Cindy's lawyer takes my call. She explains that Cindy has the choice of either serving out the minimum of her first sentence and then serving three and a half to seven years for the new charges of heroin possession, or pleading guilty and going directly to the prison drug rehab. She explains that Cindy could plead guilty because of circumstantial evidence but not admit to the charges against her. She tells me this is called an "Alfred plea."

I tell Cindy about the "Alfred plea" and that if she pleads guilty she can go directly to the prison rehab. "They will take my lithium away from me," she tells me. "And Elavil. I can't do it without medication. They might as well give me a gun, it's that serious. What good am I going to be if I get psychotic? Since I've been on lithium I've been okay. The psychiatrist when I was trying to get out said I needed those drugs."

"Maybe they will allow you to take Elavil and lithium."

"No. Not at the prison drug rehab." She names the director of the rehab and the probation officer who wrote the reports. "They would never agree to let me take antidepressants."

CINDY PLEADS GUILTY A SECOND TIME TO THE POSSESSION OF HEROIN

On October 5, Cindy phones and says she is going to plead guilty. "It's either the prison rehab or twelve and a half years."

"Where did the twelve and a half years come from?"

"The numbers change every day, seven, fifteen, twelve and a half, what's the difference."

"What about lithium?"

"I don't know." Cindy sounds tired. "That's their problem. If they take me off it I won't be responsible."

Once Cindy signs the guilty plea the circumstances of the signing no longer matter. She remains in jail and waits to be sentenced. Weeks pass. No decision is made. Cindy calls. "They want me to go back to the women's state prison," she tells me. "If I do that I'll be caught up in the system."

I want to tell her that she is already, but I don't.

"I'll have to go to quarantine, then B tier, then A tier, and then C2."

We talk about the difficulties that she had at the prison before she was released. She names the prison medical social worker. "She would love to have me back," she says.

Another call.

"I've pleaded guilty." Cindy tells me that the assistant county attorney would not accept the "Alfred plea." "She said I had to plead guilty otherwise I was not admitting that I need help."

Cindy tells me that there are other men and women in the jail who have been represented by the court-appointed lawyer who is representing her.

"She rarely goes to court. She plea-bargains. She said to me, 'Well Cindy, if this doesn't work out we can always withdraw the plea.' But if I withdraw the plea they would send me up for another seven and a half years on top of my old sentence. They are friggin' pissed with me already. She had an answer to everything I said. I talked to her for about an hour and I signed a paper that I was guilty. I didn't want to plead guilty. That's why I've been here five months. She reads me all these things. One of them was waiving my rights to a speedy trial by pleading guilty." Cindy sighs. "I'm so confused. She said that a jury would not decide in my favor. Then she said that if I plead guilty, the county attorney agreed that I should go to a long-term rehab instead of prison. I don't want to go back to prison, so I agreed."

We talk for a while.

Then Cindy says, "If they would have given me counseling when I got out of prison I really don't think I would be back in here. But I couldn't find a doctor or a counselor. I really need someone to sit down and tell me I am not a bad person. I feel I am a really bad person. I think of the bad things I have done. I think of my daughter constantly. Just shit. Stupid stuff. It really bothers me. And I've been alienating everybody. I have no friends and I want them. It bothers me that I've turned away from people in the program. I just feel I haven't any support. From you, yes, but in here I just feel alone and abandoned."

Cindy is buying the opportunity to go to a drug rehab with her guilty plea.

"I hated pleading guilty," she tells me. "I'm not a bad person. I have done a lot of drugs, but you know my crime, well actually it wasn't a crime—me doing drugs. It helped me forget. It helped me feel good. But what I was saying was that doing drugs is my only crime. I've never stolen. I have never hurt anybody. They say they want to rehabilitate you in prison but it's forced on me. I just want to feel normal. I know that the way I feel right now is not normal. It's rarely that I feel good. So this is punishment. Boy are they giving it to me. For what? It's so extreme."

Cindy's mother brings her daughter to visit her.

"She's really tall. She said, 'Mom, I wish you could get out of here and rescue me.' "

When Cindy was released from prison she was not allowed to see her daughter. It was months before her daughter's therapist was willing to consider the possibility of them spending some time together. "By then I was taking pills. I was already on that shit and I didn't want her to see me fucked up. If I'd seen her when I first got out of prison it might have made a difference."

Cindy refuses to go to the prison rehab without lithium and Elavil. "There are no guarantees. I could go in there and the judge could say he doesn't want to plea-bargain." Impasse. Cindy waits in the county jail.

On October 19, Cindy says she has asked the court-appointed lawyer if she can stay in the jail. She does not want to return to the women's state prison. "I've been here five months. By the time I have my hearing in November it will be six months. They give murderers and drug dealers bail and I don't get bail." She laughs at the irony. "I'm warehoused! How long can they keep me here without a hearing? They said they didn't want to warehouse me."

On October 20, Cindy asks me to call the court-appointed lawyer. "I don't understand anything she says when she talks to me."

The attorney tells me it will take at least eight months for Cindy to be processed through the prison. I ask her about the plea. I tell her that Cindy is confused. The attorney sounds irritated, agitated. "Cindy was not confused when she talked with me. I thought everything was settled." She is sharp, abrupt. "In future I will talk with Cindy direct. Not through a mediator."

I tell Cindy that I think my calling the court-appointed lawyer has made the situation worse.

"It can't get any worse," she says. "In five months I've talked to her six times. She sends me things. I have a whole drawer full of stuff and I don't know what it means. I just don't want to get caught up in the prison. She may think that I know things but I don't. She didn't even explain the plea bargain to me."

THE PURPOSE OF CINDY'S INCARCERATION IS TO REFRAME HER IDENTITY

When Cindy pleaded guilty she forfeited her right to a speedy trial. She waits in the county jail and wonders what the legal system is going to do with her. Weeks pass without any communication taking place between Cindy and her court-appointed lawyer.

She calls me collect each day and we talk. I am caught up in her suffering, but there is little that I can do to help her except listen. I telephone the American Civil Liberties Union, but I am told they don't take criminal cases. I telephone Legal Aid, but they are not interested. I get an answering machine when I phone a local organization that is supposed to provide legal advice.

An anonymous recorded voice explains that it will take six weeks for a representative to return incoming calls. I don't leave a message.

Cindy's court-appointed lawyer continues to persuade her to go to the prison drug rehab. Cindy resists. Then her lawyer tries to negotiate with the assistant county attorney for Cindy to be sent to a private substance abuse rehabilitation center that can cope with her dual diagnosis status—in other words a rehab that will allow Cindy to take antidepressants. Cindy asks me if I can find out about dual diagnosis rehabs. I start making phone calls. The lawyer tells Cindy that the probation officer has recommended she be sent to the prison drug rehab. Cindy calls upset. "The only reason he's pushing the prison drug rehab is because he doesn't want me to go to an outside placement," she says.

Cindy knows women who have been to the prison rehab. "In the morning everyone sits around and bitches at you and tells you what's wrong with you. It's like when you are a little kid and your parents are molding you and are shouting at you. It would be like going home and having my stepfather tell me what to do. I can't do it. It would be like my childhood all over again."

I ask Cindy if she sees any differences between the way she is being treated by the courts and the prison system and the way she was treated as a child by her mother and stepfather.

"Come on, Denny," Cindy laughs. "I've been shouted at all my life. There is no difference."

Our conversation returns to the prison drug rehab. "They mess with your mind," Cindy says. "I don't want to go there. I told my lawyer that I couldn't go without my medication. I need to take Elavil. I've been on it for fifteen years. The last time they took me off of it I shot myself."

Prison messes with Cindy's mind by denying her the medical and psychiatric treatment that she needs. A note in her prison file states that one of the goals of her incarceration is to "Rebuild—reframe Cindy's identity." To rebuild her identity the superior court and the prison system are working to "control her drug-seeking behaviors."

Cindy is treated as if her drug addiction happened in a vacuum. It is as if there is nothing that happened to her in her life that should be taken into consideration by the judge, the lawyers, the probation officer, the counselors, and the prison personnel as they work to "reframe her identity." Her stepfather never hit her when she was three until she peed on the floor, he never punched her with his fist breaking her jaw, she was never beaten about the head by one of the men with whom she lived, never fell down a flight of stairs and fractured the bones in her face. Her molars have no jagged edges that dig deep into her gums. Her neck does not hurt. There are no migraine headaches. She isn't depressed. There are no scars on her stomach where she stabbed herself three times with a kitchen knife, the bullet from the gun that she fired at her heart did not pass through her chest.

For a brief moment when she hired a lawyer Cindy's political status changed. Her life counted. But when she cannot pay her legal bills she becomes "the hypodermic." She is anonymous. An addict. She exhibits drug-seeking behaviors. She screams and no one listens. Her pain does not hurt. Her suffering is not real. She is not a person. She does not exist except as a burden to society.

Cindy waits in jail and she talks about the counseling. "I need help to control my medications and I need counseling for depression. I can't live with drugs and I can't live without them." She knows that her refusal to go to the prison rehab without lithium or Elavil is making her situation worse. She is aware that she is criticized by the director of the prison rehab for her "drug-seeking behaviors" and by the assistant county attorney for her refusal to accept the authority of the legal system. "They think I'm trying to manipulate the system. But I've been abused all my life and this is just more abuse. I need to go to a rehab that can help me use prescription drugs properly and can help me with depression and women's issues."

Each day she tells me how she is feeling. There are good days and bad days, and over time I can tell by the tone of her voice if she is in pain or suffering from a migraine headache. As the weeks go by Cindy continually complains of pains in her stomach and of constipation. "I'm so bloated and it hurts something fierce."

At the beginning of November Cindy telephones to tell me they want to do some blood tests. "Why do they want to do that now?" she asks. "I've been here all this time. It's six months. Why didn't they do them when I first arrived?"

The assistant county attorney will not consider an outside placement. Cindy is exasperated. "I can't be the only women in the state who needs to take antidepressants and enter a drug treatment program."

On November 3, a psychiatrist evaluates her. The psychiatrist is a woman and Cindy finds it easy to talk with her. "She's coming back tomorrow. I wish I could talk to her on a regular basis," she says. "She had all my records. I don't know how she got them." If the psychiatrist recommends that Cindy remain on her medication the judge won't know what to do with her. The court-appointed lawyer tells Cindy that the judge has really been taking this personally. "She said on Friday, 'He's pissed. It makes him seem like a jerk.' "

Cindy waits for the psychiatrist report. November 25, the day the supposed trial was to take place, comes and goes. Cindy waits. In December the court-appointed lawyer and the assistant county attorney are still discussing sending Cindy to a rehab that will allow her to take medication. Cindy is not allowed to have presents at Christmas.

"Not even some cigarettes?" I ask.

Cindy laughs. "I'm not allowed to smoke."

January 1993. The assistant county attorney continues to insist that Cindy be sent to the prison rehab. Cindy continues to refuse. Her lawyer argues on Cindy's behalf that she be sent to an outside placement where she can continue to take medication for depression. She continues to be warehoused.

Cindy is given a copy of the report written by the psychiatrist. The underlining in the excerpts below is in the original report:

Reasons for the Evaluation: Cynthia presently takes multiple psychotropic medication. We are to determine whether these medications are needed and what behavior changes would occur, if any, were she not medicated.

Interview: Cynthia looked older than her stated age of 35 years. She was taller than average, of slight build, and seemed of average weight. She appeared well groomed, neat, and tidy. She has no observable abnormal mannerisms.

She scored 28 (perfect score was 30) when taking the mini-mental state examination.

Her speech was fluent, production slow and steady. Her vocabulary seemed average. She related quite well, with good eye contact. There was no apparent thought disorder.

Although her facial expressions appeared dull, she displayed a wide range of emotion. Her affect was appropriate. There is a prevailing sadness.

The psychiatrist reviews Cindy's use of antidepressants, her use of alcohol, and her dependance on drugs. Then she presents her analysis:

Summary and Recommendations: Cynthia is a 35-year-old Caucasian female, single, separated from her daughter, and experiencing mood instability, persistent migraine headaches, and neck pain. Her childhood environment was one of unhappiness, poor nurture, and physical abuse. Her biologic father left when she was two years old, and she grew up with an abusive stepfather and alcoholic mother.

There seems biologic loading for mood disorder.

Cynthia started on alcohol at age ten, and used marijuana at thirteen. She was also medicated with psychotropic and anxiolytic drugs at age sixteen. Her use of psychoactive substances continued, which included prescription as well as illicit drugs. <u>The outcome is increasing dysfunction over time</u>, such as <u>failed relationships, inability to care for her daughter, loss of job, financial difficulty, and legal problems</u>.

Many people who abuse alcohol present with symptoms identical to those of a Major Depression. The overwhelming majority of these symptoms <u>are alcohol-induced and resolve spontaneously within four weeks of cessation of drinking</u>. The intense sadness tends to be temporary and to disappear without antidepressant medication. Cynthia <u>remained depressed despite sobriety for three years</u>, and antidepressant medication. This indicates presence of primary Major Depressive Disorder with secondary alcoholism.

Review of records and patient's account revealed that in later years, subsequent to these depressive episodes, is the <u>occurrence of manic equivalents presenting as irritability, low frustration tolerance, leading to anger</u>. There is also strong evidence of <u>emotional lability</u>, going from <u>being happy, to irritability, to depression, in minutes or hours</u>. Cynthia's multiple use of drugs led to exaggeration of preexisting depressive symptoms, including suicide attempts.

Her <u>migraine and neck injury requiring painkillers</u> make drugs easily available for abuse. These appear to be a <u>perpetuant that sustains the habit</u>, since these drugs may trigger urges to return to the primary drug, or a substitute when the agent of choice is not available.

With this backdrop, and evidence of <u>marked cyclicity</u>, the use of <u>lithium</u> for maintenance therapy is justified. <u>Lithium decreases the number and severity of manic episodes</u>, and the number of depressive episodes. Lithium is also known to have <u>lesser efficacy in the treatment of depression</u>. In Cynthia's case, <u>where depressive episodes are not adequately controlled by lithium, coadministration of antidepressant agent is a necessity</u>.

At the end of the report the psychiatrist states:

> As Cynthia begins to substitute people (plan of taking her daughter back, AA and NA support groups) for drugs, her dependence on substances will hopefully vanish.

Cindy is watching me read. "What do you think? Do you think it will make any difference?"

Naively I respond, "It's going to be hard for them to ignore what the psychiatrist has written."

Meanwhile Cindy continues to wait.

On February 7, I visit Cindy at the jail. She is still waiting to be sentenced. She's gained weight but she does not look healthy. There is a puffiness to her face that reminds me of the swollen faces of the few pregnant women I've known who are suffering from toxemia.

We sit at a long table. Cindy is on one side wedged between two large men wearing prison green. She expresses her discomfort at their proximity with looks of hostility—first at one then the other—but the men don't see her as they hold hands across the table with their visitors who are sitting on either side of me.

Cindy has telephoned the lawyer who had helped her when she petitioned the courts to obtain her release from prison. "He was surprised to find out that I haven't been sentenced. He said I might end up doing time."

"How much?"

"I don't know." She shrugs her shoulders, smiles a nonsmile. "Seven to fourteen." She laughs.

We talk about the prison drug rehab. "I'll do time first," she says. "I can't stand the pain."

She has told me all this before but it seems to me that with each repetition she expands her own understanding of the difficulties that she faces in taking prescription drugs. "But if I take the medication I can't control it. I end up taking more and more." She leans forward and opens her eyes wide. "How are they going to help me deal with that? If they put me in prison for five years do they think when I come out I will be able to cope without drugs?" She whispers loudly. In the noisy visiting room I have difficulty catching her words. "How long do they think they have to lock me up to stop me using? If they put drugs in front of me right now, I'd use them." Cindy smiles. Her eyes are wide open and she holds up her hands and wiggles her fingers feigning delight. "I'd use them." Her voice trails off and I cannot hear her.

She puts her hands flat on the table and presses her lips together, and as the moment passes, the sadness returns to her face. Her eyes are closed. "Everything's gone. There is nothing left. I haven't had an attitude like this for three years. Longer. I don't care any more. I just want to use."

Cindy is quiet. Neither of us speaks. "I can't stand not knowing," she says. "How much longer will I have to sit here while they decide what to do with me?"

She is rubbing her neck, leaving red marks.

"Your neck looks swollen."

"It hurts to swallow. When I lie down I feel as if I am being strangled."

The psychiatrist had noted that Cindy's thyroid was swollen in her report.

"Ask to have it checked."

Cindy looks at me as if I will never learn.

"Drug-seeking behaviors." Again she smiles.

The next day Cindy telephones me. "Guess what. My attorney says that there is a drug program in the next state that she thinks she can get me into and the assistant county attorney has said okay. She just wants it in the paperwork that if I mess up I have to be brought back up here to do time." Cindy is convinced that this turn of events is because of the report written by the psychiatrist. She's upbeat.

Two weeks later Cindy telephones me. The court-appointed lawyer has told her she can't go to the out-of-state rehabilitation facility. Cindy says that she doesn't feel good. She tells me that she has been to the emergency room at the local hospital because of arrhythmia. "They don't give a shit, Denny." Her voice is dull and flat.

"Are you okay now?"

"No. Do you know that when I went to the hospital because my heart was arrhythmic the nurse covered over her badge so I wouldn't see her name. Why would she do that? What did she think that I was going to do?"

Cindy asks me to telephone the drug rehab to find out why she can't go there. I telephone the facility. I am told that there are only four beds allocated for women who are incarcerated and that they are already filled. The person with whom I speak also says that the facility is not set up to receive out-of-state funds. When Cindy telephones to ask me why she can't go to the rehab, I relay what I have been told. Cindy is angry with the court-appointed lawyer. "Why would she get my hopes up?"

A hearing is scheduled at the superior court on March 1.

"I'm going before the judge without a plan." Cindy sounds anxious. She rushes on, "I'm going in naked. I guess the judge will ask me if my attorney has done her best and I am going to say no. It's insanity. They said last summer, we don't want her in prison we want her in a rehab. My lawyer is downright nasty to me. Three months ago it was just going to court. Then it was rehabs. Now it's we're just going into court. In November they wouldn't do anything until I had blood work. Then it was a psychiatric report, but when they got that they still didn't do anything."

On February 23, Cindy telephones and says she's talked to her lawyer. "She doesn't even have a list of possible rehabs." I have been networking trying to find a rehab that will take Cindy. One of the facilities that I telephoned sounded promising so I give the name of the institution to Cindy so that she can pass it on to her lawyer. When Cindy calls again I ask her if she's given the information to the lawyer.

"Yes, but she said it was third-hand information."

CINDY'S SUPERIOR COURT HEARING IS POSTPONED

At the superior court on March 1, I wait for the hearing at which Cindy is scheduled to be sentenced. A man in a dark gray suit comes through the metal detector and walks down the ramp to the waiting area. Walking behind him is a young girl who looks fifteen or sixteen. They sit down at a table in the waiting area and talk.

Another man walks down the ramp and speaks to the man in the gray suit. The man in the suit says he's brought his daughter for the—he uses Cindy's last name—case, then returns to his conversation with his daughter about parole violations.

More people pass through the metal detector. A woman who looks like a lawyer jokes with someone about the sentencing hearing. The man in the gray suit calls her by her first name, and I realize she is Cindy's lawyer. I have not met her in the ten months that she's represented Cindy. She asks the man in the gray suit what he's doing at the courthouse.

"We're here for the sentencing," he replies.

Cindy's lawyer smiles. "What, in the"—she says Cindy's last name—"case?"

He nods.

"This is not a popular case," she tells him. "Her reputation precedes her."

A man with no teeth comes down the ramp, and Cindy's court-appointed lawyer walks over and talks with him. They talk about Cindy, about the prison rehab, about removing Cindy's medication for depression and bipolar disorders. Then Cindy's lawyer leaves the waiting area.

Cindy's brother arrives and sits next to me. We talk but mostly we listen to the conversations taking place around us. At some point a small woman with a large briefcase arrives and sits down at a table by herself. She opens the case and takes out a folder and reviews some documents. I wonder if the woman is the psychiatrist who evaluated Cindy, but Cindy has not described her so I have no way of knowing. The probation officer arrives and he sits with the man with no teeth. Their conversation is about medication and drug rehabilitation.

After about an hour the court-appointed lawyer comes back and tells the man with no teeth that the hearing is postponed. "The judge wants to get her into a rehab. There will be a hearing in one week."

The man with no teeth stands up. "This is bullshit. Am I supposed to postpone my dental surgery again?"

The probation officer is also on his feet. "Who is going to pay for the rehab?" he asks in a loud voice.

Cindy's lawyer tells him that the judge wants the state to pay. The probation officer does not conceal his anger. "No consequences again." He shakes his head as he starts walking up the ramp out of the waiting area.

CINDY IS HOSPITALIZED WITH AN INTESTINAL BLOCKAGE

On Tuesday, May 11, Cindy is rushed by ambulance to the local hospital. She has an intestinal blockage.

On Wednesday morning they operate.

Cindy usually telephones me every day, so when I do not hear from her I begin to worry. Several days pass. I telephone the jail and am told that she has been to the hospital but that everything is fine. I am not told that Cindy has been admitted nor that she has had emergency surgery.

I telephone the jail again. They say Cindy is fine.

On May 20 Cindy telephones. "I've been in hospital. I've had an operation."

"Are you okay?"

"I kept saying, where are you Denny? Why don't you phone?"

"I did phone. They kept telling me you were okay. I thought you were back in prison."

"No. I didn't have nobody. *Nobody.*" Cindy's voice is tight and strained. "I wanted to talk to you. They rushed me out in an ambulance. They cut me from my crotch up past my belly button. I have about a twelve-inch incision. They gave me morphine the first day. I told them that was not a good idea. I tried to phone you, but they wouldn't let me make any phone calls."

"There was no one with you?"

"No. I haven't seen anybody. I was there in that room all on my own, just lying in bed watching television. I started writing down what was happening to me, but I couldn't bring it back here because they would read it. I want you to put it in the computer. I'll phone you tomorrow or Saturday."

"Why did they operate?"

"I don't know. Before I went in I was in such pain. I was puking shit and the guard said it was just nerves. Motherfucker."

"Do you know what they did to you?"

"No. They took out some of my intestines, I think. I don't know. And now I'm up front. They won't let me go back to my cell. I wouldn't eat my dinner last night, so they are punishing me because I threw up and I'm in pain. When I stop puking and I stop hurting, they will let me go back to my cell. They are punishing me because I hurt." Cindy tells me that she is in a cell with no furniture. "They can see in all the time, and the toilet doesn't flush. I have to ask a guard to come and flush it for me."

I've had major surgery twice in the last two years. I cannot imagine having surgery on my own.

Cindy talks about the months of pain she's suffered because of the blockage. "They wouldn't listen to me because they thought I was trying to get drugs. Whatever is wrong with me it is drug-seeking behaviors."

The next day Cindy is taken back to the hospital. She is returned to the jail later in the day. "The lieutenant came in and yelled at me because I ate some Life Savers and had some ginger ale. He yelled at me and said I was trying to manipulate the system by trying to make myself sick. He said, 'You keep this up and we can put you somewhere else.'" Cindy is crying. "I am so frustrated. I think I've been under so much strain this last year my body is shutting down." She talks about the lieutenant. "He stopped my canteen." She explains, "You have to fill out a paper and you can get soda and shampoo and I can't get that anymore." Her voice is high. She sounds nervous, anxious, as if she has a fever. "You know what he is pissed about? Because I had to go to the hospital today."

"Have you heard from your lawyer?"

"No."

"Does she know you're sick?"

"Yes. I talked to her secretary."

"Do you know what the holdup is now?"

"The rehab they are trying to get me into costs more money than she thought it was going to so she is trying to put a motion in to get more money."

"I didn't know there was a given sum of money."

"I didn't either."

I ask Cindy when she last spoke with the court-appointed lawyer.

"I don't know. I am so angry with her. My blood pressure is back up and I take pills for it and it is still up. My stomach is torn apart. My lower staples didn't hold so it is open."

"Do you have a dressing on?"

"Finally. Yesterday. They sent me out without dressings. They are dressing it once a day. I haven't had it done since yesterday."

"Were the nurses okay with you?"

"Some of them. Some not. I definitely know this body is not going to take this stress and strain. I think they are just pushing it too far and nobody wants to do anything. I mean it has been almost a year now and all that's happening is, it's getting worse. I still haven't been sentenced. I have to sit here and wait."

She talks about the probation officer who wrote the presentence report. "He's on everybody's ass. The secretary told me he is still insisting that I go to the prison rehab without my medication. I went without it in hospital for five days and it was like a roller coaster for the last two days. Finally the day before I left they let me take it. Before that I was on a liquid IV so I couldn't take it."

"Did you write down that they wouldn't let anybody contact me?"

"Yes. Being in there just drove me crazy, not to be able to talk to anybody. They should at least have let me use the phone. They treated me as if I was an axe murderer, with the guns and stuff and the old people staring at me and stuff, it was unbelievable. Every time I had to go for a walk the guard came with me." Cindy is sobbing uncontrollably. "All I am being is warehoused—for a probation violation. Everything is threatening. If I don't do this, I get threatened. I was punished for eating Life Savers. I hate it here. I hate it here. This is the worst thing, and they expect me to sit back and say it is okay but it isn't, I can't handle it any more." She calms down.

"I hate crying. I don't want them to see me crying."

"Do you want me to see if I can talk to your lawyer?"

"Would you phone her and ask what is going on? I think I've been too laid back. They couldn't do anything worse to me. You've got to keep calling her. God forbid that I get sick again because they will put me down front in a tiny cell that is no bigger than a bathroom. Next time I'm not going to tell them I am sick, because all I do is get punished. Last night when I was throwing up I had to keep banging on the door to get their attention because the toilet doesn't flush. They had to flush."

The outside placement that Cindy is told she can go to refuses to take her.

Cindy cries, then she whispers loudly in a voice that seems to want to shout.

"I am worried about my mind. I forget things. I feel so stupid when I am talking. You put a person in this situation and it is very mind damaging. I just want to get on with my life. First get the help that I need. What they are doing to me by housing me in this little tiny cell I don't know. And now I am worried that they are going to send me back to prison. The jail doesn't want me. If I go back to prison I have five years ahead of me. I don't understand why they want to send me to the prison rehab. There has to be a place that will take me. I do need counseling. I do. I don't know what to do anymore. It is a wondering game every day. Wondering if somebody is going to take me. Wondering what will happen to me. I know I am going friggin' crazy. I am worried that they are going to throw me back into prison. Now the probation officer knows that the rehab didn't take me so this is the ace in the hole. My lawyer is just going to give up and I will have to go to the prison rehab."

The next day Cindy telephones. She says she thought about writing a letter to the judge but decided against it. "It will only piss him off."

"I'll continue to try to find a drug rehab," I tell her.

I telephone the Office of Drug and Alcohol Prevention (ODAP) at the State Department, and I speak with a substance abuse counselor. The difficulty is finding a rehab facility that will take dual-diagnosis patients. Most rehabs are not set up to deal with men and women recovering from addiction who need to be medicated to control depression. Eventually I put together a short list of facilities that might be willing to take Cindy. I read the list to Cindy and tell her about each facility.

"Will you give it to my lawyer?"

I telephone the law office. The court-appointed lawyer isn't available. I give the names and telephone numbers of the facilities to her secretary. I ask which rehabs are being considered as possible placements for Cindy. She names the rehab that refused to accept Cindy.

"Since then?"

"She hasn't contacted any more," the secretary tells me. "I'm sure the list will be helpful."

CINDY IS SENTENCED AT THE SUPERIOR COURT BUT THERE ARE NO WITNESSES

On June 7, Cindy is brought to the superior court for a sentencing hearing. She has been in jail for three hundred and seventy-five days. Cindy is expecting to be sent to an outside placement where she can be treated for manic depression as well as drug addiction. The court-appointed lawyer says she has found a substance abuse facility.

"She said if I plead guilty I will be sent to a rehab," Cindy tells me. "I won't have more than another month in jail. I don't have a choice. I have to plead guilty."

Cindy's brother arrives at the courthouse with one of her sisters. They come and sit in the waiting area with me. Cindy's brother talks about the house he is renovating. "There are plenty of summer jobs opening up," he says. "Cindy could find a job and live with me."

The small woman with the large briefcase who was at the canceled hearing passes through the metal detector and walks down the ramp. As before, she seats herself at a table, opens her briefcase, and begins to read. This time I go over and introduce myself.

She is the psychiatrist who evaluated Cindy. We talk about the hearing. The psychiatrist shows me the books that she has brought with her—*Substance Abuse and Psychotherapy, Alcoholism and Clinical Psychiatry, Psychiatric Disability: Clinical, Legal and Administration*. She opens the book on *Psychiatric Disability*, searches through the pages, and locates some highlighted passages that she intends to use to support her argument that Cindy is suffering from a bipolar mood disorder and major depression as well as polysubstance addiction. "This woman has suffered so much," she tells me. Then she holds the book up in front of her face and whispers. "But they won't listen to me. I am a woman and I am colored." The psychiatrist is from the Philippines.

I introduce her to Cindy's brother and sister. We sit together and talk while we wait. A counselor who works at the prison arrives. I do not see the probation officer or the man with no teeth—which surprises me as I had anticipated that they would both testify.

Cindy's lawyer comes down the ramp and walks over to where we are sitting. She is wearing a turquoise knit skirt and a mostly turquoise madras shirt with a brightly colored ceramic brooch of a cat pinned at the neck.

She tells us that Cindy is "downstairs." Then she says that if Cindy does not go to a rehab she is facing nine and a half to fifteen years. The counselor from the prison is reassuring. "The system is really trying to accommodate her," she tells us. The court-appointed lawyer leaves and joins the county attorney and the assistant county attorney in the judge's chambers.

We have already waited about an hour. It is another hour before the court-appointed lawyer reappears. She hurries over to where we are sitting.

She leans forward. "The judge said, 'I don't care what the testimony is I am still going to send her to prison.' " She stands up straight and looks at us as if waiting for a reaction.

"Can he do that?" I ask.

"He's done it," she says and leaves.

I write what she has just told us in my notebook and I ask the psychiatrist to verify what I have written. Carefully she writes her full name. Looking troubled, the psychiatrist asks for my telephone number and she gives me hers. We agree to keep in touch. The counselor also gets up and goes. Cindy's brother and sister remain seated.

"Are you going to stay?" I ask.

"I want to know what they are going to do with her," her brother says.

Stunned, I try to work out the implications of what the lawyer has just said. For almost thirteen months Cindy has been held at the county jail. During that time she has never had the opportunity to explain to the judge what happened to her when she was released from jail. Her journals have been used against her and she has not been able to object to their use or to explain the entries that were read into the court record. The affidavit from the man who said that the heroin found in her apartment belonged to him has never been used. The psychiatric report that states categorically that Cindy is suffering from a major form of depression will never become a part of the official court record.

In my head I go through the documents that have been used, the probation reports, the prison recommendation, the report of the sheriff who searched her apartment, toxic texts that are presented as objective reality but that distort the "truth" and do not accurately portray what has happened to Cindy.

We continue to wait. We watch the clock and wonder if we will have to come back after lunch. It is almost an hour before the court-appointed lawyer returns. She says she has been back in the judge's chambers. The hearing is about to take place. Then she hurries back up the ramp to one of the small courtrooms that can't be seen from the waiting area.

"How can they have a hearing without witnesses?" I ask. It's not really a question. Fed up, I am just being cynical. We hurry up the ramp after the lawyer.

In the courtroom Cindy is sitting next to the court-appointed lawyer. The new county attorney—a woman who has recently taken over the case— is sitting at another table with a man whom I presume is the new assistant county attorney. The judge enters the courtroom and we all stand.

The judge reads docket numbers. He speaks quickly, and I am already lost. I catch him when he says, "This is not a negotiated plea. The state is going to recommend something, and the defendant is going to recommend something else."

I ask myself, if this is not a negotiated plea why are there no witnesses?

The judge tells Cindy to stand and he speaks directly to her. "Do you give up your right to a jury?"

"Yes." It is only a month since Cindy had major surgery. The incision the surgeon made when he removed part of her intestines has not yet healed. She is white faced, her hair is drawn back, and she stands with her hands, palms down, on the table.

The judge is speaking rapidly. "Do you give up your right to witnesses?"

"Yes, Your Honor."

"Are you satisfied with the services of your attorney?"

"Yes, Your Honor."

I feel sick.

"To the violation. How do you plead?"

"Guilty."

The judge is writing.

Cindy is swaying. Just her fingertips are on the table.

The judge asks her if she waives the right to read the indictment. Cindy hesitates. Later she tells me that she didn't know what the judge was asking her. She leans over and speaks to the court-appointed lawyer.

It is the lawyer who responds, "Yes, Your Honor."

Cindy tells me later that the lawyer appointed by the superior court never mentioned the indictment to her. "I have no idea what it contains. When I get out of prison I'm going to go to the courthouse and read it."

The county attorney describes the search of Cindy's apartment. Point-zero-five grams of heroin were found. The county attorney recommends that Cindy be sentenced to seven and a half to fifteen years in prison. She speaks of showing the community and the defendant that this behavior will not be tolerated.

I close my eyes. It is the language of the probation report.

Cindy's lawyer stands. She is hesitant, inarticulate. She tells the court that Cindy uses her addiction as a coping mechanism. She talks about her brutal childhood. She uses the word brutal twice. She explains that efforts have been made to get the defendant into a rehabilitation facility but that she hasn't been accepted.

For violation of probation, Cindy is sentenced to 375 days in jail—the amount of time she has already served. The judge then sentences her to not more than seven and not less than three and a half years. He states that Cindy can petition the court for admittance to a long-term drug rehabilitation facility. He says that such an arrangement will have to be approved by both the probation department and the court.

The court-appointed lawyer gives Cindy some papers to sign. We stand. The judge leaves. The guard says, "Quick," and Cindy's brother and sister go over and put their arms around her.

"Will you visit me?" she asks them. She is crying.

I follow the court-appointed lawyer out of the courtroom and ask her about the sentence.

"This is exactly what we hoped would happen." She is brusque. "Cindy will be sent to a rehab. She won't have to stay in prison for more than a month or two."

"What if the probation department won't let her go?"

The lawyer looks annoyed. She tells me that she doesn't have time to talk to me. She turns her back and walks away.

CINDY IS SENT BACK TO THE WOMEN'S STATE PRISON

On June 11, Cindy telephones me. "They've got me in quarantine. They're going to take me off all my medications."

"Can they do that?"

"There's a psychiatrist coming in to evaluate me to see if I need lithium and Elavil."

"When?"

"I see the psychiatrist next Monday." She talks about the prison. "It's going to be hard time if I have to do it in here. This place is a joke. I hate it."

She talks about the prison social worker. "She grins each time she passes me. I ignore her."

I ask Cindy if she has heard from the court-appointed lawyer.

"No. She refuses to take my calls."

We talk about the hearing.

"She was giving me papers to read in the courtroom. I didn't know what was happening. I just said what she told me to say. I kept having to say guilty, guilty, guilty."

We talk about rehabs. Several look promising.

"Can you call the Washington House for me? Get some information about the place?"

"Sure."

Cindy tries to be optimistic. But the effort is too much for her. "I'm just tired. I think they have made me worse. This is mental cruelty."

She laughs. She tells me that when she was at the superior court, she spoke to the lawyer who represented her when she was released from prison. "I thought he was just being friendly, but he's charged me for the time he spent talking to me. I've got a bill from him."

On June 14, Cindy tells me that the psychiatrist has just told her she doesn't need medication. "He said he has no proof of me being bipolar. He said, 'You're a drug addict.' He said, 'I don't see why you should be on medication.' He's taking me off lithium and then he's taking me off Elavil. He got right in my face and yelled at me. He said, 'What are you taking Flexeril for?' He made me feel like an asshole. 'If these pills were working you would never have taken drugs.' I said, 'I didn't want to come in here and argue with you.' He said, 'That's very interesting.' He kept referring to the psychiatrist who was here before. I told him 'that psychiatrist said I should be medicated.' Oh God. I'm really miserable. I'm so angry. I could choke that son of a bitch. I told him I'm manic and he said, 'I don't see anything to indicate that you are manic.'" I can hear someone talking to Cindy. "I gotta go. The psychiatrist wants to see me again. I'll call you tomorrow."

I call the court-appointed lawyer. She is out of the state. I ask her secretary to tell her that Cindy is being removed from her medication and that I am worried about her. "Someone needs to intervene."

Cindy phones again. "The psychiatrist is taking away my medication. I get one hundred mil of Elavil tonight and fifty tomorrow. He said, 'You have three choices, the infirmary, a mental institution, or stay here without meds.' He called me back in because he found more records. I told him I wanted my medication. He said 'Want? Want? You don't need it.'" Cindy is crying. "Oh God. Get me out of here. I can't do this. He said, 'Make sure' "—she is sobbing—'make sure you behave.' I had to sit there and tell him I'll be okay or they'll lock me up. And if I wack out they'll put me in an institution. He said he has no record of me being bipolar."

I ask Cindy if she has a copy of the psychiatrist evaluation that she can give him.

"No, they've packed all my papers away. Can you call her?"

"As soon as we finish talking."

"This asshole wouldn't give me his name."

I call the psychiatrist who I met at the superior court. She tells me she will send a letter to the prison doctor expressing concern that Cindy is being removed from her medication. On June 15 the psychiatrist writes:

It has come to my notice that discontinuation of lithium and Elavil has been contemplated in treatment of the above captioned.

Enclosed find a copy of my psychiatric evaluation report on Cynthia. The summary and recommendations took into account an extensive review of available past records and data from individual interviews. The analysis and recommendation in relation to diagnosis and treatment for Cynthia are explicitly stated.

There are clear undeniable indications calling for her current medication. Taking her off medication is unwarranted. Discontinuation of medication will, with great certainty, result in a relapse of either manic or major depressive episode. Either one of these could push Cynthia again into serious risk of suicide. I strongly recommend maintaining the current medication to prevent serious consequences.

That same day, Cindy talks again about her meeting with the psychiatrist. "He was threatening," she says. "If I don't cooperate they'll put me in a mental hospital. I'm frightened."

I remember when Cindy was hospitalized before and I was told she was all right. "Make sure you call me every day," I tell her, "that way I'll know you're okay."

"I waited in jail for a year so my medication would not be taken away. My mother takes Elavil. They took her off it two years ago and she wacked out. I don't know where they found this guy. There is nowhere in my records that it says I should be taken off my medication. He says two years is long enough."

We talk about the prison rehab. We are convinced that Cindy has been taken off her medication so she can go to the prison rehab. If she is unmedicated there is no reason for her to be sent to an outside placement.

"If I wack out it's going to be lock-up," she says. "They'll say, you're violent, get out of here, and they'll send me to a mental institution." Cindy is crying. "I've gotta go. I'll telephone you tomorrow."

She calls again. "The psychiatrist has signed a document and he said 'I'm going to sign this and if you act up once you'll go to state prison to the psychiatric ward.' I'm fucked. I don't feel good and I can't start crying."

On the morning of June 16, Cindy tells me that she has been trying to see the regular prison doctor. "She's here today but they told me I can't see her until next week. I went down to medical and the nurse said I had to put in a request to see the doctor and then she said, 'You have to come to sick call first.'"

Cindy talks about the psychiatrist taking away her medication. "I don't know what they expect. I could understand if it made me high but it doesn't. They won't even give me an aspirin."

"The doctor should get the psychiatrist's letter this morning."

"But they won't let me see her. When I saw the psychiatrist here I told him that the last time I was taken off my medication I shot myself. He said, 'Yes, I read that and how were you feeling that day?' "

"You've got to hang in."

"I know. If I lose it they'll lock me up in the infirmary. You get a bed and a toilet and if you're lucky you get a book."

On July 1, Cindy tells me that the court-appointed lawyer won't take her calls. "She's blocked my calls. There was supposed to be a hearing before the first. I get no letters. No telephone calls. Nothing. I'm going crazy."

Cindy calls me collect every day, sometimes we talk for an hour, sometimes she calls twice or three times. In between I make other calls to rehabilitation facilities that don't take out-of-state patients, that are not set up to deal with dual-diagnosis patients, that cost too much, to substance abuse counselors who have no advice except to tell me that there is nothing they can do if "the matter" is being handled by the courts, to friends who are lawyers who are amused that I am naive enough to expect justice from the courts. I am tired. Cindy hears it in my voice. Instead of me encouraging her, she encourages me.

"Hey you! Go take some time off with David."

"I might take a couple of hours off."

"No. You take more than a couple of hours. Go hang out with your husband."

She makes me laugh.

"Are you okay?" she asks.

"Yeah. I'm okay."

"I'll call tomorrow. Take the day off!"

July 17. "I went to sick call. They won't let me see the doctor. They've told me I can't see her until the end of the month."

On June 18 Cindy tells me that she has an interview at Washington House but that the state has refused to transport her. "I'm being medically watched. They said the reason they denied me the Washington House is because I could get drugs there. That's bullshit. I could get drugs here." She talks about the court-appointed lawyer. "I told her I've had it and she said, 'So you don't want your hearing?' Then she said she'll be glad when the case is over." She recalls the time she was in court, and the court-appointed lawyer's promise that Cindy would not spend more than a month in prison. "I knew this would happen if I came in here. I feel like shit. I waived my rights when I went into court. I had to say whatever she wanted me to say."

Cindy calls again on the evening of June 18. She tells me she is writing a letter to the court-appointed lawyer. "I can't get her to understand," she says. "If anybody acts up they are locked up. One girl was locked up for forty-five days. Three girls in my room have been to the infirmary. They've all been locked up. I was only supposed to stay here for one month. She told me, 'One month, maybe two, and you'll be out of there.' There were things the judge was saying to me and she was telling me what to say. All they do is degrade me, degrade me, degrade me. But I haven't given up yet. But you know there is only so much a person can take." At the end of the conversation, Cindy tries to be upbeat. "I really want this to work and it can work. You have to want it or it won't work."

"It'll work. It has to. Call me tomorrow."

"Yeah. Don't worry. I'll call."

On June 19, Cindy says she has talked to her mother. "She didn't say a thing. She just asked me what I'm going to do. None of my family want to help." We talk about the court hearing, Washington House, Cindy's medication. "I don't feel good today," she tells me. She is no longer taking Elavil or lithium. The conversation focuses on the conditions in the prison. "There are six people in my room. It's small and there's no air. There's no light in the evening except for the TV. There's just enough room to walk to my bed between the footlockers and chairs." She talks about the women who share her room. "Two of them have been in the psychiatric ward and one in the infirmary. It's the sick room. All I do is lie on my bed. I can't stay out of bed for more than forty-five minutes."

Cindy tells me she has written to the psychiatrist who evaluated her when she was in the county jail. I remind her that the psychiatrist has sent a letter to the prison doctor. "I don't know if she's got it. I'll ask her when I go to see her. I don't know what I'll do if they won't let me go to Washington House. I feel like I'm under so much pressure. Like an explosion waiting to happen. This is supposed to help me?"

On the evening of June 24 Cindy calls to tell me that the court-appointed lawyer will not speak to her. "She won't take my calls. I called twice. They've blocked me off."

I tell Cindy I'll call the superior court to find out if a hearing has been scheduled.

Cindy has talked to the prison social worker. "I asked her how long I will have to wait if they send me to prison drug rehab. She said, 'Nine months,' and she just kept walking."

I tell Cindy that David and I played hooky and went to see *Jurassic Park*. "We went to the two-fifteen matinee."

"You need to do things like that more often," she tells me.

During many of the telephone calls Cindy talks to me about her life. She is trying to fit it all together, searching the past for a way to cope with the present. She talks about the events that were taking place when she shot herself and when she stabbed herself. She tells me about her recovery before she was sent to prison, going to meetings, speaking about her addiction, encouraging other drug addicts to stay in the program, going to more meetings, getting a sponsor, making a telephone call and asking for help.

"When I was using I was afraid to go out. I'm back to that. They have to force me to go outside. I'm so angry."

On June 28, Cindy writes to the judge. She asks me to spell *Honor* and a few other words she's used. In the letter she apologizes for letting the judge down. She talks about her need for a dual-diagnosis program and of Washington House, a facility that can provide her with psychiatric help as well as drug rehabilitation. She tells him that her court-appointed lawyer has given up on the case. "Well, I just wanted to write you a letter. This is my last chance to say anything, although I haven't been able to talk since this mess started. Your Honor, I don't want to be forgotten and be left sitting in prison."

Cindy talks about writing the letter. "Once I started writing, it just sort of came to me. I wanted to try to hit the points. It is like answering some of the bad things that they are going to say." She is quiet for a moment. "I just want the judge to think about what has happened to me," she says finally, in an empty voice. I think she knows that her letter is unlikely to make a difference.

The conversation turns to the county attorney's quoting from the probation report.

"The probation officer called it a big-city drug in his report." She laughs. "I came up here to get away from it. But it was here. I met people who were using it and dealing. I started using again within a month. That's how I got started again. Here. In the city."

Cindy continues to wait in prison for an outside placement. She asks for her journals to be returned to her. The court-appointed lawyer says the district attorney has refused to return them. Cindy tells me she has seen the prison doctor. The doctor has not received the letter from the psychiatrist. "She looked through all her mail. She hasn't received it. She's a straightforward person." Cindy tells me that she likes the prison doctor. "But she's under orders from the prison psychiatrist. I don't think she is allowed to give me any medication."

I ask the psychiatrist to send another letter. She sends me a facsimile of the recorded delivery receipt. The letter arrived at the prison on June 17 and there is a clearly identifiable signature on the receipt.

On July 8 Cindy is screened for an outside placement. Her court-appointed lawyer goes with her. She returns to the prison and waits. And waits. "I get no letters. No telephone calls. Nothing. There is supposed to be a hearing."

"I'll call the court."

The person who speaks to me at the superior court states that there is no need of a hearing.

"But the judge said if she could get an outside placement there would be a hearing to see if she can go."

Once again I've irritated the person who is speaking with me.

"It's all been taken care of."

I apologize. "I'm sorry. I know I'm being a nuisance."

"Yes you are." She hangs up.

The next time Cindy calls she tells me she has received a letter from the court-appointed lawyer, asking if Cindy wants me to represent her and telling her to respond within five days.

"Can you represent me?"

"No, she's being sarcastic. She knows I can't."

On July 27 Cindy receives another bill from the lawyer who represented her when she got out of jail. "I owe him $4,000, and $2,000 of that is interest."

I ask her if she has heard from the court-appointed lawyer.

"No. Not a word."

We talk about recovery. Again Cindy tells me that all she has ever known is drugs. In my notes I write that she is going to need a lot of help to build new ways of coping. She talks hopefully of going to Washington House. We joke.

At some point during every conversation we laugh, at ourselves, about Cindy's smoking, my eating Grapenuts while I'm working at my computer, diets, craving food, about different addictions, my compulsive work habits. Cindy tries to get me to take a day off. "You've got to stop working so hard," she counsels me. "Take a day off. Go out and have some fun," she says.

"I am having fun," I tell her. We both laugh at the absurdity of the situation.

We talk again on the next Monday. Cindy has received a copy of the motion written by the court-appointed lawyer in which she petitions the court for Cindy to be sent to Washington House. Cindy reads paragraphs from the motion and we discuss what the court-appointed lawyer has written. We are both impressed.

Cindy is told that the hearing will take place on August 11. "I hope they let me say something," she says. "I've been writing stuff down."

"Is your family coming?"

"My mother isn't, but my brother said he would try to get there."

I telephone the psychiatrist who evaluated Cindy when she was in the county jail. She says that she has not been asked to testify. I ask her if she will write a letter to the superior court judge stating that Cindy is suffering from a mood disorder that requires medication. She does:

> The above captioned has a long documented history of co-existence of mood disorder (bipolar disorder and major depression, recurrent with multiple parasuicide), and substance abuse disorder (alcohol and psychoactive substances).
>
> It has been a common error in the past to regard these disorders in isolation, neglecting the social context of the involved individual.
>
> In recent years, it has been recognized that treatment of the underlying emotional disorder is crucial to the success of any substance abuse remediation. Fortunately, there are now some existing programs that are aware of and responsible to this well-recognized presence and special need of individuals with dual diagnosis.
>
> Cynthia needs psychopharmacologic treatment for her mood disorder. There is a current and also long-term risk of suicide with no medication. Addressing the substance abuse problem should not hinder the delivery of assistance for a condition that needs continuing medical attention.

I make a copy of and put it in an envelope with a copy of the letter that the psychiatrist wrote to the prison doctor stating that Cindy needs to continue taking lithium and Elavil.

PRACTICING MEDICINE WITHOUT A LICENSE AT THE COUNTY SUPERIOR COURT

On August 11, I take the letters to the superior court. There are people in the waiting area at the superior court, but no one is there waiting for Cindy. Lawyers talk with their clients at tables. There are mothers waiting with young women, and a man who looks like a biker, but no men without teeth or lawyers with their children hoping to catch the show.

I wait. I am concerned that the hearing will take place in one of the small courtrooms that I can't see from the waiting room. How will I know?

I continue to wait. After about thirty minutes I get up and speak with a uniformed court official. He tells me that Cindy is downstairs in a holding tank. I tell him I have some documents that are relevant to her case. He says the court-appointed lawyer is with the county attorney in the judge's chambers. "I'll take them in to her."

I tell him that I am worried about interrupting their meeting.

"Will they help her?" he asks.

"They might."

He smiles and holds out his hand. I give him the envelope. I wait. Twenty minutes pass. From where I am sitting I can see the man in uniform who took the envelope. I ask him if he will tell me when the hearing is about to take place.

"They've been in there for about ten minutes," he says.

Later Cindy tells me that she asked the court-appointed lawyer to tell me that the hearing was about to start but the lawyer refused.

I open the door and walk in. The county attorney is speaking. She states that Washington House is a ninety-day program that can be extended. "The defendant would do better, in the state's opinion—or a more appropriate program would be the prison drug program, which is a year in different phases." She mentions a letter from Washington House. "They were not aware that she was on Flexeril and they weren't aware that she had a prior failure when she was out."

Later I obtain the letter to which the county attorney refers—and which is addressed to her personally—from the superior court records. In the letter no mention is made of Flexeril, which is an opiate-based muscle relaxant. The drug mentioned in the letter is Elavil, a nonnarcotic antidepressant. In addition, no mention is made of Cindy's "prior failure when she was out." The writer questions Cindy's minimization of the reasons for being reincarcerated—"possession for personal use but not for distribution." Cindy was quite clear that she did not talk about possession for distribution during the Washington House interview. In all the conversations I had with Cindy she never talked about distribution except in the context of the presentence probation report—and then she said, "I always tried to make sure I had enough. I was always frightened of being without it. Why would I sell it when I needed it?" No, more likely it was the county attorney—who stated in court that she spoke with counselors from Washington House on the telephone—who introduced the erroneous idea that Cindy possessed the heroin for the purpose of distribution. And what was not mentioned by the county attorney—and was not introduced into the proceedings by the court-appointed lawyer—is that Cindy is described in the letter as appearing to be "very sincere in expressing her willingness to go to any lengths for her recovery." The writer goes on, "Even with these reservations, we feel our program can adequately meet her treatment needs."

The county attorney continues. "Given the lack of security and the relative brevity of that program and the focus on adolescents, although defense counsel maintains she would be separate from them. But given that, and as well as her manipulative and addictive propensities, the more appropriate placement would be in the prison drug rehab. Anything less than that will set this defendant up for failure. She has had chances before and she has shown that she can't control her dangerous addiction. The state therefore requests that the motion be denied." She concludes by asking the court to allow a drug and alcohol counselor for the department of corrections "to say a few words."

The woman is middle-aged, heavyset, and soft-spoken. She says good morning to the judge, states her name, and tells the judge that she has a master of science degree and that she is employed by the house of corrections as a court referral officer. "I have had the opportunity to go over Cynthia's case and also to do some investigation into the rehabilitation of Cynthia. Washington House is set up and licensed for a ninety-day program. They will repeat that process if a client is resistant to treatment. That's why it is so structured."

The letter from Washington House states that the program is three to six months but can be adjusted to fit individual need. Later, I telephoned Washington House and I was told that it has a six-month adult drug and alcohol treatment program and that the clients are reevaluated weekly. The person with whom I spoke stated that the information provided to the court was "misinformed."

"It is my professional opinion," the court referral officer continues, "and I haven't interviewed Cynthia, but I have read her files and I have read the various expert opinions that she presents as a long-term parallelmatic addicted to opiate substances. Given that fact, the recovery for a person such as Cynthia must be very, very structured over a significant length of time. It is my professional opinion that people addicted to opiates have lost all social skills and must be *habilitated* and not rehabilitated."

Wipe out. I can't take notes, the tape recorder is on, I just try to take in the scene. Cindy is sitting with the court-appointed lawyer. The court referral officer is standing next to the county attorney. She speaks as a lawyer would from the floor of the courtroom, not as a witness who has walked over to the witness box and been sworn in. She speaks with the authority of a lawyer, gives a medical diagnosis, and prescribes a course of treatment as if she is a doctor, and *she never interviewed Cindy*.

Cindy is slumped in her chair. She seems to be listening but she does not react when the court referral officer speaks. She is alone. Her family have not come to support her. Her brother never showed up. There are no witnesses. The psychiatrist who evaluated Cindy was not asked to testify. I am the only person in the courtroom other than those who are participating in the event. No objections are raised by Cindy's court-appointed lawyer as to whether or not the court referral officer has the necessary medical qualifications and expertise to evaluate Cindy's medical records.

The court referral officer is still speaking. "I understand that Cynthia has some women's issues. Also as far as the dual diagnosis goes there is a tendency among substance abuse counselors—those who are certified and licensed by various states—to say, yes, indeed there is dual diagnosis among addicts. About five percent of the population is bipolar or manic and five percent of addicts are bipolar or manic depressives. The tendency in treating is to triage, in other words you treat what is going to kill her first and what is going to kill her first is her addiction. You must treat her addiction and after a year of not using mind-altering substances—" The court-appointed lawyer does not object. She does not point out that Cindy has been drug free for more than a year. The court referral officer is on a roll. "—because there are mood swings and there's learning to reengage, and if you did brain scans you'd find that there is a certain chemical imbalance in someone who is recovering."

Objection! The court referral officer does not have the medical qualifications to perform brain scans or to interpret them. But there are no objections. The court-appointed lawyer does not object.

The court referral officer continues. "After about a year, you know, nine months to a year, to reassess, and if that person needs things like lithium or an antidepressant, is to indeed to prescribe them."

Objection! The court referral officer does not have the medical qualifications to discuss the prescription of medications! But the court-appointed lawyer makes no objections—even though she has on the table in front of her the report written by the psychiatrist who states that Cindy has a long-documented history of bipolar disorder and major depression recurrent with multiple parasuicide. The lawyer does not object—even though the psychiatrist writes of the "common error" of treating drug addiction in isolation. She does not object—even though the psychiatrist states categorically that Cindy "needs psychopharmacologic treatment for her mood disorder." The court-appointed lawyer does not object. She is passive, as if the decision has already been made, as if she knows that it won't make any difference if she objects.

The court referral officer continues, "Statistics say that one out of a hundred alcoholics gets sober and one out of a thousand heroin addicts gets sober. And that's kind of frightening and it needs aggressive treatment. Thank you, Your Honor."

The court-appointed lawyer stands. In a tired voice she says she has received from an unidentified source a copy of a letter from the psychiatrist who evaluated Cindy when she was in the county jail. She states that she would like it to be part of the record. The judge acknowledges having read the letter in his chambers before the hearing. Pathetically, the lawyer continues. "I'll just put on the record that obviously there are lots of schools of thought." She says that the court referral officer has one school of thought, the psychiatrist another. "Her theory is that—can't treat the—you can't treat the emotional disorder subsequent—separate from the substance abuse disorder, you have to treat it in concert." That's it. That's all she has to say.

She tells the judge that Cindy would like to address the court. In a voice barely audible, Cindy talks about prison drug rehab. She tells the judge that if she goes there she will not be able to take Elavil for depression. She says that if she goes and can't manage without it, then she will have to return to the prison to serve out her time. "I have tried before and I have not been able to go without it. It is not a drug that gets me high. I can think with Elavil. It is for depression, and I suffer from depression. I know I have a lot of problems to work on. Washington House talked to me about the medication and the drugs, how they could help me along with that to learn about both, not just one, as in-prison drug rehab would do. The director of the prison drug rehab told me that the prison drug rehab is solely for drug addiction. Washington House is willing to help me work on family issues, a lot of women's issues that the prison drug rehab does not do. I would be seeing a counselor. I would have my own counselor there. Plus there would be a psychiatrist there who would come in once a week. So. I have been going without medication. I said yes I will go in and try to do my best to the best of my ability to go in there and do the counseling and see how I am without my medication but—" Cindy stops. She is on the verge of tears.

She composes herself and then continues, her voice trembling. "Yes I do need a lot of structure, but the Washington House seemed like they really cared and they were willing to deal with all of the things I need. Not just drugs. I guess I do have a problem with medication. I know that. And that's why I need to be helped with that too. Not just the drug addiction. I need both. If it is a long-term program because if I just deal with drugs, when I get out the problems are still going to be there." She is crying. Cindy tells the judge she wrote some things down that she wanted to say but doesn't have them with her. "So I would like it if you could really think about it. I would really like to go to the Washington House. I would get a lot more out of that and learn more out of it. And I am willing to stay there as long as they want me to stay. I mean until I'm ready to go back out. And it is all women and it just feels like it would be a lot more caring there, and I think that's the most important part of it. Thank you, Your Honor."

The judge speaks. "The court will take it under advisement."

"All rise."

The judge leaves. I stay to talk with Cindy.

"Did I do okay?" she asks. "I'm not sure I said everything that I wanted to say."

The court-appointed lawyer interrupts. "I want to talk to my client."

I leave, following the court referral officer down the stairs. "Now I can go back and start my real day's work," she says, looking back at me, smiling pleasantly. At the bottom of the stairs, as she heads along the corridor toward the probation department, I stop and write down what she said.

On August 13, Cindy calls. "The judge ruled against me. I can't talk. I'm going to lie down and have a cigarette."

August 17. "Now I'll have to play the game. I'll play the game. That's what it is, a game. You can't fight the system but I'm not going to walk out on this. I'm mad. Real mad. This past year has totally fucked me up. This makes me want to do drugs." Cindy is crying. "I'm fucked. There's nothing left of me. I'd like to do a bag right now."

HOW HUMAN RIGHTS VIOLATIONS TAKE PLACE THROUGH THE INACCURATE INVENTION OF AUTHORITATIVE TEXTS

Since 1989 I have tried to support Cindy in her struggle to resist the legal system's punishment of her for being a heroin addict. To support Cindy in her struggle I have worked to gain some understanding of how the legal system has classified her as a "felon." I have tried to discover how her life has been officially reinvented in authoritative texts and how these toxic forms of literacy have been used to incarcerate her.

I have viewed the official documentation pertaining to Cindy's addiction—to both prescription and street drugs—within the context of her everyday life. I have tried to understand what is happening to her, what is going on in her life, what she thinks, what she feels, what she does. I have tried to stand side by side with her, to imagine her pain, to come as close as I can to her memories of the events in her life that shape her existence, to conceive what it must have been like to be beaten as a child, to understand what is it like to be incarcerated, to be out of control, high, detoxing, having bad thoughts, craving drugs, attempting suicide.

Juxtaposing the life that Cindy has lived with official versions of her life, I have tried to understand the ways in which the actions of the courts, combined with the activities of the state and local prisons, have not only critically affected Cindy's ability to cope with her addiction but have also limited the opportunities that she has had to overcome the prejudicial responses by social welfare agencies and medical institutions to her personal situation.

There is no doubt in my mind that Cindy has become locked into configurations of institutional abuse that have made it impossible for her to recover from her addiction. I have no qualms in stating that Cindy is a victim of human rights violations that have been publicly sanctioned through official texts. Her life has been criminalized by the distortion of the record, by the misrepresentation of events, by the fabrication of information, through the ineptitude and incompetence—some might argue the sheer bloody-mindedness—of those who represent the American justice system.

The distortion of the record began with the presentence report written by a probation officer for the superior court judge after Cindy was arrested in 1989 for the federal offense of receiving heroin through the mail. When I first met Cindy and she said that the probation officer had written that she was selling the heroin she received in the mail, a member of the community—who was in recovery from twenty-nine years of hard-core addiction—laughed and said to me that the twenty bags Cindy received would have only lasted her a couple of days. "She's using enough to knock out a bull elephant."

But it was still difficult for me to imagine how she could use twenty bags for her own consumption in such a short time. My only frame of reference was the "drug busts" reported on TV, when the camera zooms in on kilos of cocaine hidden in the cargo of a plane or piled in plastic bags on a coffee table in someone's living room after a police raid. I knew Cindy for several months before I found out that the twenty bags contained a total of only one gram of heroin, the amount of sugar substitute in a single Sweet 'n Low packet. If you use a knife to divide up one packet of the sweetener into twenty small piles, you have Cindy's twenty bags—enough heroin to last her for two days.

Cindy's medical records state that she was using seven to ten bags of heroin a day. At most, in her advanced stage of addiction, the heroin would have lasted her three days, and yet in the first probation report she was accused of selling the heroin that she received through the mail, and the superior court judge stated at the beginning of the hearing at which she was sentenced that she was "charged with possession of a narcotic with the intent to sell." Even though the judge then went on to state that the charge was "now possession," the accusation that she was selling heroin hung in the courtroom and became a part of the official record.

I ask Cindy about the informer. "Why did he tell the police you were selling heroin in the city?"

"We used to get high together," she says, sounding bitter. "Sometimes he'd give me heroin and I'd give him some if he ran out."

Cindy continues, sounding as angry with herself as she does with her so-called friend.

"He knew I was getting heroin through the mail. I told him I was getting some. Then he got arrested so he turned in my name. He thought it would help him get off. He told them about me even though he knew I wasn't selling."

Cindy tells me that when she was in the prison rehab she met the informer—who was sent to prison even though he informed—and although the men and women were not supposed to speak to each other, she asked him why she turned her in. "One day I went up to him and I said, 'Look, I could have caused a lot of trouble for you, but I didn't. There was no need for you to do that to me.' I asked him why he did it, why he turned me in. He just threw up his hands. He didn't deny it. He didn't say anything. Then he tried to shake my hand." Speaking slowly, carefully pronouncing every word, she says again, "He tried to shake my hand."

"What did you do?"

"I walked away. What else could I do."

I ask Cindy another question. "What were you going to do when you'd used the heroin that you got through the mail?"

"There was another ten bags on the way."

"What happened to them?"

"The police got them the following Tuesday." Cindy pauses for a moment. "I think I got arrested on the Friday. I telephoned my friend to tell him not to send anymore but he had already gone and got it. The stuff was in the mail. He sent it regular mail, which he didn't do very often, and it arrived the following Tuesday. The police took it from my box."

"What happened to it? There is nothing in the public record to say that there was a second mail delivery."

"It's unaccounted for. I only got charged for the first twenty bags."

In August 1991, more than two years after Cindy was arrested, the allegation that she was selling was resuscitated in the second report written by the probation officer. In the report he reminds the superior court judge that an informer told the police "that the defendant was a junkie and was going to sell."

"Why would I sell it?" Cindy asks. "It was nothing. It would have lasted no time at all. I needed it. I have done a lot of drugs, but I'm not a bad person. I did drugs to help me forget. It's the only way I've ever felt good. I wanted the heroin for myself. I was terrified of not having any. I stockpiled it when I could but it never lasted me very long."

Despite the fact that there was no evidence of sales and that the amount of heroin that Cindy received through the mail was consistent with her own use, the implication that she was selling continued to dog her. In the subsequent report, the probation officer refers to the original presentence report when he reminds the judge that "the conclusion of the presentence investigation emphasized the seriousness of the offense and the need to send a message of deterrence to the general drug subculture as well as a message of protective assurance to the community in general." The "message of deterrence to the general drug subculture" was that drug dealers will receive severe sentences if they try to sell heroin, and the "message of protective assurance to the community in general" was that drug dealers will be imprisoned and will be kept off the streets of the city.

This interpretation of the text is supported by my own unexpected reading of a portion of the original presentence report when I visited the superior courthouse to review Cindy's court records on November 10, 1993. The clerk who usually handled my request to see the files was out of the office and another clerk assisted me. On previous occasions the probation reports were removed before the files were given to me. This time they were not. I moved through the numbered documents from the back to the front of the file. Inside the cover was a brown manilla envelop without a number. I opened it. Inside was the original prison report, of which I had a copy. I leafed through the pages to see if there were any papers that I had not seen. There was a three-or- four page biographic description of Cindy's childhood that was new to me so I skimmed it. It was not until I read the first paragraph on the next page that I realized that what I was reading was probably a copy of the first probation report.

Panic.

I stopped reading but that last paragraph echoed in my head. Feeling stupid at my response to the situation, I took out a pencil and began writing. I copied the paragraph I had just read and then put the report back in the envelope, moved to another section of the file, found documents that I needed for my files, and asked the clerk to make copies. The clerk who was normally in charge of the files returned and asked the woman who gave me the files if she had removed the probation reports.

"Did you read the probation report?" she shouted at me.

"No," I lied. Except that I didn't read the report. What I had read were sections of a copy of the report in the envelope with Cindy's prison papers. And I stopped reading when I realized that the document must be the presentence report. Here is the paragraph that I copied:

> In addressing the disposition, one begins first with the seriousness of the offense. Not unlike finding toxic waste in one's community, there is a sense of shock to the local community when there is an arrest for possession of heroin. With the sense of shock, there comes a strong community expectation that there should be zero tolerance for such a hard-core drug surfacing in the local area.

And so the myth that Cindy was selling heroin was invented, and remained the most compelling reason that the court could establish for the severity of her sentence. The lack of evidence of any intent to sell and her conviction only of possession were subsumed under the more serious earlier allegations.

Many of my subsequent conversations with Cindy focused on the way her drug addiction had been criminalized. We talked about what was written about the events that were taking place as we tried to understand what was happening to her. While I can present to you documents that establish a paper chronology of her "case," neither Cindy nor I were privy to the documentation as it was produced, and she is still not allowed to have copies of some of the documents that critically affected the official decision-making process.

For a fact there are some documents that have been written about Cindy that she has never seen. Also, documents to which she should have access have been withheld from her. For example, Cindy has asked for her journals to be returned to her, but her request has been denied. Even now, when she is living in a halfway house with no court hearings pending, her diaries still have not been returned.

In my analysis of the official texts as they have been used to determine what is to be done with Cindy, I have learned that there are specific documents—such as the probation reports—that contain the central themes of her criminalization, and there are other texts that have been discarded because they do not "fit" with the official account of her "felony." Such documents remain unauthorized, prohibited, and illegal, in the sense that written interpretations that present contradictory evidence are kept out of the "legal" record.

Stated another way, the record is distorted because critical documentation is excluded so that it does not interfere with the "legal" decision-making process. The psychiatrist's evaluation of Cindy's long-documented history of major depression as well as a substance abuse disorder never became a part of the official record. It was never used in the courtroom, and on the occasion when the psychiatrist came to the court to testify on Cindy's behalf the court-appointed lawyer stated, "The judge said, 'I don't care what the testimony is I am still going to send her to prison.'"

No alternate explanations were allowed to detract from the official record.

The doctor who supplied Cindy with prescription drugs was never questioned in court. The pharmacy records were not included in the superior court files. The plastic bags of prescription containers were used in the courtroom for effect, but no one asked how Cindy obtained so many pills, no one asked if the pills the doctor gave her potentiated her addiction, no one questioned how he was paid for the office visits. There was no investigation, and no consideration given to the possibility that he might have been getting sex for his pills. Even when a private lawyer represented Cindy, the role the doctor played in creating the conditions for her use of street drugs did not become a part of the official story. And, even though there is a possibility that *he* is a threat to the community—in the city there are stories of other young women who visit him—his professional status protects him. He remains immune. He still practices medicine with impunity.

To ensure Cindy's pariah status as a drug addict, events were misrepresented. When the women's state prison sent a report to the superior court that was described as "an accurate report of the information contained in the subject's offender record," that report was *in*accurate, *in*complete, and distorted the record. Even when the lawyer that Cindy hired to represent her established the inaccuracy of the information at a court hearing the report remained uncorrected in her official file at the county superior court. The fabrication that Cindy lost one hundred and twenty days of "good time" was still a part of the official record.

Finally, at the last superior court hearing, the court referral officer was used to maintain the official record. She testified in court even though she had never interviewed Cindy. The court referral officer maintained the record by providing medical opinions—even though she did not have the medical qualifications or expertise to discuss major depressive or bipolar disorders. The information she provided was inaccurate or just plain wrong, but there were no objections to her testimony's becoming a part of the official record.

By the time the court referral officer testified, the official documentation that controlled Cindy's life had a life of its own, and no one objected when testimony was fabricated to maintain the record. The official version of Cindy's life—as it was described in authoritative texts—had become a reality. The text represented truth, fact, actuality.

The "legal" version of Cindy's drug addiction had become unquestionable.

Officially, Cindy's life was a disaster. She had to be punished for her addiction, deterred from using drugs and from selling them. She needed to be imprisoned to learn to live without drugs, *h*abilitated not *r*ehabilitated, for, as the court referral officer stated, drug addicts have no social skills.

The irony is that Cindy appeared to live out the official text. It became a reality. When she was released from prison she used drugs and the cheering team abandoned her. The probation officer, the assistant county attorney, the court-appointed lawyer—who behaved for the most part more like a prosecutor than a public defender—and the judge appeared to be right.

LEARNING FROM CINDY

What Cindy teaches us is that in the official text they got it wrong. Cindy is a political prisoner. She is a political. As a person she doesn't exist. Drug addicts have no social worth. They have lost their humanity. The story line of the official text was constructed to "fit" the dominant political myth of our time that drug addiction is a form of law-breaking activity for which users must be punished.

In this way we abdicate responsibility. In denial, we don't have to consider how Cindy's family encultured her into using drugs. We don't have to question how Cindy's medical condition became rewritten as criminal behavior. If her medical records were discarded and the psychiatrist's report was struck from the record, we cannot be held accountable. When the psychiatrist writes that she observed a "prevailing sadness" in Cindy we are under no obligation to help her. When Cindy tells us "my growing-up years were terrible, my father hit us, and sometimes I get real angry and just want to yell" we don't have to listen. She is a drug addict. We don't need to know that she was in so much pain that she deliberately shot herself in the chest or that she stabbed herself in the stomach or that she has accidentally overdosed on heroin more than six times. It has nothing to do with us that her life has become increasingly dysfunctional. It is not our responsibility to examine the official subtexts of her life.

After Cindy was arrested, she tried to recover in the community, but the prison system destroyed her newly emerging social skills. The superior court judge released her, and she was left to reestablish her everyday living situation without the help of any social agency. In spite of these difficulties, Cindy tried again to recover from her addiction. She was ready to rewrite her life.

When she was first released from prison, Cindy presented at a conference with me. She was energized by the possibilities of speaking at meetings, enthusiastic about helping children, and articulate about working to help communities understand the problems of men and women who are suffering from addiction.

Cindy embraced the possibilities but she quickly learned that her life had become encoded on computer screens, and that decisions about what was going to happen had been made on paper. She had become abstracted in official documentation. Social agencies and medical facilities used print to deny her access to the services she needed. What happened to Cindy was determined through texts, and her life was determined by those who controlled the paper.

She was socially isolated, economically dependent. Her life had been edited, and any rewrites were no longer feasible. There was no opportunity for her to participate in the recovering community that had rallied in her support when she was first arrested. For some members in the program, her sobriety was a symbol of their own recovery. But when she was incarcerated, she became a painful reminder of their own pariah status and of how close they themselves had come to being punished for their own "criminal behavior." These indoctrinated members of the community blamed her for the criminality of her addiction. They refused to help her.

By the time Cindy moved back to the city after she was released from prison, she was already in a downward spiral, and nobody cared what happened to her. Her court-mandated recovery was not working and she was locked into a bureaucratic configuration of abuse that made it impossible for her to take responsibility for her life or to control her addiction. When she needed help she could not ask for it for fear of being reincarcerated.

"Remember, before I went to prison?" Cindy reminds me. For a moment her voice is light. "How I talked at meetings? I thought I'd make it back then." Then the dullness returns. "Now I know that I won't. There's nothing left of me. I exist. I have no energy. I filled in the forms for voc rehab but there is nothing I want to do. I just want to lie on my bed and forget everything that has happened to me."

Cindy explains. "If you're made to do something, you are not going to put everything into it." Speaking of the judge she says, "If he does not let me address my problems with pills and family and my daughter and growing up and all of that, how am I going to recover? You can't just deal with my drug issue. I'm just going through the motions."

She continues. "What is the sense of living if you are sick and depressed? Why go around being sick and miserable when you can take a pill for the pain? It is abnormal for me not to take anything. I hate it because I feel so shitty. In prison they tell me 'you'll be all right if you keep off your pills,' but all I do is lie in bed. What kind of life is that? I lie in bed all day. Isn't straight supposed to be better? I was happier when I was using drugs."

In an attempt to punish and then *habilitate* Cindy, the criminal justice system has taken away her reason to live. She has been habilitated into criminality. She has nothing. Nobody. The criminal justice system, through official documentation, has reconfigured the abusive relationships that she suffered as a child, the social welfare system has supported the legal system in this endeavor, and we have compounded her difficulties by our refusal to recognize the subtexts that control her addiction.

As I write Cindy is in a halfway house waiting to be paroled. She is going to return to the community. She works the six-to-midnight shift at Dunkin' Donuts. The rest of the time she spends on her own, her eyes vacant and her affect flat. But sometimes when I talk with her on the telephone we joke at the absurdity of her situation.

Cindy says, "Do you want to hear something funny?"

"What?"

"This man came up to the window and ordered coffee at Dunkin' Donuts. I'd seen him before, because he often drives through. He's always nice to me. Well, anyway, I was busy and I forgot to give him his change so he came in and started talking to me. Just before he left he gave me his card and said if he could ever do anything for me to give him a call. Like I said, I was busy so I didn't look at his card until I was locking up. He's the chief of police!"

I laugh. "He likes you."

"Yeah. But what would he say if he knew I was a convict!"

The joke is no longer funny. "You're not a convict."

"Come on, Denny, I'm a convict. A drug addict and a convict."

"Not to me."

On July 27, 1994, I visit Cindy at the halfway house at the men's state prison. We sit and eat the soup and sandwiches I have brought with me. The manuscript of this book is on the table. I have printed out a list of the sub-headings so that Cindy can get an idea of the way in which I have documented the last four years of her life. She moves between the side headings and the manuscript, talking about the events in her life that I have tried to capture.

"There's something else that needs to be in here," she says, looking at me steadily. "Something I don't think I told you."

I smile at her, anticipating what she is going to say.

"The first time I was in prison I used heroin."

"I know." I explain that in the court records there is a letter that her mother wrote to the judge in which she told him that Cindy was using when she was in prison.

"It was after the hearing. I didn't think I was going to be released. I just didn't care anymore. I couldn't take it anymore. I used it to block out the pain. Finally, I decided to kill myself. I had a large amount brought into the prison and I was going to use it to kill myself."

"How much is a large amount?"

"A gram."

We both smile at the irony—it was a gram of heroin that got Cindy locked up in the first place.

"What happened?"

"The judge called me back to court and I was released."

"Did you use after you got out of prison?"

"No. It was December before I started using again."

"What about the eight months before you went to prison? Were you using then?"

Cindy looks surprised at my question. "No. I used a few times when I got out of the rehab but after that I was into the program." Cindy looks intently at me. "Being in the program meant something to me. I was getting a lot out of it. I worked hard. I didn't want to use drugs anymore." Her expression changes. She smiles, but her face is etched with grief.

"Now I go to meetings and get nothing out of them. I can't relate. I don't speak. Prison has left me with nothing."

I have been making telephone calls on her behalf. I talk about helping her to find an apartment, a doctor, a counselor who will help her.

"Denny," Cindy stops me. She sounds desperate. "I'm back where I started. I've been having bad thoughts all week. All I want to do is use. It will only work if I can find some reason to live."

3

"FILE" IS LIFE SCRAMBLED

ONE OF CINDY'S LAWYERS SPOKE OF HER "ANIMAL INTELLIGENCE" and of the instinctive way in which she fought to survive. To the lawyer she is a nonperson. She is one of more than a million who live in our jails, their lives scrambled.

Stripped of her humanity she becomes a social integer, a statistic, aggregated on a bar graph, published in an official report, reduced to a sound bite on TV, a line of print by the national press. *"Eighty percent of prisoners in the state jails are drug addicts and alcoholics."* Cindy is a factoid in a local newspaper.

She is a felon, an addict, a welfare recipient. She is an indigent who can't pay for her medical treatment. We revile her with our pejorative ascription of terms. She costs us money, ups our taxes, and adds to our Medicare and Medicaid payments. We never consider how she was harmed, how she was abused as a child, poisoned by her physician, tortured in prison.

We are hostile. Punitive.

Her punishment alleviates our anxiety, our vulnerability, the uncertainty that we have about our own lives. We ignore the possibility that by jailing Cindy we are contributing to the criminal economy. We do not consider that she is an addict in a country that has made addiction an industry. It does not occur to us that her welfare status entitles bureaucrats to keep their jobs, enables them to push more paper, to create more regulations, and to process more forms. Death by paper is quiet, painful, and very slow.

Written off by society, Cindy has become a facsimile of a person, an abstraction hidden in obscure lines of print, concealed in the language of official forms—and we are deluded into believing the veracity of what is written, the objective information about her situation, the facts as they are presented. Cindy teaches us that there is no "objective information" and that the "facts" are complex constructions, political acts, that impound our thinking and shape our existence.

In Washington there is talk of moving to an "opportunity society." Opportun*ity* or opportun*istic*? More prisons, harsh discipline, drastic restrictions in welfare and Medicaid, new limitations on the qualifications for Aid to Families with Dependent Children (AFDC), more regulations, stipulations, constraints, controls, and guidelines. Nothing is new. Republican or Democrat, the bureaucratic institutions remain the same. More money, less money, nothing changes, the American psyche remains intact, the poor are undeserving, we blame the individual, we take no responsibility for the current situation. If Cindy would only stop using drugs, if very young women would only stop having children, if ghetto men would only stay in school and get jobs.

It's a question of morality, what William Bennet described in 1990 as "psychomachia," the struggle between good and evil for the possession of the human soul," a belief that reverberates some five years later when *Newsweek* questions whether it is time to bring back shame, a sense of right and wrong, sin, yes SIN—the fire and brimstone of the conservative right.

The arguments are persuasive. Who among us would argue against the fundamental importance of knowing right from wrong? Who would question the need for each one of us to take personal responsibility for the life he or she lives? But who's right and who's wrong? And what opportunities do people have to take personal responsibility for what happens to them in their everyday lives? Such concepts as "shame" and "sin" are abstract, open to interpretation and far removed from the reality of the lives that are lived. When Cindy took personal responsibility, detoxed herself from both legal and illegal drugs, and began to rehabilitate herself within the community, the county attorney said that "while what the defendant has proposed may be rehabilitative, it ignores the deterrent punitive aspect that society has the right to expect."

In the years in which I have worked with men and women who live in the margins of society, I have seen them endure countless indignities, innumerable insults, and relentless scrutiny as they struggle to take personal responsibility for themselves and their families, and I have watched as various governmental agencies, in conspiratorial companionship, systematically undermine the efforts that they are making. Defenseless, the men and women with whom I have worked are destructible—and in the end corruptible. If toilet paper, soap, and toothpaste cannot be bought with food stamps, then the food stamps will be sold. Welfare recipients "cheat" to survive the paper machinations of the bureaucratic organizations that create the very patholo-gies they criticize.

Cindy teaches us that we have to get beyond the money-making moral indignation of opportunistic politicians and the greedy rush of disingenuous hosts of radio and TV talk shows into the *details* of the lives of the men and women *and children* who are incapacitated by the subtexts of political rhetoric. Moral arguments may make money—especially in book royalties—but they tell us nothing about the ways in which those with power and privi-lege enculturate large segments of society into poverty. It is only when we examine the texts as they are used politically that we can begin to understand how official documentation is used by federal, state, and local agencies to turn poverty into a bureaucratic industry.

There are connections between the lives that people live and the ways in which their lives are officially reconstructed on paper. It is possible to juxta-pose the political activities of the time with the events that were taking place in the lives of local people—the homeless, sick, and poor—whose lives quite literally depend on what is written in official texts. The political rhetoric af-fected the lives of those who were—and still are—disenfranchised, and the events that were taking place in the city when Cindy was first jailed foreshad-owed the mean-spirited national agenda of the political right, whose rhetoric is punitive in its composition and deadly in its effect. The official lives of Sam, Laurie, and Kathryn are characterized by denial, abuse, and neglect, and contrast sharply with the life of the city manager whose official life became a part of the public record when the mayor and the city council tried to take away his job. The manager, a gentle gray-suited man who made his fight pub-lic, had power and privilege. He was familiar with the functions and uses of official documentation. He knew how to interrupt the text.

Reflecting on the city's reaction to the manager's challenge provides us with the opportunity to gain a more in-depth understanding of the ways in which official texts can be used to the benefit of those who control them. Such reflection also provides us with a chance to consider the ways in which tax dollars are spent. City taxpayers paid almost $200,000 in legal fees during the legal battle surrounding the firing of the manager—a sum of money quite probably proportionately in excess of what Los Angeles has paid for OJ.

This leads us to ask some important questions. Whose lives do we value, and on whom are we willing to spend our tax dollars? Why are we will-ing to pay the legal expenses of the city manager in addition to the legal ex-penses of the city, but when Laurie has uterine cancer we cripple her with radiation because it is *cheaper* than surgery? Why do we sign petitions, hold rallies, and go to meetings when the city manager is fired from his job, yet do nothing to help Laurie when she is crippled and the state tries to take away her welfare payments? What chance does Laurie have without our indignant energy? Why are we unable to grasp our own negligence? How did we become so complacent?

We are told what we know.
We believe what is written.
We no longer question.

WINTER IN THE CITY

New England is bitter in the winter. In the northern lakes regions and in the foothills of the mountains, the ground is frozen until the middle of April, and sometimes snow still falls in early May.

The winter of 1990 is particularly bitter. The economy is in a deep freeze. The state's jobless rate is reported to be well above the national average, and between September 1989 and September 1990 the number of families receiving assistance rises by a staggering 46 percent.

People are fearful and nervous. This particular city's jobless rate is the highest in the state and continuing to rise. By January 1991 it will reach 11 percent, and more and more people will be forced to ask for financial assistance. Throughout 1990 layoffs are reported across the board, in manufacturing, retail, and service industries: factory workers, store employees, wait staff, cooks, and cleaners. Workers earning minimum wage and fighting poverty work hard to survive, intensely and intently living their own lives.

To make matters worse, on January 29, 1990, six right-wing council members, including the mayor, are sworn into office and immediately begin to cut services. The councillors call themselves the *straight arrows*. They are so-called fiscal conservatives whose campaign of parsimonious rhetoric fed on the economic insecurities of the electorate and the people's pessimism about the future.

During the winter of 1990, this far-right political party is frigidly working hard to reduce or eliminate benefits for the people who need them most—especially the unemployed.

Without employment, workers apply for assistance. Some of those who qualify for benefits receive as little as $32. The lucky ones get as much as $168. The average is $132 a week.

Many whose employment has been temporary are not eligible. Desperate, they ask the city for help but there is less money for assistance. Emergency aid is given only to those without assets. Citizens have to be destitute before they can receive support from the city—and even then many are turned away.

Pleased with his "budget cuts"—he prefers "fiscal restraint"—the mayor talks of "setting the tone for the state." He is too modest. The policies he puts in place set the tone for the nation.

Newt's "Contract with America" is an extreme example of toxic literacy.

A leading columnist for a national newspaper writes that the citizens of the city have declared war on themselves and lost. In biting prose, he writes about the cuts in services and the effects of the cuts upon the lives of those who are rejected by the city. He argues that if the city is to continue to die within its means, it will be necessary to make further cuts in expenditures. "There being nothing left to cut in the schools," he reasons, "the straight arrows will be forced to turn to other frivolous expenditures: the Fire Department and the Police Department. . . . And when this happens," the journalist writes, the city's "defeat of itself will be complete. For when the teenager who is home from school alone accidentally sets the house on fire, no one will come. And when the drugged-out gang of sixteen-year-olds vandalizes the church, no one will come. And when a seventeen-year-old dropout mugs a straight arrow supporter who has profited from the tax cuts—when this self-sufficient youth rips the necklace off the lady's throat, leaving her bruised and afraid—then it will be long past time to consider an old eastern European proverb: *What use are pearls if they choke me?*"

The newspaperman's predictions are correct. But it is the children who are the first to be choked, not the ladies wearing pearls. Teachers are fired, kindergarten classes are eliminated, and some of the poorest children in the state can no longer go to school. In a city with no well-child program or prenatal clinic, those who suffer first are the young already living in the margins of human existence.

In 1990, the number of families in the city who need assistance almost doubles—the numbers are far in excess of the increases for the state—and the number of homeless men, women, and children rises dramatically.

Children are disenfranchised.

The homeless are not recognized.

When a man who is homeless dies, a local paper, as if not to offend the local citizenry, reports that he lived in "various locations" around the city. No one is offended. No one notices.

But there *is* alarm from local citizenry when there is an increase in the number of suspicious fires. Between September 1990 and March 1991, a dozen fires are ruled arson and they are under investigation. This catches the electorate's attention—especially since the mayor and his straight-arrow councillors have cut the budget of the fire department and there are fewer firefighters to fight the fires that are set. "With a 22 percent reduction in manpower and a 600 percent increase in workload we are told to be more innovative!" says a spokesman for the fire department, angry and frustrated with the city council. The next day more firefighters get termination notices.

When there is also an increase in crime, the electorate becomes concerned that the police department budget has been cut. There is talk of harsher punishment and more prisons. Stories of the state's shock treatment program for prisoners are featured prominently in the local newspaper. There is a picture of an inmate at the state prison whose head is being shaved while a sergeant points a finger at him and screams in his face. The prisoner is in an experimental program that guts egos in order to build character—character being "what you are when nobody is looking at you."

At the same time these severe cuts in services are being made by the local straight arrows, the state legislature is also drastically cutting funding for health and human services. In a regional newspaper a member of the Action for Decent Care Coalition is quoted as saying, "The state literally balances its budget on the poor." The conservative governor proposes a $30-a-month cut in AFDC. A twenty-five-year-old mother with three children who is studying to be a nurse receives $516 in monthly welfare payments. The reduction would mean that she would have to house, feed, and clothe her children on $486—at a time when it is difficult to find housing for under $400 a month.

In the newspapers the governor prefers to talk of "choppy waters" and "high seas" as he balances the state budget with the $118 million dollars in federal Medicaid funds that he says offsets the 30 percent drop in the business tax. "Everyone has to take some pain," the governor pontificates as he tells the workers in the state welfare offices to take some unpaid days off. In the city the number of state welfare caseworkers has already been cut. There is an increasing backlog of federal and state paperwork and the people are piling up.

A caseworker from the state welfare office in the city talks about the problem. "We're in a tough position. Everything we do is by policy. This is the way it is supposed to be and there is no getting around it." She looks tired. If she sat in the waiting room in the welfare office you might mistake her for a recipient. Poorly paid and poorly treated, she is in the bureaucratic line of fire. But she is a lifeline to the people. Even as she says she is "burnt" she helps them with the forms that will determine whether they are eligible for assistance. "Either you are eligible or you are not, and that's the hardest part because you want to help them and you can't. That's the most frustrating part of this job. It takes time to process the forms. We wouldn't be so bogged down if it wasn't for all the paperwork we have to do. We used to be able to take time and get involved but there are fewer caseworkers and they increased the caseload."

She talks about the people without jobs. "One of the things that is happening is that people who are laid off are running out of their employment benefits, so after that they become eligible for our programs. The other day I drove by unemployment and the line was out onto the sidewalk. When they have finished there, they come here. When they get here, it's so busy it could take four hours just to see someone. Then they go on to the city welfare office if they need emergency assistance."

The caseworker talks about the homeless. "You tell them to go to the city. You say, 'Have them help you find a place to live,' but there isn't any place. There is no shelter. According to people around here we don't have a homeless problem. The caseworkers in the agencies know there is a homeless problem. I had a person come in and tell me that she had stayed in a room in which twenty other people were living. You never hear about it. The city must know, they must know where these people are, they must see them." If they know, they are not going to admit it. In a conversation with a caseworker at city welfare I am told, "People have a misconception of homelessness. There simply is not a homeless problem in this state."

The state welfare caseworker ends our conversation, "In the city, either you have money or you don't. There are very few people in the middle." She looks troubled. "Unfortunately, I think that people in this area pretend that we don't have any problems, that this is the perfect little community." She shakes her head. "But it isn't."

CAUGHT IN THE BUREAUCRATIC CROSSFIRE

Sam is standing on Main Street. It is March 3, 1990, eleven days before Cindy is sentenced to three and a half to seven years in prison at the superior court and a month after the conservative straight arrows were sworn into office. The day is icy cold. Gusts of arctic air take away the breath of anyone who ventures out on the street.

Nobody notices Sam, who is looking down at the sidewalk, moaning quietly to himself. His hair is long, greasy, and matted. It hangs down on his shoulders, and every so often a blast of frigid air blows it forward so that it adds another layer to the straggly nicotine-stained beard that covers his face.

Sam is wearing a green oversize army field coat. Underneath the coat he has on a torn jean jacket, a flannel shirt, a sweatshirt, and two T-shirts. Two pairs of trousers, stiff with dirt, are layered over sweatpants and long underwear. Beat-up workboots and two pairs of worn-out socks cover his feet.

All these clothes give Sam bulk, but underneath the many layers he is painfully thin. There are sores all over his body. The skin on his back has been repaired with skin grafts. Ridged and furrowed, like wax, it is pale and pulled tight. His arms are covered in homemade tattoos, including FUCK YOU.

Sam's hands are thrust deep into the pockets of his army field coat. He is panhandling for beer money, but his hands are blue so he clenches and unclenches them in his pockets as he shuffles his feet to keep warm. Sam is confused. He is painfully cold and yet he feels hot. He starts to sweat, tremble, and then shake. He needs a beer. He rocks back and forth, moaning, as he detoxes on the street. Sam is disorientated. People continue to pass him by.

A hard-core addict who talks at AA meetings about his twenty-nine years of violent drug and alcohol addiction hurries past. Sam is sobbing. The man, who is fighting his own need for a drink, turns and shouts, "What the fuck's wrong with you?"

A year later when I ask Sam to describe that day he writes, "I was living on the streets. I didn't have any money for food, clothing, or housing. I was hopeless. I had been to all the social agencies and couldn't seem to get any help whatsoever. I had a hard time making out forms. I couldn't remember too many things. My brain was dysfunctional. City welfare wouldn't give me any help, nor the state welfare, because I was an alcoholic. I was tired of living the way I was but I didn't know where else to go. My life was a shambles."

The man who shouts at Sam is helping me with my research on the ways in which literacy is used by official agencies in urban areas. He takes Sam to the apartment of the same young woman Cindy is encouraging to overcome addiction. (Remember how Cindy would rub the young woman's back and say, "Keep coming kid"?) This young women is also working with me on the literacy project. She cooks spaghetti for Sam and he sits in her kitchen and eats it.

He tries to speak, to explain his situation, but his speech is fragmented.

The sounds he makes are distorted, disconnected, speeded up, slowed down, gibberish. He repeats phrases over and over as if he is trying to hold on to what he wants to say. His face is flushed and feverish. He tries to tell them he is sick, that he keeps having seizures.

"Do you want to go to the hospital?" the young woman asks loudly, as if dementia has affected his hearing.

"Yeah," Sam says. "But . . . but . . . but . . ." Sam has trouble speaking, but eventually the literacy workers understand. Sam doesn't think the hospital will treat him. The literacy workers take Sam to the hospital and he is denied treatment. His blood alcohol is recorded at 183 at 1:28 P.M. In the triage notes the nurse writes that Sam entered the hospital "requesting detox. Last drink of beer at 9 A.M. Presents shaky." " 'I had a seizure this morning,' " she quotes Sam as saying. " 'I need help to stop drinking. I live on the streets.' "

The doctor in emergency tells the literacy workers that Sam has been to the hospital sixteen times to detox. He refuses to provide Sam with medical assistance and it seems that while the nurse records that Sam is in the emergency room, there are no notes made by the doctor of this visit. The literacy workers write in their notes that the doctor said he didn't feel that Sam was "sincere enough."

They take Sam back to the young woman's apartment to wait until he is sober. Sam takes a shower, but all he has to put back on are his dirty clothes. The smell of sweat, dirt, and feces fills the tiny apartment. Sam sits at the kitchen table, drinking coffee and smoking cigarettes. Much of what he says is muddled. He has a hard time remembering. He spends his nights in a hallway of a warehouse and keeps his "things" in a cupboard at the top of some stairs. He can only go into the warehouse in the late afternoon, and when the building is locked he remains inside throughout the night. He spends most of his days walking around downtown panhandling for beer money. Sometimes he goes into one of the buildings on Main Street, climbs the stairs to the first floor, and looks out of the window at the people and cars passing by on the street. He goes to the library every day. "I like to read the papers," he says, "but mostly I sleep."

Sam talks about the death of his brother. He becomes agitated and cannot get the words out. He repeats over and over "let me speak . . . let me speak . . . let me speak."

Sam explains that on Tuesdays and Fridays he goes to the Salvation Army for a hot lunch. Because they are closed the rest of the week, Tuesdays and Fridays are sometimes the only days that he eats.

The literacy workers take Sam to an AA meeting, and then, not knowing what else to do, they take him back to the hospital. It is more than twelve hours since Sam has had a drink. They hope that it is long enough for his blood alcohol to have dropped below .10 so that the doctor in the emergency room will treat him. He is still hot and his lungs are badly congested. They are concerned because as Sam detoxes, he seems to be having more seizures. His eyes go vacant and start to shimmer, and he doesn't respond when they speak.

There is another doctor on duty in the emergency room. In the hospital record of this second visit the doctor writes about Sam's social condition but very little about his medical condition. He gives new meaning to "socialized" medicine:

> 33 Y-O W ♂ enters requesting detox. States he wants to straighten out. Dependent on ETOH—can't hold a job. Denies legal problems. Denies drug use. Brought in by friend who found him "shaking." Has been drinking up to a case of beer per day for months maybe a year or two. Panhandles for drinking.

The doctor also states that Sam had just been discharged on February 28, 1990, after five days of detoxification. Sam denies that he had just been in the hospital, and the records show that it was the previous year—in February 1989, not 1990—that Sam was hospitalized. There is no documentation in Sam's hospital file to support the doctor's statement. The doctor ends his notes by writing:

> Pt has historically had poor motivation for follow-up and medication compliance. . . . Recommend that he return in A.M. ETOH free. . . . Detox nurse recommends out-pt detox.

The doctor does not order a second blood alcohol (ETOH) reading, and even though the literacy workers argue that Sam is no longer drunk, the doctor insists—without medical evidence—that he is still intoxicated. Sam is again refused treatment at the hospital.

The doctor gives the two literacy workers a packet of Librium and tells them to take Sam home and detox him there. The literacy workers explain that they themselves are in recovery from drug and alcohol addiction and that they have not been sober long enough to be given drugs. The doctor merely repeats that if they really want to help Sam they should take him home until he is sober.

They take Sam back to the young woman's apartment. He is sweating and shaking and coughing up green phlegm. Sam lies down on the couch, confused and disorientated.

"Let me speak . . . let me speak."

On March 5, 1990, Sam is finally admitted to the hospital.

TAKE ME TO THE MORGUE, I WANT TO DIE

Sam's hospital records are convincing. Officially he is a hopeless case. In the records, he is portrayed as a chronic alcoholic who asks for help but then keeps on drinking. He appears recalcitrant, rebellious, and his life is characterized as unmanageable. In the records of Sam's hospital stay in February 1989 the final diagnosis is ethanol abuse, myopathy, malnutrition, chronic bronchitis, and dementia. In one of the reports of this hospitalization a doctor states that Sam "came in for about the 16th hospital visit." Another doctor begins, "This is the (?) 15th" admission. What the reports don't say is that Sam's hospital "visits" include those occasions when Sam goes to the emergency room and is sent to jail or denied treatment.

When Sam went to the hospital on September 29, 1989, he complained of seizures, and in the triage notes the nurse wrote, "he is requesting to die," and she added that Sam asked them to "take him to the morgue." Sam's blood alcohol was 476 MG/DL. The doctor noted that Sam was suffering from acute alcohol inebriation and that he was depressed and suicidal.

In his instructions he wrote, "To jail for protective custody—suicidal, depressed and intoxicated. Mental health evaluation in the A.M." The nurse wrote of this visit to the emergency room, "CPD notified pt is intoxicated/suicidal—needs to go to CJ for PC."

Sam was described as "agitated." "I'll jump in the river tomorrow," Sam shouted at the doctors and nurses as he was taken to jail by the city police department. "Pt. removed from department by CPD." There is no record of any mental health evaluation in the morning. Sam was released from jail at 6 A.M., walked the two miles back downtown, and resumed his life of living on the streets of the city.

On November 25, 1989, desperate for help, Sam went again to the emergency room and his records state that he requested detoxification. His blood alcohol was reported at 332 MG/DL. He left the hospital without treatment and remained on the streets throughout the winter.

On March 9, 1990—the time when we pick up Sam's story—he is released from the hospital and once more returns to the streets. In Sam's discharge summary the final diagnosis is given as "(1) Chronic alcoholism, and (2) Seizure disorder by history." In the summary, the doctor notes "This is the 17th admission for this 32-year-old male asking for detox. He detoxed without incident and arrangements were made for him to be ultimately transferred to the Chemical Dependency Program at Dorset House." The doctor states that Sam is "to keep in touch with AA and our counselors if there is any difficulty arranging this placement." Sam does keep in touch with AA but he hears no more about the placement.

In an accompanying report another doctor—who also begins "This is the 17th hospital admission"—notes that Sam has "been getting drunk on a regular basis." The doctor ends by stating that the "likelihood of rehabilitation is low due to his many previous attempts unsuccessfully." Sam is sentenced but the sentence is unfinished.

Sam Is Offered a Bus Ticket to Leave the City

On March 9, five days before Cindy is sent to jail, Sam is back on the streets. He is released with a prescription for Antibuse and the telephone number of the city welfare office. He has twenty-two cents in his pocket.

He walks to the Salvation Army to ask for money so that he can fill the prescription he was given at the hospital. It is Friday, so he eats lunch in the Salvation Army's soup kitchen before he walks downtown to the city welfare office. Later, at the apartment of the young woman who is working with me on the literacy project, Sam talks about what happened when he went to city welfare. "I asked them if they could help me with getting a place. They said they would if I could find one." Sam is flushed and he hesitates as he speaks.

He has trouble getting his words out. He gets halfway through a sentence, then repeats, stops again, and repeats. He is agitated. "They tried to give me a bus ticket out of town," he says. His bloodshot eyes open wide. "They wanted to send me to a homeless shelter in another city. I've lived here all my life. They're not going to get rid of me by buying me a bus ticket!"

He talks of the rooming houses he has visited. "I went to one place but there were no rooms available. I also went down to another place and she said she would keep me one night and I tried to get her to let me stay the weekend and she said I could but that I would have to be out on Monday morning. So I went back to welfare and they gave me an application to fill out but, but, I had a hard time because I can't remember dates."

Sam telephones the Salvation Army and a local Catholic church from the young woman's apartment, trying to find a place to stay. He has no luck. He goes to an AA meeting and asks for help. A man who has known Sam for years says that he can stay with him for a few nights while he looks for a place to live. Sam stays the weekend with the man from AA and then he is back out on the street.

"Why did you leave?" I ask.

Sam explains that when he told welfare that he was staying with a friend, they wanted him to get some forms filled in. "He didn't want to do the paperwork. I left because I didn't want no trouble."

In the days that follow Sam shuffles back and forth between the state and city welfare offices. On March 12, Sam goes back to the city welfare office. He is given some more forms. He complains that he has already filled them in. He is given another form and is told to take it with him. "When you get a landlord, give this form to him. We can't help you until he fills it in." The caseworker makes another appointment for Sam on March 14, and she tells him to go to the state welfare office to ask for assistance. "We'll help you with food until you get food stamps from them."

Sam leaves the city welfare office and walks across the street to the state office of health and human services. He is given a six-page form to fill out. He speaks with a woman who tells him she is his caseworker. She goes over the application that he has just filled in and reads him his rights. Then she tells him that he needs to make an appointment to see if he is eligible for vocational rehabilitation. She gives Sam pamphlets to read and tells him that he might be eligible for Social Security disability benefits.

On the way out Sam stops to read the job descriptions posted on the bulletin board in the waiting room. Each description is followed by a telephone number. "Those numbers are bullshit," Sam says. "I'm not qualified for anything up there. They just put them there to look good."

Sam is still living on the streets. Sometimes he stays in the warehouse, occasionally with friends. He eats sandwiches, drinks chocolate milk, and he makes staying sober his top priority. He goes to AA meetings—one at the hospital in the morning, one in a church at lunchtime, one of a variety of meetings in the evening. He visits the library where he reads advertisements for rooms to rent in the classified columns of the local paper.

"How many places have you called Sam?"

"Probably six or seven. I just call for rooms because welfare will only pay eighty-five dollars a week. One guy said he don't take welfare. Some of them want references." Sam is concerned about moving into a rooming house where there's a lot of partying. "If I go to a place where I don't think I should be, I know I'd end up drinking again, I know it." Sam's face is serious. "I'd rather just sit in the warehouse and look out the window."

Sam continues to call.

"You'll need two references and a deposit."

No answer.

"I'll want to see your rent receipts."

Busy.

On the evening of March 17, Sam goes to an AA meeting. At around 10 P.M. he heads down Main Street onto First Street, looking for a place to stay. He is going to ask a friend who used to drink with him if he can spend the night. Without any warning, Sam drops to the ground, hitting his face on the curb as he falls. Sam says, "I remember I was somewhere on Second Ave. or maybe I was still on First Street. I must have had a seizure. I don't remember anything else."

In the local paper there is mention of medical assistance being given to someone on First Street at 10:15. The police say Sam was on his feet when they arrived. He said he was "all set." An ambulance had been called, but the officer on duty canceled it because the dispatcher thought Sam was just looking for a place to stay.

Sam has a cut on his head and a black eye. His ribs are bruised and he has a gash on his leg. He is coughing up blood and when he learns that the police were called he laughs, "They probably thought I was drunk!" Sam says he didn't want any trouble. "I just walked off up the street. I didn't want to be thrown in jail." It is over a year before I begin to understand why Sam worries so much about the police throwing him in jail.

On March 20, Sam is caught in the warehouse where he has been sleeping. The man tells him he can stay there at night as long as he minds his own business and doesn't start any fires. The only problem is, he is going to start locking the building at four-thirty in the afternoon. If Sam wants to go to an AA meeting he will have to find somewhere else to sleep.

On March 21, Sam goes to the city welfare office. The literacy worker who accompanies Sam writes in his notes that Sam is "anxious" and "almost pleading" as he asks for help. Again Sam is offered a bus ticket out of town, to a shelter for the homeless in another city. "They're not going to get rid of me that easy," he says. "I'm sick of the runaround. I don't want to go to welfare anymore." Four years later Sam still talks about the two bus tickets that he was offered by city welfare. On March 22, the warehouse where Sam spends his nights is locked up. Sam is locked out. It is bitterly cold. He looks for somewhere else to stay.

On March 23, Sam goes back to the city welfare office. He is told that he owes the agency $524.21 for assistance he received in 1984 and 1987. Sam is angry. "They said I'd have to pay them back," he shouts. "How can I pay them back? I don't have a job."

Later a caseworker at city welfare tells me that welfare recipients are required to pay back the assistance that they receive. However, because the jobs program run by the welfare office pays only minimum wage, the longer people are in the jobs program the further behind they get and the more money they owe. Eventually they become indentured to the city.

Sam spends the night at the apartment of an AA member. Sam is up most of the night walking back and forth saying "fuck it" over and over.

I ask Sam if he will keep a journal.

"Okay," he says. "But it's the same old story. Not much is happening."

On March 24, Sam writes in his journal, "Went to AA meeting at hospital. . . . Hung around town not doing very much. Thinking about where I was going to spend the night. I ended up in three different buildings in hallways."

March 25. "Was up early with not much going on in town—5:30 A.M. or around that—so I found a hallway with heat cause it was cold outside. Went over to the store to get some cigs at 7:00 A.M. . . . Waited for 5:30 to roll around so that I could go to Salvation Army for church and supper. After supper I went to congregational church AA meeting."

On March 27, Sam returns to the emergency room. In the triage notes the nurse writes that he is complaining of chest pains and has a productive cough with bloody drainage. The doctor diagnoses "bronchitis/pleurisy" and notes "past history of alcoholism." He prescribes erythromycin for a full ten days. Sam leaves the hospital and is back to living on the streets. He says that he is not going back to welfare and for a few days he stops going to AA meetings.

IF YOU LEAVE A QUESTION BLANK, YOUR APPLICATION WILL BE AUTOMATICALLY REJECTED

By the second week of April Sam has lost interest in trying to get help. His food stamps are late, and when I see him he has not eaten for several days. He says he spends his time attending AA meetings and reading the newspapers at the library. For six days he goes to the state welfare office, and for six days he is told to "come back tomorrow."

On Friday he is told to come back at nine o'clock on Monday morning. On Monday morning he is told to come back at two o'clock. At two he is told to come back on Wednesday. On Wednesday he is told that his food stamps are still not available.

Sam is sitting at the kitchen table of the young woman who cooked him dinner the night you first met him. He is talking about welfare. "There was a mother in there yesterday," Sam says, "with five children. How is *she* supposed to manage without her food stamps? How do they think she is going to feed her children?" His hands are shaking and beads of sweat are running down his face. "She waited all morning to speak to someone and then they told her to come back tomorrow!" Sam is making small noises. His eyes are vacant, his legs are twitching, and he does not hear us when we speak.

"Are you okay? *Sam, are you okay!*"

He starts making sounds as if he is taking part in a conversation. At first what he says is incomprehensible. Then it becomes clear he is still talking about welfare. He starts to speak. Stops. Starts again.

We think he is trying to tell us again that he hasn't received his food stamps.

"Food stamps?"

"Say it," Sam says.

"Food stamps."

Sam begins again but still cannot finish the sentence. "Say it," he says, "say it."

Later, Sam tells us that he thinks he had a small seizure. "I get them when I think about things I shouldn't think about," he says.

"What were you thinking about?"

"Not having my food stamps," Sam says, anxiety etched on his face.

We take Sam in my car to the state welfare office. As we climb the stairs Sam's mood brightens. "It's different coming in here with someone," he says. "I don't like coming on my own." He goes up to the glass window and asks the receptionist if his food stamps have arrived. The receptionist sorts through a stack of envelopes until she comes to one with his name on it. She hands it to Sam through the small counter-level half circle cut out of the glass. Sam looks visibly relieved.

"Why were his food stamps so late?" I ask the receptionist.

"We're shorthanded, because of the budget cuts. It's taking us longer to process the information and put it in the computer."

On April 28 the headlines on the front page of the city's local paper confirm what she says: "Welfare Budgets Feeling Pinch of Heavy Demand." "Increased unemployment has put more stress on state social service programs, causing delays," the article states. "AFDC applications that were taking six weeks can now take as long as twelve weeks."

But it is not until January 1991 that the Legal Assistance Agency becomes actively involved and is reported to be considering suing the state. "We just can't let our clients wait much longer," the local paper quotes a spokesperson for the agency as saying. "They need more people to process the applications." The same article notes that some caseworkers have been working overtime without pay to "eliminate the tremendous backlogs in processing welfare and food stamp applications."

While we are at the state welfare office I ask if Sam can meet with his caseworker to see if he is eligible for the Social Security disability benefits that he was told about when he visited the office in March. We sit and wait.

After a long delay Sam's caseworker comes out to talk with him. She tells him that she can't help him, that he needs to see another caseworker who deals with disability benefits. She says that this other caseworker is at lunch but she will see him when she gets back. She gives Sam some more forms to fill out and returns to her office. It is 11:20 A.M. We sit together and help Sam answer the questions and fill in the blanks on the new forms that he has been given. The first form is an "Initial Jobs Appraisal." Sam reads the first question out loud. "*What would you like to do for work?*" He looks puzzled. "I don't know," he says.

Then there are a series of questions that focus on the applicant's work history. Sam can't remember all the places he has worked or the dates of his employment. He explains to us that he sometimes did odd jobs but that for the last six years—the period he has been living on the streets—none of his jobs have lasted more than a few weeks. Sam writes, "Don't remember dates."

"*Do you want more schooling?*" Sam hesitates. He says he isn't sure that he is capable of going back to school. I suggest that he write what he has just said. He does. "I don't know if I am capable enough."

He reads the last question. "*Are there any problems you have to fix before you can go to work, school, or training?*" Without hesitation Sam puts an X in the yes box. He writes, "Have to find out why I have seizures."

There are several other forms, including one that Sam has filled out before, but he fills it out again just to make sure. Then he gets up and gives the forms to the receptionist.

Sam sits back down and we wait for the caseworker who deals with benefits for people with disabilities. And we wait. It is 1:10 P.M. Just as Sam looks as if he is getting ready to leave, a tall, neatly dressed woman enters the waiting room through a door that leads to back offices. She smiles at Sam and introduces herself as his new caseworker. Then she asks us why we are with him. I tell her about the city literacy project and of our interest in how Sam can get the assistance he needs from the state and from local welfare agencies in the city.

The caseworker has in her hand the forms Sam has just filled in and we wait while she looks through them. She asks Sam why he has filled in the job appraisal form. Sam looks confused and answers with a shrug of his shoulders.

"It's not applicable," the caseworker says, "you didn't need to fill it in."

We follow the caseworker through the back door, along a narrow corridor, and into one of the small cinderblock cubicles where caseworkers interview clients. The room is barely big enough for two chairs and a table, but the caseworker is accommodating and she allows us to borrow some chairs from another cubicle. We crowd into the room.

Sam sits on one side of the table, the caseworker on the other. We sit to the right of Sam with the backs of our chairs against the wall and the sides close together.

The caseworker begins by telling Sam that there are more forms to be filled in. Sam looks anxious but the caseworker smiles and says that she will help him fill them in. She reads the questions on the first form and she writes Sam's answers in the appropriate places.

She asks me to verify that Sam is a resident of the city and I sign my name in the appropriate space on one of the forms. The irony of the situation is not lost on us. Sam has lived in the city all his life and I have never lived there. Later we joke about the inequity of the situation but none of us thinks it's funny.

The caseworker asks Sam for his address. "I don't have one," he says.

"I have to put an address," she tells Sam with a look of inquiry on her face.

We ask her several times why she can't just write that Sam is homeless. The caseworker smiles and looks as if she understands our frustration. Calmly she tells us that the form will not be processed without an address. The caseworker persists. She asks Sam where he has been sleeping and after some discussion Sam tells her that earlier in the winter he was sleeping under a friend's porch and he gives her the address of his friend.

The caseworker writes down the address.

"What about before that?" she asks Sam. Sam looks up at the ceiling as if he is trying to remember. We wait.

Sam gives the caseworker the address of a house with an attached garage where he hid late at night and slept for a while before leaving early in the morning. Sam says he slept in the garage in the late summer of the previous year but that when the weather turned cold they locked it up and he could no longer get inside. Without commenting, the caseworker writes the address of the house on the form.

The questions then change to finances. "Does anyone give you money on a regular basis?" "Cigarette money," Sam says, and then, deadpan, he says, "Coffee money and it's a hit." The caseworker writes, "No."

The caseworker reaches the question about "members of household." She writes, "Lives alone."

"Why not write homeless?" we ask. "If he's homeless, he's homeless!"

The caseworker explains that it is important to distinguish between people on their own and families. This seems somewhat illogical. "A family could be homeless," she clarifies. None of us thinks much of this explanation.

When all of the forms have been filled out, the caseworker gives Sam two forms—one for mental disabilities and one for physical disabilities. "It takes six to nine months to process the forms," she tells Sam. She explains that she is not sure which form is appropriate and that if he fills out the wrong one he would have to reapply, which could take another six months. "You'd have to wait over a year before you received any benefits."

The caseworker tells Sam to take the forms with him and have his doctor fill them out. She shows him the sections of each form that he is supposed to fill out himself. "Answer in ways that it is going to help," she tells him. "Every question has to be answered." Then she cautions, "If you don't know, guess and put a little question mark beside your answer. If you leave a question blank, they will automatically reject your application."

Later, I ask Sam what questions he would ask if he was given the opportunity to construct the forms. "I'd get the basics, Social Security, stuff like that," Sam says, and then without hesitation continues, "Then I'd ask, What's going on? What seems to be your problem? I wouldn't ask them anything else. Just how they've been surviving. I'd find out what they want for help, and go from there. I mean you don't need tons of paperwork just to find out something. I don't think that it is necessary."

We talk about the addresses fabricated on his forms. "That's unnecessary." Sam speaks with conviction. "It's simple and sweet. If I'm homeless what else can I say. I've lived in this city all my life. Okay. But I'm on the streets and I do not have a legal residence. So in other words she was lying. I did not stay at those places. I mean I'm sleeping under a porch. So what? That isn't a street address. And I shouldn't have been there because if his mother had known she'd have thrown me out for sure."

I'M A FUCKIN' MIRACLE

On April 13, Sam finally has a place to live. However, living in the rundown rooming house is not easy. The rooms are filled with drinkers and Sam is determined to stay sober. He says he has to be careful to stay away from the men and women in the rooming house. Still, Sam is happy. "Today was the greatest day of my life," he tells us with tears in his eyes. "It's a beautiful day!"

Sam gets a haircut and he washes his clothes. He looks younger, his mood changes, he laughs, jokes, and welcomes us when we visit him. He cleans his room, washes the floors, and rearranges the furniture. He talks of getting a pillow for his bed and a rug for the floor.

Each day Sam goes to AA meetings, visits the office that I have opened for the literacy project, and stays sober. He is optimistic but his troubles are not over. He complains the rooming house is dirty and that tenants are drinking and drugging. But what really upsets Sam is that tenants are stealing the food that he buys with his food stamps. He has been hungry most of his life, he has less than thirty dollars a week for food, and he doesn't have money to replace it if it is stolen. Angry, Sam looks in the classified section of the paper and tries to find another room.

On May 2, Sam writes in his journal that he saw a room advertised in the paper. "Got there about 9:45. The room was rented. Said stop back in a week. Went over to the Salvation Army. Got some food. Home at 10:30. Watched TV. Left for AA meeting. Went to the church but it was closed so I walked to the library and then came home."

Sam clocks each day. May 3. "Up and dressed ready for another day. 7:20. Read first step. Left for hospital meeting 7:50. Got there at 8:20. Left meeting at 10:00." He ends, "Watched a little bit of TV. Tried to do some thinking but I didn't know what to think about. Had some pain in my chest and down my left arm. I'm not going to tell anyone because they probably think I'm just trying to get attention. I did get my sixty-day chip tonight. That felt good. Got to bed about 12:30."

In his journal Sam talks about "stupid thoughts." He tells us that he keeps thinking about killing himself. "I don't know what to do. I need money. I need medicine. What the fuck am I supposed to do. I keep getting dizzy. I think about killing myself but it don't do no fuckin' good. I don't want to bullshit myself. I never had a fuckin' life. I think about shit like that. My head hurts. I go home and cry and cry. I feel I depend on too many people but if I didn't I don't know what I'd do. I'd be back out on the street."

June 3. Sam has been sober for three months. "You're looking at a fuckin' miracle," he tells us. "I'm a fuckin' miracle standing right here."

On June 5, Sam goes to court to appeal a DWI conviction that he received over a year before we met him. He tells the court that for the first time in his life he is sober, and I testify on his behalf, sharing with the court the changes that have taken place in Sam's life since I first met him. His appeal is denied, and he is sent to the county jail.

During the time that Sam is incarcerated, I visit him regularly. Once I attend an AA meeting with him. Sam tries to keep upbeat, but he says he is having difficulty with his attitude. He complains that the AA meetings are a joke and that nobody takes them seriously. He says it is hard for him to work on his sobriety while he is incarcerated.

On July 29, Sam is released from jail. He says he is no longer going to take his Antibuse, and he complains that he has a bad attitude. He seems to have lost his determination to stay sober, but he does not drink, even though he no longer attends so many AA meetings. He is not sleeping, he has nightmares, crazy thoughts are constantly running through his head. He starts going to mental health.

On August 29 Sam writes in his journal, "Same ol shit. Different day. Went to mental health, came home for a few then down to probation. Came home took a nap, thought things would be a little better but I guess not. Went to an NA meeting."

September 4. "I did my laundry took a hike to the library and stopped and picked up a sandwich. Checked the mail. No news. What's new? Sat around watched a little TV. Went to AA meeting at congregational church. Almost feels like it's going to fucking snow or maybe I've just lost a few more marbles, could be either one."

In September Sam moves out of the rooming house in which he is living. He says that the people rooming there are drinking and fighting and that he would rather live on the streets than live there. He has no place to go.

He starts visiting the social agencies again but this time he says he is comfortable going on his own. He stays with a friend for a few nights and then he finally finds a room at a rooming house that has a reputation for being well run—it is the rooming house that Sam wanted to live in when he first got sober but he was turned away. This time, to show the landlord that he has changed, he asks the local Roman Catholic priest—who often helped him when he was drinking and living on the streets—to write a character reference for him.

The rooming house is a large Victorian house with additions. It has long corridors of rooms and a small kitchen with a microwave, sink, and refrigerator. The sink is always filled with dirty dishes and cockroaches crawl around the floor.

"Don't open the refrigerator," Sam warns me. He pulls a face. "Something died inside."

Sam keeps his room clean, keeps to himself, and says that he tries not to bother anyone. He is still having trouble sleeping, and he often talks about his dead brother. Mental health tries to solve the problem by giving him pills.

THAT'S MY MONEY, I EARNED IT LIVING ON THE STREETS

On October 15, Sam finally receives a check from Social Security. It has taken six months for him to be approved for disability benefits, but his first check includes retroactive benefits for which he was eligible but did not receive. Sam opens a bank account.

On October 25, the city council holds a public meeting to talk about issues affecting the community. I decide to attend and I ask Sam if he will come with me. We are the only ones there. When we walk into the conference room of empty chairs, two members of the city council—a man and a woman, both straight arrows—are sitting behind long tables at the front. Sam gets two chairs and pulls them up to the table and we sit down opposite the members of the council as if waiting for a meal. Sam starts talking. The mayor arrives. "This is the longest I've been sober," Sam tells him.

"How long?" one of the council members asks.

"Nine months," Sam tells him. "Last winter I slept in a closet in a hallway."

"Where'd you get your beer money?"

"Panhandling." Sam explains that he doesn't eat much and that the Roman Catholic church sometimes helped him out by giving him vouchers for food. He tells the council members about the rooming house in which he is living. "Try staying sober in a house full of drunks," he says.

Sam talks about the difficulties he experienced getting help from welfare. "I couldn't fill in the forms," he says by way of explanation.

"Can't you read?"

"I can read. I just had difficulty answering the questions." Sam gets conspiratorial, he leans forward and lowers his voice. "They offered me a bus ticket out of town."

"Why did they do that?" the woman council member asks.

"They wanted me to go to a shelter in [he names another city]."

"I've visited that shelter," the woman tells Sam. "It's really very good."

Sam looks dumbfounded. She doesn't get it. "Try living in a shelter," Sam says, moving back from the table.

Outside, after we leave, Sam looks immensely pleased with himself. "That was interesting!" he says, lighting a cigarette. He runs through the conversation. "Just because I was homeless they think I can't read." He is walking toward the car. "They wouldn't think twice about sending me to a shelter."

On October 27, Sam moves into a furnished apartment—two rooms— on one of the streets he lived on when he was a child. It is his first home in six years.

He wants a thirteen-inch TV with a remote control "in case someone comes over. If I have a remote I won't have to get up to change the channel." He also says he wants a blue telephone.

The young woman who is working for the literacy project takes Sam shopping. He buys a $12 blue telephone and pays $90 for a microwave oven. But the TVs are too expensive, so he shops around before he finds one he can afford. Sam pays cash for the TV and the salesperson carries it out of the store for him. Sam is pumped.

At a five-and-dime he buys a set of pots and pans for $12 and a wall clock for $5. He talks loudly and jokes with the salesclerks and other customers. He tells them that he has a new apartment and a new TV. People respond to him, they smile and nod their heads. Sam forgets that the people he meets are the people who passed him by when he was panhandling outside the store.

At the checkout a woman cuts in front of Sam.

"Hey! Get to the back of the line!"

Sam laughs.

The woman moves to a different register.

Back at his apartment the young woman helps Sam unpack. She sets up the microwave while Sam sets up the TV. When I visit, Sam talks nonstop. He shows me his new place and his new things.

He spends much of his time cleaning. His apartment is spotless. It smells of Comet. He scrubs the floors, washes the walls, and scours his sink. He washes the shade on the ceiling light and the blind that covers the window in his apartment door. Sam is scrubbed pink and smells of deodorant. Every day he showers and washes his clothes. He buys new boots and covers them with a waterproof spray before he wears them. Sam is happy. He has dry feet and a place to sleep.

Sam contemplates the possibilities. He talks about rehabilitation. Not drug rehabs, but rehabilitation into the community. "There's nothing that I know of to help you do that," he says. "If you're an alcoholic and you get drunk they have one place to rehabilitate you and that's jail." Jail is a recurring topic of conversation. He worries about getting sick. He tells me that when he is sick, they send him to the county jail.

Sam keeps to himself, lives quietly, and tries to keep himself occupied. But when the city learns that Sam has received money from Social Security, the welfare director informs him that he has to repay the money they had given him for rent—including the money he received in 1984. The hospital and the doctors send him letters about the money he owes them—even though the bills for his Social Security disabilities medical evaluations were supposed to be paid by the state welfare department.

One day while Sam is at the literacy project office, he telephones the billing department at the hospital to tell them that he is not responsible for the bill. He tries to explain that the bill was supposed to have been paid by the state welfare office. When the woman won't listen to what he has to say, Sam yells into the phone. "What are you gonna do? Come down here and take my color TV?"

Later, when I suggest that Sam could consider paying the bills out of his settlement money, he becomes agitated. "That's my money," he says. "I earned it living on the streets."

Sam's medical bills are turned over to a collection agency. More letters, then telephone calls. An employee of the collection agency tells him to go out and collect soda cans to pay off his doctors' bills. Then Sam is turned down for Medicaid. "How can they say I'm disabled and then say I don't qualify for Medicaid?" he asks. "How am I supposed to pay for my medication? After my rent is paid, all I have to live on is fifty dollars a week."

Sam talks about starting over and of learning to live sober. He talks about going back to school, but he isn't sure what he would study. Joking, he says he would like to be a race car driver or a kamikaze pilot, but most of the time he just quietly wonders what he could do. He says he'd like to try to get a part-time job but he can't because he'd lose his benefits. He talks about the jobs he has had, of the severity of his seizures, and of the third-degree burns he has on his back from the time he fell off a garbage truck. "Who's going to employ me?" he asks. "I'm nothing but a liability."

Sam feels trapped. There's no such thing as *partially* disabled, no give and take, no counseling, no rehabilitation. He is off the streets but there is no opportunity for him to reestablish himself as a productive member of the community.

So, Sam works for me. Every day he reads the local papers and cuts out articles that he thinks are relevant to my work—many of the newspaper quotes that I have used in this book were taken from articles that Sam cut out during the time that he worked for the literacy project.

At first Sam is nervous. "I might do it wrong. I don't want to fuck up."

"There's no way you can do this wrong," I try to reassure him.

"I could." Sam's eyes are wide. In all seriousness he continues, "I could fuck up a wet dream."

At the end of the first week, he tells me that he has come up with a number of categories that he thinks are applicable to the project. He explains that he looks for articles on the homeless, on drug addiction, and on education. He cuts out articles about the local economy, about city government, about police arrests, and about schools. He searches for articles that have something to do with literacy, sometimes cuts out national articles that might be relevant.

Sam takes his work seriously. He tapes the articles squarely to yellow notebook paper and records all the bibliographic information. As he becomes more confident, his categories expand—state politics, local politics, the straight arrows, welfare, drug cases, unemployment, "Panel of Experts Probes String of Suspicious Fires," "Mayor Wants City Council Exempt from Parking Regulations," "Jobless Rate Highest in State," "Welfare with Dignity."

Sam comes to my office and I visit him at home, but he is lonely. The community literacy workers have been accepted in a local community college and are no longer around. He goes to the corner store but rarely farther, except to an evening AA meeting. He cleans his apartment and washes his clothes. He reads the papers, cuts out articles, and learns how to program his TV—he puzzles over the instructions for several days as he works to understand the various functions of the button codes. "I worked out the sleep button and the time button first," he explains. "It gave me a headache."

Every day he reads the Big Book—the AA bible. He also reads other recovery books, some of which he orders from magazines. Sam keeps track of his appointments with social agencies and doctors on a monthly planner, and he writes down the cash he spends and his monthly expenses.

Most of the time he sits at his kitchen table listening to police broadcasts on the radio scanner he bought when he first got his disability settlement. It is the only activity that piques his interest. He spends hours figuring out the codes and he keeps a scanner log with the call-in numbers for all the local police and fire departments. "I learn something new every day," Sam says, excited that he can decipher the police codes. "I don't know what but I learn something." He even learns how to pick up radio calls from Texas and the Midwest and passes more time trying to locate the places of the broadcasts on a map of the United States. He uses the telephone directory to work out the different time zones.

Sometimes when Sam retells his story, he sounds as if he still has hope. "You're looking at a miracle," he says again, as if to remind himself. "I'm a miracle, standing right here."

Occasionally Sam works at the drop-in center for alcoholics and drug addicts that Cindy visited during the few months she was out of prison. But the center—two rooms filled with worn-out furniture and a television set— is a thirty-minute walk from Sam's apartment and as the temperature drops he stops going.

Sam is increasingly isolated. Every day is a challenge. He tells me that he doesn't know how to make friends, for as long as he can remember he has only had drinking buddies. Frustrated, he says he even has to learn how to make love. "Someone is going to have to teach me," he says. "I've never done it sober. It scares me."

On Christmas Day, 1990, Sam comes to my house to spend the holidays with my family. "Hey Santa Claus!" Sam says as he undoes his Christmas stocking, "It's good to see you sober!" When he is asked to distribute the presents from under the Christmas tree he shakes his head. "I don't know how to do that."

But my children encourage him, and he gets up and finds presents for all those who are sitting around the tree. "Merry Christmas," he says each time he gives someone a present.

"Merry Christmas, Sam."

The day after Christmas when I talk with Sam on the telephone, he says that he has taken the ribbon from one of his presents and wrapped it around his dresser mirror.

There were walnuts in his Christmas stocking. "I opened them with my screwdriver," he says. "I ate the nuts. Then I glued them back up."

"Why did you do that?"

"It'll remind me of Christmas," he says.

But then the conversation changes. Sam sounds anxious and his voice is strained. "I feel as if I've fallen off the edge of a cliff," he tells me. "I worry about everything. There's always something going through my mind. I've got no momentum. My back is aching and I have pains in my legs." He ends by saying, "I've just got to learn to live a sober life."

IT'S NEVER BEEN
BETTER THAN THIS

Sam writes in his journal about seeing his counselor at mental health. "He got me wound up. I was having a real good day until I went to see him." The counselor prescribes more pills. Doped, Sam talks slowly, his words are slurred. He is irritable and often sounds confused. "I can't remember anything," he says.

"What medication are you taking?"

Sam pulls the prescription out of his pocket. Pamelor. He says he is also taking Desipramine. Both are antidepressants. The documentation that comes with Desipramine states that "extreme caution should be used when this drug is given [to] patients with a history of seizure disorder, because this drug has been shown to lower the seizure threshold."

Sam says he thinks he has had some seizures. He says that one day last week he came to on the floor of his kitchen with a bump on his head. "I think I hit it on the sink when I went down." But he doesn't know.

The warning for Desipramine users also states that "*in patients who may use alcohol excessively, it should be born in mind that the potentiation may increase the danger inherent in any suicide attempt or overdose.*"

On the calendar that Sam keeps he writes "2 pills, 3 pills" before he crosses off each day. By January he is taking three or four pills a day.

Sam is not sleeping. He talks a lot about his twin brother, who was killed in a car crash, and about his three sisters, who still live in the city. "We were brought up by our grandparents. Our mother didn't want anything to do with us. She was crazy and always in and out of the state hospital. She hated us kids, especially me and my twin brother. She beat the fuck out of us all the time."

He talks about his family's drinking. "My father liked his booze. My mother never drank but she used an awful lot of pills. I used to sip my father's beers. Hell, I grew up around booze. When me and my brother were little kids our grandfather used to give us eggnog laced with rum."

On other occasions Sam talks about being shut up with his brother in a room with a stone floor and no heat. It was winter and his mother took their clothes off and locked them in the room. Remembering being locked in the room Sam becomes morose. "We were locked in there all night," he says. Then he laughs and says something funny, shares a story about his brother, or tells about some trouble he got into when he was young.

He complains about the price of his medication. "It's supposed to help me sleep but it doesn't. I might just as well have a beer," Sam reasons. "That would help me mellow out."

He talks about reaching the best point in his life. "It's never been better than this." It's a negative statement and he apologizes, although it isn't necessary. "It's just that I can't remember a time when it was any better."

Sam's counselor at mental health tells him that he has to pay $25 a week for his services. Sam is livid. "I told him to go take a fuck on a flyin' donut!" He is talking quickly, he is agitated, he gets up and sits down as he speaks. The mental health payments added to rent and medication would take all of Sam's SSI benefits, leaving nothing on which to live. For a while he continues to go to mental health but he refuses to pay. He is morose, morbid, he talks about death, dying, and says he is having bad thoughts.

On February 15, 1991, Sam forgets to get a paper and so the next day he goes to the library to read it. While he is there he copies an article for me: "Advocates Worry Kids Will Suffer if Program Dies." In upright cursive writing Sam carefully duplicates the text. "In his budget speech Wednesday the governor proposed replacing the program for CHINS, or children in need of services. . . . But no new program has been developed—and the new budget goes into effect July 1. . . . Elimination of the CHINS program will save the state about $4.25 million each of the next two years."

"I thought it was important," Sam tells me. "One of those kids could be me."

Sam stops taking his medication. "It's not helping any." Sam is defensive. "It gets me all confused. I might just as well have a beer."

Sam starts drinking. He still visits the office of the literacy project and sits and talks. He is mellow, talks easily, and smiles. But within a short period Sam's drinking is out of control.

In March he stops going to mental health. By the beginning of April he is never without a beer. He drinks until he passes out, wakes up shaking, and gets another beer. "I don't want to drink," he tells me. "I'm emotionally fucked up. I've got a lot of problems. I just don't have the knowledge to go out there and make it work. I know I'm doing the wrong thing but I'm not doing wrong to society." Sam desperately wants me to understand.

"Drunk or sober we're still friends," I tell him. I don't know what else to say.

"It seems this is the only life I know. Going to meetings isn't going to help me with personal things. I sit here and try and read the paper and my head goes round and round. My whole life from being beat on is messed up. My problems came as I grew up. But I'm not going to jail. I haven't done anything wrong."

Naively I reassure Sam, "Nobody is going to send you to jail."

"I'm not a bad person," he tells me. "The other day I gave my Pepsi cans to a guy on the street. He said, 'Thanks Sam,' and I was glad to help him." Again he tells me, "I'm not a bad person."

I'm Like a Book with the Pages Closing

Sam sees old friends. They visit him in his apartment and drink. He gets the money from his settlement out of the bank and he spends it on his friends. Old drinking buddies—"friends" who have not spoken to him in years—and members of his family come and see Sam. He buys them booze and loans them money. Sam stops eating. "I'm a sick fuckin' puppy. I'm so nervous I can't sleep. I'm hallucinating. I've got the DTs. I'm like a book with the pages closin' and I can't get it open."

Sam says he keeps seeing his twin brother, who was killed in a motor accident. "The cops are on a high-speed chase. I wish it was me. I'd hit the tree. I wish I was with my brother tonight. I can't go to sleep because he's talking to me."

The "friends" with whom Sam is drinking are fighting. Sam is on the fringe of the dispute, but he is frightened. "I'm sitting here waiting for my door to be banged down." His voice is trembling. "I feel I'm going to get my head blown off," he says.

Sam is congested, is having difficulty breathing. He is pitifully thin and although I suspect that he is dehydrated his forehead is glistening with perspiration. "Can I take you to the hospital?" I ask.

"No. I'm not going to jail."

I don't take him seriously. "Of course not," I say, dismissing the possibility. "I'll take you to the hospital and wait until you are admitted."

"It won't work," Sam tells me, "I'll stay here."

On Monday, May 13, I drive Sam to the hospital. He is feverish and has trouble breathing. I pick him up just before three o'clock in the afternoon. He sits down in the small office of the receptionist and she asks Sam about insurance. He explains that Medicare will pay for his hospitalization.

In triage a nurse takes his temperature, pulse, blood pressure, and other vital signs and asks him why he has come to the hospital. Sam explains that he is congested and that he is having trouble breathing. He tells her that he can't eat, that he is depressed, and that he wants to stop drinking. The nurse makes notes. "Looks and acts sober." She draws blood. She directs us to a waiting room where we sit and wait.

At 3:44 P.M. a nurse telephones the doctor in charge of medical. He recommends that Sam be referred to mental health. A counselor at mental health suggests that Sam be placed in protective custody or be admitted to the hospital.

Sam is taken to an examination room and an ER doctor listens to his chest and talks to him. The examination takes no more than a few minutes. In the hospital records, the doctor's diagnosis is stated as acute bronchitis, acute and chronic alcoholism, and depression.

More telephone calls. At 4:45 P.M. the head of medical—who I am told is also a recovering alcoholic—recommends that Sam be put into protective custody.

At 5:40 P.M. a nurse asks Sam to come to the front desk. From behind the counter, she tells Sam that the doctor will not admit him and that he wants him placed in protective custody.

"I'm not going to jail." Sam is alarmed. He looks trapped. "No way. I'm getting out of here."

I ask him to wait. I talk with the nurse. "If you won't admit him I want a letter stating the reasons for your refusal." I tell the nurse that it is dangerous for Sam to detox without medical supervision because of his seizures.

Patiently the nurse explains, "We telephoned mental health. Mental health said that they wouldn't give Sam a psychiatric examination until he was sober and that he should be put into protective custody or go to medical. Medical will not accept him because they want a psychiatric evaluation first." She suggests I talk to the doctor in charge of the medical unit who has refused to admit Sam to the hospital. When she calls him, he says he will phone back in ten minutes.

Sam is upset. "Wait," I tell him. "Don't leave yet."

The head of medical telephones. Smoothly, he explains that the nurses get upset when he admits alcoholics to the medical ward. There is no doubt in my mind that Sam needs medical care. "If you refuse to treat him then I want a letter stating why."

The doctor becomes less friendly. I tell him that Sam is severely congested, that he hasn't eaten in over a week, and that he is chronically depressed. I remind him that Sam has seizures and that it is medically dangerous for him to detox on his own. I am out on a limb. I do not have the medical qualifications to diagnose Sam's physical or mental state, but he is sick and he needs help. He needs antibiotics, fluids, detoxification, medical assistance to alleviate his depression. He is no longer just a participant in a literacy project, we are friends, I care about him and I advocate for him as I would for any member of my family.

"I want it in writing that you have denied Sam medical assistance."

"I'll admit him," the doctor tells me, "but not because you're threatening me. I'll do it as a good Samaritan act, but you tell Sam that he is not to cause any trouble."

We return to the waiting room. It is 6:00 P.M. and I am watching the clock. I promised to stay until Sam was admitted but I have to attend a school board meeting at 7:30. My son has finished all his high school requirements in three years and wants to graduate. The school board in its infinite wisdom has ruled that he can have his diploma but that he is banned from the graduation ceremonies. The rationale? He is not a part of the graduating class and so he cannot participate in their graduation ceremonies. I am going to ask the school board to reconsider their decision.

At 6:15 P.M. I tell Sam I have to leave. "They are probably arranging for a bed," I reassure him. "The doctor agreed to admit you."

"I don't like waiting on my own. How do you know they won't change their minds?"

"They won't," I tell him. "I have to go." Taking the doctor at his word, I leave Sam waiting for a bed on the medical ward.

The school board agrees to let my son march in the graduation ceremony but refuses to let him take part in any of the other graduation activities. We cannot attend the dinner for graduating seniors and their parents because even though he is graduating, he is not a senior. Give me strength. For a short while I forget about Sam.

On Tuesday Sam calls. He is drinking.

"Where are you?"

"Home."

"What happened?"

"I waited and I waited and I waited and I was getting nervous and it was after seven o'clock and I said well there it is it's after seven o'clock and so I got up and walked out the door and home I came and jail I went."

"Jail?" I'm trying to take this in. "They sent you to jail?"

"I walked out. I stopped at the store. I talked to the girl over there. I got home at about seven-thirty."

Sam said he listened on his scanner as the hospital called the police and the police went to the hospital before going to his house. "I told them, you have no right coming in here!" Sam talks loudly, almost shouting. "I tried to tell them that I was all right but they didn't want to listen. Then the other cop came and that was it, they took me to jail. I was here when the hospital called the police and said I was missing. They said I was missing and I was supposed to be admitted. So when the cops came, they knocked on the door. I had one beer and I had finished that one and I had opened another one. I'd been listening to the scanner all the time and I was getting ready to take off so they wouldn't find me. I hadn't had a drink from noontime to seven-thirty." Sam talks rapidly. "Anyways, they knocked on the door and I said, I'm all right, and they said, We're just checking on you, and the other cop pulled up and the cop who was already here came in and I told him he didn't have any right to come in and he said they were just checking on me to make sure I was all right. Then he asked to use the telephone and I said sure."

"Do you know what he said on the phone?"

"No. I didn't pay attention. He was talking to the station."

"Then he said to the other cop, well, we've got to take him 1038. And I said what in the fuck is going on!"

"A 1038 is what?"

"To jail! They also said 202, but I don't know what that means. I was all right. I was just sitting here reading my paper. They said they were taking me into protective custody and I was in my own fuckin' house!"

"Did they handcuff you?"

"They handcuffed me, took me out, and put me in the van. The van is all stainless steel and it's all enclosed and there are no seatbelts. If I had been drunk I could have fallen off and banged my head. I was talking like I am right now." Sam is talking rapidly, none of his words are slurred. "When I got there they asked me all kinds of questions and shit and that was it. In the morning I asked them if they would call me a taxi and they said they couldn't and I was shaking like a fuckin' leaf. They had me right in a cell. It sucked and I didn't do nothing wrong, you know, I don't like going to jail that makes me want to get the fuck out of here. I said, Why don't you take me to the hospital? I don't need protective custody. I need help. They said, 'You're going to jail.' Straight to jail for doing nothing fuckin' wrong."

"How much have you drunk today?"

"I don't know, I'm fuckin' pissed. I'm not going to get over it easy. I didn't do nothing wrong why should I be behind locked doors? I was behind one—two—three—four locked doors! Okay! All concrete. I couldn't even flush the toilet!" Sam voice is strained. "And I didn't know whether they were going to let me out or not!" He sounds frightened.

"Did they give you any medication for your bronchitis?"

"No. Nothing." Sam is calming down, he speaks quietly with resolution. "I'm not going there again. I don't care. I'm not going to fuckin' jail again for nobody. Dead or alive I'm not going to fuckin' jail. It's very, very depressing, I live behind locked doors and I do not have the freedom that you are entitled to *for doing nothing.*"

In the hospital records it states that Sam's admission status was canceled at 7:20 P.M. The extended notes state that I expressed concern that Sam was suicidal. On this particular occasion I did not think Sam was suicidal—we had arranged to go to the hospital earlier in the day because Sam was having trouble breathing. There have been times when Sam has been actively suicidal and I have intervened but this was not such an occasion. I was genuinely worried that Sam had bronchitis or pneumonia and that if he was left to detox without medical supervision he might suffer from seizures—which I knew could be extremely dangerous.

In the notes made in the emergency room at the hospital a nurse states that the "police have found Sam—I called and told them that the doctor wants him put in protective custody. The dispatch will inform the officer and call back." Another note. "Pt in his house. They will put him in protective custody." Finally, "Mental health will see pt first thing in AM for further evaluation."

Sam was not treated for the acute bronchitis from which he was suffering. There were no antibiotics, no care, and the next day there was no evaluation made by mental health.

LIVE AND SUFFER OR DIE AND BE HAPPY

Sam is without hope. "I can't cope with life," Sam tells me. "I've got a gash on my head. Must have been a seizure. The only time people come around is when they need money or a favor. Good ol' Sam, he's good for five bucks."

I just listen.

"The hospital says I owe them money from the night they sent me to jail." Sam's voice is strained. "I'm not going to pay them to send me to jail." He speaks rapidly. "The welfare sent me to the clinic. The clinic sent a bill collector fuckin' thing. The hospital said they demand that I pay them. It sucks. If I have to run, I'll run. Life scares me. I should be fuckin' dead."

I talk with Sam about trying to find another hospital that will agree to provide him with medical care.

"No!" Sam sounds appalled by my stupidity. "I'm not going to jail. I'll stay home and drink until I fuckin' die."

Sam is caught between a rock and a hard place. He is angry, confused. He needs help but he can't ask for it. Whenever we talk he tells me that he is not going back to jail. "I can live and suffer or die and be happy," he tells me. For Sam there are no other choices.

Sam stays inside his apartment. He rarely goes farther than the corner store. He tells me he is afraid that the police will pick him up if they see him walking on the street. I try to reassure him. "I'm not taking the chance." Sam shakes his head.

On July 10, Sam writes in his journal, "Didn't do much. Took out the rubbish. Sat around. Listened to the radio. Walked down to the store." July 13. "It's boring. Hopefully someone will stop by. Just sitting around." July 19. "Up. It's 1:30 A.M. Having a brew. It's still pretty warm in here and it sucks. Got back up at 5:30. Went back to bed then got up around 8:00. Just sitting around having a few beers. Took a nap. Went to the store. Didn't get to bed till midnight. It was a boring day."

Sam stops writing. He drinks himself into a stupor. For the rest of 1991 Sam's life stays the same, and even though I do manage to get him into a hospital in another part of the state he has no hope for the future. In his heart Sam knows that whether he is drunk or sober, it makes no difference—except that he sometimes buys beer at the store and sometimes he buys soda. He is still stigmatized, ostracized, alone, lonely, living in exile, desperate for friendships, companionship, and love, for a sense of purpose and an opportunity to participate in the everyday life of the community.

Still, he keeps busy. October 29, he writes, "Read the paper then had to get over to the store to get some soda. Did some housecleaning. Went back over to the store to get the paper. Lay down for an hour. Went to an AA meeting. Finished the paper and cleaned out the frig. It's now after midnight. Time to call it a night."

On November 10, Sam cuts out an article that was in the local paper about Carolyn Chute. In it a professor of literature is quoted as saying, "I think she wants us to understand that these are people who are struggling, but they are still proud."

November 29. Sam receives a letter stating that Medicare has "denied payment for all services." He is informed that he has "now met $0.00 of the $100.00 deductible for 1991."

On December 5 he receives a letter from the local hospital to remind him that he has not paid the bill for May 13, the day the doctor in charge of medical sent him to jail:

Failure to send payment in full will result in your account being placed with an outside agency who will continue collection efforts. If you own property, our attorney will be asked to put a lien on your property so that we will have security for this balance.

The letter is sent to Sam in triplicate. "Failure to send payment"— "FAILURE TO SEND PAYMENT"—"FAILURE TO SEND PAYMENT"!

"I'm not paying them to send me to jail," Sam tells me. His voice is flat. He speaks in a monotone. He no longer sounds angry, just worn-out, beaten, but even though he says he has no hope that his life will change he keeps struggling to live.

On December 13 he writes, "It seems like everything comes down all at once. I try not to let things bother me but there's times when I just can't put things aside. It's hard for me to explain. It seems like there isn't a day that goes by without something bothering me, so I have to do something or else I could find myself in trouble."

By the middle of December Sam has been sober for two months. He gets his sixty-day chip from AA. He wants to drink but he searches for a reason to stay sober. On December 15 he writes, "Tonight's meeting was real good. Part of it was about trying to accomplish or set goals that don't happen and that's how you are apt to say fuck it and down you go. It hit home with me."

Nothing changes. Sam is trapped in the monotony of his life.

New Year's Eve. "Today ought to be an interesting day, hopefully today will be a little better than yesterday. Went and got the paper. Listened to the radio. Took a shower, now I've got to clean up the house. I can't get into trouble if I stay home. I'm just going to sit back and listen to the scanners and some tapes. Washed the floors. They look a little better. Somebody up at Laurel Cove is armed with four guns and is ready to have a shootout with the law. They've got some state troopers coming now they're blocking the place off. Less than an hour for the new year then I'm hitting the sack. Happy New Year."

Sam's entries in his journal become shorter, his handwriting less steady. February 2, 1992. "Took a shower and watched the tube. There's nothing to do and I don't feel like going out. Lay down on the couch and fell asleep watching TV. It's been a long day."

The next day Sam buys some beer. The struggle is over. He drinks himself into oblivion. By February 20, I am once again trying to persuade him to get medical assistance. It's flu season. Many people in the city are coughing and wheezing. The lack of food leaves him vulnerable. I think he has bronchitis.

Sam agrees to let me take him to the hospital. This time I give him my word that I will not leave until he is admitted for treatment. I drive to Sam's apartment. Sam says he has changed his mind. "I'm not going to jail. That's what they will do to me. Send me to jail."

I stay for while and we talk. I take him to the store so he can buy some orange juice and chocolate milk. I encourage him to eat. Each day we talk on the telephone. Sam is disorientated, losing touch with reality. He says he can't read. "I sit and read the words but I don't know what I'm reading, I forget what I am doing."

"Are you eating?"

"No, I can't eat."

"You've got to eat."

By February 26 Sam has not eaten for over a week. He talks about joining his brother, about dying. He buys tequila and vodka and drinks them straight.

Sam telephones. At first he is incomprehensible. He says he can't breathe, that his chest hurts and he needs help. It's snowing. The weather forecast is for "significant snowfall." It will take me hours to drive to the city. I ask Sam if he will go to the hospital if I telephone the head of medical and get him to agree to admit him. Sam is hesitant. I persuade him.

"Okay."

I telephone the doctor. A recording instructs callers to try again after seven o'clock. I call back and talk with the doctor. I remind him that the last time Sam tried to receive medical treatment at the hospital he was sent to jail. I tell him I want some reassurances that if Sam goes to the hospital the medical personnel will not send him to jail.

The doctor is not unfriendly. I tell him that Sam is having trouble breathing and that he says his chest hurts. The doctor reassures me that if Sam needs medical treatment, he will admit him to the hospital. It's not much of a reassurance.

"I want your word that you won't send him to jail."

"We won't," the doctor says. "Tell Sam not to give us any trouble."

I telephone the emergency room and tell the person on duty that Sam is coming up to the hospital and that the doctor in charge of medical has given his word that Sam will not be sent to jail. The person is distant and her voice is disapproving. I give her my telephone number and ask her to call me if I can be of any assistance.

While I am on the telephone to the hospital emergency room, Sam phones mental health. He tells a counselor that he is suicidal, that he is drinking himself to death. Later Sam tells me that the counselor said, "What do you want me to do about it." The counselor at mental health calls the police.

I telephone Sam. A policeman answers the telephone. I tell him I have spoken with the doctor and that the hospital is expecting Sam.

Reflecting on what happened next, Sam says, "All I remember is having oxygen in the ambulance and then at the hospital they said I had a blood alcohol of point five one. They called the police and said, 'Get him out of here.' "

The hospital records state that when Sam arrived he was complaining of chest pains and he was asking to be buried. His blood alcohol is recorded at 510 MG/DL and in the diagnosis it states that there is a possibility that he might have pleurisy. When I ask a physician friend about the level of Sam's blood alcohol, he says, "If that was you or me we'd be dead. Even for an alcoholic it's high. Your friend is lucky to be alive."

At 9:35 P.M. I receive a call from the hospital. An emergency room nurse asks me to come and get Sam. "Otherwise he will be placed in protective custody." My husband has just arrived home. It is snowing so hard it took him an hour to drive the last ten miles to our house. The visibility is so poor that on one occasion he drove off the road. "I can't get there," I tell the nurse, "and even if I could I don't have the medical qualifications to take care of Sam."

"If you refuse to take him he'll be sent to jail."

The conversation is ugly. I am angry with the nurse and she is angry with me. I remind her that the doctor I spoke with promised that if Sam was sick he would receive medical treatment.

"Will you come and get him?"

"I can't."

"Then he will spend the night in jail."

At 10:10 P.M. Sam is picked up by the police and taken to the county jail.

I telephone the city police station. I tell a lieutenant that Sam is too sick to be sent to jail. He is sympathetic. He tells me that the hospital is "a real problem" for the city PD. He says that the hospital calls them on a regular basis and that they have no alternative other than to pick people up and take them to jail because that's the way the regulations are written. "We often pick up people who should be in hospital but instead they are sent to jail."

Sam spends the night in jail. In the morning he is put out on the snow-covered street and once again he walks home.

I get a message to Will, a recovering drug addict I am also working with and you will meet. I tell him what has happened to Sam, and he says he will try to get him into a crisis center in another city. Will takes Sam to the crisis center but it quickly becomes apparent that Sam is too sick to be there. Sam is taken from the crisis center to the hospital, where he is diagnosed as suffering from pneumonia.

In the report of this emergency room visit the doctor states:

Mr.___ [Sam] is a 35-year-old gentleman who had a blood alcohol level of 500 a couple of days ago. He was taken to the police station after being discharged from a hospital to the north of here. He hasn't been drinking since then. He has been in the crisis center. He comes in with what I think is quite obviously alcohol withdrawal. . . . He is quite tremulous, quite anxious, quite hyper-alert. . . .

I would feel more comfortable hospitalizing this patient, because I am quite concerned about his alcohol withdrawal, and what probably represents a small pneumonia. The gentleman is quite adamant that he prefers not to be hospitalized.

I will be giving him Librium and erythromycin. However, I told him that if his condition worsens, he should reconsider, and be taken to the Emergency Department. He is lucid. I think he is competent to make these decisions.

"Why didn't you stay in the hospital?" I ask Sam.

"I was worried they would send me to jail."

"How did you get home?"

"I walked. It was really cold out there."

Sam walked about ten miles before he managed to get a ride downtown and then he walked home from there.

"I like that hospital," Sam tells me. "They treated me really nice. It was different you know. Go to the hospital up here and all they do is put you in jail. They don't care. If somebody goes up there for help they should be treated, not sent to jail."

At the beginning of March Sam buys soda.

March 9, 1992. "Got my house cleaned up. Watched a little TV. Had something to eat. I still feel kind of light-headed. I think it's because of my meds cause I haven't had nothing at all to drink in over a week besides Pepsi and ginger ale. I've got a lot of things going on in my head. I just hope I can keep myself together and stop worrying about what I'm going through."

March 12. "It's 8:30. I got up and took my pills and had a smoke then went back to bed. Did some laundry. Had a can of corn for my supper. Went over and got a bottle of soda so I wouldn't run out. It sucks. It went up 50 cents since this afternoon. Watched some TV. Went to bed after the news. Called it a day."

March 27. "The wind woke me up this morning. I was up at 5:30. There seems to be quite a bit of flooding and tree limbs down. Went over and got some soda. Been reading my hot rod magazine but now it's time for my radio show." This is Sam's last entry.

I talk with him on the telephone. "I have a lot of problems," he tells me. "I need help but mental health won't see me and the hospital won't treat me."

Sam is right when he says that these medical institutions won't treat him, but they do send him bills. Mental health is dunning him for the $25 payments they charged for his weekly visits to the clinic—during which they pushed prescription dope that exacerbated his alcoholism and quite possibly increased his suicidal tendencies. Letters from collection agencies arrive regularly—some of them written in an all-cap bully text that lifts off the page and shouts at Sam.

THE ABOVE NAMED CREDITOR HAS REFERRED YOUR ACCOUNT TO THIS FIRM FOR IMMEDIATE COLLECTION. WE WISH TO RESOLVE THE MATTER AMICABLY IF POSSIBLE.

OUR CLIENT HAS EXTENDED SERVICE IN A PROMPT AND PROFESSIONAL MANNER AND HAS THE RIGHT TO EXPECT A SIMILAR RESPONSE FROM YOU. WE FEEL CERTAIN YOU INTEND TO HONOR THIS OBLIGATION. THEREFORE, WE ARE REQUESTING THAT YOU TAKE THIS OPPORTUNITY TO SETTLE THE MATTER ON A VOLUNTARY BASIS. ALL ACTION TO PROTECT OUR CLIENT'S INTERESTS WILL CEASE IF PAYMENT IN FULL IS RECEIVED WITHIN SEVEN DAYS. YOUR CHECK, MADE PAYABLE TO THE CREDITOR, SHOULD BE MAILED AT ONCE TO THE ADDRESS ABOVE.

Sam has no money. He is behind with his rent. The owner of the apartment in which he is living says she is going to evict him. He goes downtown to sell his jacket. "Too small," he says when I see him the next day.

He smiles. In his hand is a can of beer.

I tease him about being so tiny. We laugh, but the reality is that he is malnourished and underweight. We talk about his life, the year that he was sober.

"That was worse than this," he says. "Then I cared. Now I don't."

"What would it take right now to get your life back together?"

"I could never get my life back together," Sam tells me. "I could probably get sober again but I don't know how, you know, because I'm not going to end up going to a hospital and end up in jail again. I'll sit and drink till I die before I go to jail, because that really fucking sucks. In plain English that really is totally bullshit."

LEARNING FROM SAM

Sammy teaches us that official texts are used to do in the individual. In the introduction to this book I quoted from a play by Tom Stoppard. "For the politicals, punishment and medical treatment are intimately related. I was given injections of aminazin, sulfazin, . . . which caused trembling, fever, and the loss of various abilities including the ability to read, write, . . . and button my trousers. When all this failed to improve my condition, I was stripped and bound head to foot with lengths of wet canvas . . . *and still my condition did not improve.*"

For Sam, punishment and medical treatment are intimately connected through official texts. At first we treat his condition by using our bureaucratic agencies to maintain his status as a political—we relegate him to the streets by making the processing of official forms so complex that Sam is unable to fulfill the textual requirements that we use to determine whether or not he is eligible for assistance. Stacks of forms are used to punish him for being homeless. When he has the audacity to come to our office sick with a fever, coughing and wheezing, we still refuse to provide assistance. And when he keeps coming we offer him a bus ticket out of town.

TWICE.

When that fails we offer him instead thick piles of forms to fill in, forms we can discard if he doesn't answer every question.

We abdicate responsibility. We send him from one agency to another. We withhold his food stamps. We make him wait for emergency housing. Deny him medical assistance. Send him to jail. *JAIL HIM!* Send him medical bills for his incarceration. Bully him. Threaten him. And still his condition does not improve.

"*Of course not. That was not the point of the exercise.*"

I know, Stoppard's doctor had no interest in improvements.

"*No, and we are not interested in improving Sammy's lot in life.*"

"*We gave him SSI—what more does he want?*"

"*He is socially indebted to us for the money that he receives.*"

It's a bribe. The money we pay to keep him off the streets is a bribe.

"*Did you really think that we wanted to provide him with an opportunity to participate in the community?*"

He is among the most vulnerable in our society and we've rejected him.

We don't want to be bothered by him.

But his name is Sam. *Sam. SAM!* We know him. He has feelings. He has morals, principles, values, virtues as well "sins." Sam teaches us that he is traumatized by the pathology we ascribe to him. He is terrorized by his hospital "treatment"—rendered helpless, disorientated, unable to speak, to read, write, or button his trousers.

"Don't tell me—and still his condition did not improve!"

No. It did not improve.

But when we remove the filthy clothes that he wears when he lives on the streets we find his jeans and T-shirt are freshly washed. He is clean, cleanly, neat, tidy, he no longer has to struggle for words—*let me speak, let me speak*— he is articulate, capable of thoughtful conversations, of expressing opinions, he has feelings, he hurts, and he is kind. He needs kindness, he needs love.

Sam personalizes the lives of the homeless that we step over on the street. Gathered together all we can do is count them and publish our findings in some official report. They are anonymous, without feeling, dehumanized—but knowing Sam helps us understand that we are the ones who have lost our humanity.

At an international literacy conference I have lunch with one of the professors with whom I studied when I was working on my doctorate at Columbia. In many ways his work is similar to my own and I can talk to him. It is the end of April 1991, a month after Sam was last sent to jail when he had pneumonia, and I have been working every day in the city, without a break, for over a year. I talk about Sam, but what has happened to him is too much for me. In the middle of the restaurant, I cry. I am watching Sammy die, slowly, painfully, as we "treat" him with such contempt that he can no longer find reasons to live. I am traumatized by what we are doing to him. My old professor listens to me and we continue to talk without making much of my tears.

Back home I read the newspapers, listen to news broadcasts, and try to deconstruct the public dialogue—the self-serving moral platitudes of politicians and the parasitic verbiage of talk-show hosts, all of whom have turned the politics of the disenfranchised into a commercial enterprise—and I am ashamed.

Ashamed by my silence. Ashamed of my own inactivity. Will someone please tell me why nobody cares what happens to Sam?

"What's the point of your question. Who cares?"

That's the point—I CARE. *I CARE!* He is no longer a statistic to me.

Irritated by my advocacy, a friend chastises me. "You can't change the system," she tells me, in denial of her own duplicity.

"FUCK THE SYSTEM!" I say. No, I can't change "it," but I can hold it accountable.

In January 1995, Sam telephones me several times a week. He has bronchitis and needs medical assistance. On January 12, he calls and tells me he is "not good." He says that he has not eaten in nine days. I tell him he's got to eat, that he needs to see a doctor. We both know that without Medicaid or Medicare the only way he can get medical assistance is to go to the hospital.

He dismisses the possibility. "I'm not going to jail." Sam is adamant.

I am living in another part of the country and there is nothing I can do to help him.

Sam doesn't call for several days and I am concerned about him. Reluctantly, I telephone one of the lieutenants in the city PD who has known Sam for years—another policeman who expressed concern to me that the prison is used as a hospital. The lieutenant says that he will stop by and see Sam.

The next day the lieutenant calls and says that Sam is okay. Sam calls. He is angry with me. "I'll try and eat," he says. "But I'm not going to let the cops take me to the hospital. All that will happen is that the cops will be told to take me to jail."

Several weeks pass and I don't hear from Sam. Then he calls. "I've just got out of the hospital," he says. His voice is weak and he has trouble speaking. He says he spent four days and nights in the intensive care unit suffering from pneumonia and congestive heart failure. "I thought I was a gonna," he says. "The doctor told me he didn't think I was going to make it. If my sister hadn't come around and found me I would be dead." Sam laughs. "Even then I told her I wasn't going to the hospital, because I didn't want to end up in jail. But she made me go. Otherwise, as I said, I'd be dead."

When Sam's sister arrived at his apartment his legs were so swollen he couldn't pull up his trousers. "He still wouldn't go to the hospital," she says, "and the hospital said if he didn't want to come they weren't going to come and get him. So I told him that he either walked down the stairs or I'd put him over my shoulder and carry him!"

Sam lives quietly. "I'm doing the best I can," he says. He calls me collect every week.

He is nervous about the activities of the members of the House of Representatives. If the Republicans have their way, he will lose his Social Security disability benefits and be back on the streets.

If this happens we must accept responsibility.

IRRADIATING—OR IS IT ERADICATING?—LAURIE

On December 8, there is an article in the city paper about Medicaid. The Medicaid chief for the state is quoted as saying, "We've been through this many times before. They are trying to shift the costs back to the state." He predicts that the state will continue to "get clobbered by Congress" and concludes that programs will have to be cut or the state will have to come up with the difference.

At the same time doctors working in the state express concern about the increasing difficulties they are experiencing in providing medical care for the poor with the money provided to them by Medicaid.

On January 14, 1991, in an article in the city newspaper, a physician declares that Medicaid is "a severely flawed federal policy that provides for physician reimbursement at a rate insufficient to cover the cost of care." In the same article another physician is quoted as stating that "we cannot set aside the fact that physicians' offices are businesses with fixed costs that must be paid."

The federal and state arguments about who pays and doctors' contention that medicine is big business are the reasons Laurie was irradiated. We crippled her. It was cheaper that way.

I met Laurie in late spring 1991, after she had received radiation treatment for cervical cancer. Her boyfriend, Will, who is recovering from drug and alcohol addiction, was participating in the literacy project. He talked about Laurie. He said that she wanted to get a GED and we offered to help. For a while the young woman who worked for the project helped Laurie. Then when the young woman went to college Laurie continued her work with me. I visited Laurie's home on a regular basis and I learned what happened to her when she was diagnosed with cervical cancer.

To understand what happened to Laurie you have to know a little about her everyday struggle to raise her three children. Remember what is happening in the city, the high unemployment, the straight arrows cutting services, and the governor's decision to reduce state funding for programs that provide food and housing for the poor.

EVERYONE WANTS TO PASS THE BUCK

On December 14, 1990, Will visits the office of the city literacy project. He is talking fast, walking around, agitated, irritated. He has an attitude. He is fed up with being given the runaround by social agencies. He needs oil to heat his apartment and he has just lost his job.

"I got laid off Friday." He tightens the black bandanna with white polka dots that he wears around his head. He has on a black Grateful Dead T-shirt on top of a long-sleeve undershirt; jeans; and boots. He is tall and thin, scrawny, too energetic to get fat. "So I go to town and tell people I'm poor so

I can get help." Will says it as if he hates it, as if he is stating the obvious, as if it should never have to be said.

"But it's an impossible task." He is angry. "I went to city welfare and then to state welfare. They just ask for copies of whatever and it takes them a while to figure it out. By then it's Tuesday and I've spent two days running around and nothing has happened." Will's voice is raised, but I don't think he realizes how loud he's gotten.

"So Tuesday I go with Laurie to Community Action and I tell them that I have a little bit less than an eighth of a tank of oil." Community Action gives Will and Laurie some forms to fill out. The forms have to be processed before they can be helped. Will goes back to the city welfare office. "I'm told that I need an appointment. I tell them I need one as soon as possible, that I need help now but the earliest I could get an appointment was Thursday!"

Will is shouting. "I said, 'Well I'll be out of oil by then,' and she goes, 'There's nothing I can do until Thursday.'"

He goes back to Community Action. "When I got there the woman behind the desk said she told me that Laurie needed to come back at a quarter to nine tomorrow, before they were open." He shakes his head—Will is persona non grata with social agencies, it is Laurie who has to fill in forms. "The kids have to be at the bus at a quarter to nine. Laurie would have to leave at eight o'clock to walk downtown by a quarter to nine!

"Laurie went to some churches and she called up the Salvation Army. They said to go to Community Action. Laurie went and they told her there was a problem with her application." Will wipes out. "So Laurie phones welfare and the director says he's busy, and tells her to call back. She calls back and the other caseworker is totally obnoxious to her. She was really rude to her, so I didn't go in for my appointment on Thursday morning. I couldn't see where it would do me any good." Will shakes his head. "All I would do is blow up on these people." He speaks quietly. "Nobody cares if you have a house with kids and you don't have oil. That really bothers me. Everyone wants to pass the buck," he says. "I'm tired of talking to them. I'm fed up with it—you know, the runaround."

Will says that he only worked for three months so he isn't eligible for unemployment benefits. "I can't collect." It's a recurring pattern. Will finds minimum-wage employment in the summer, gets laid off in the fall. He doesn't work long enough to be eligible for unemployment benefits. While he is working, Laurie loses her welfare benefits for herself and her children. Two of her children are by a previous marriage, but Will is the father of Ricky, her youngest son. For reasons they never figured out, Ricky is not eligible for such services as Medicaid, and Will is totally left out of the configuration. When

Will is laid off, it takes Laurie months to get her benefits reestablished. Will frantically tries to find work. But this year there is no work.

The difficulties Will and Laurie face are exacerbated by Laurie's ill health. She has never recovered from the radiation treatment used to eradicate her cancer in June 1990. Will needs to make sure the house is warm, but he knows that if they turn the thermostat up they will run out of oil more quickly and that some heat is better than no heat at all.

"It's really cold," Will says, shaking his head. "But the heat's not gonna be up. It will have to stay at sixty degrees. Laurie complains but I won't put it up."

Right now the temperature is subzero and all Will is trying to do is get some more oil. He calls city welfare from the literacy project office. "I forgot my appointment Thursday, I was too busy running around trying to get oil." Will listens. "All right." He listens. "That would be good." He is conciliatory. "Sorry about missing that appointment. I'll come in on Tuesday at one." Will puts down the phone. It's clear by his face what the phone call cost him.

LOST IN THE SHUFFLE OF LIFE

On February 3, 1992, Will and Laurie come to the literacy office. Laurie is a small gentle woman with natural red-gold hair. Usually she is as calm as Will is agitated. By this time, I have known Laurie for almost a year. Laurie is constantly sick. She rarely leaves the house, and she goes very few places without Will. But today is a good day. Laurie says she feels okay and she is relaxed as we sit in my office.

Will does most of the talking. He has been trying to obtain funding through vocational education to go to college to be a youth counselor. He has been visiting schools to talk about alcoholism and drug addiction and he would like to work with young people. But his counselor at voc rehab has closed his case. "I feel like I've proved myself with my test scores. I should be in school but he wants me to get some kind of training. He was trying to get me not to go to school. He wanted to get me on-the-job training." Will is upset.

"So he closed my case. I just called up today to find out he had closed my case. I missed my last appointment in December, because the last time I saw him he told me I had to go see another doctor and get another checkup on my lungs. As if he hasn't got enough! He told me to get more letters. I told him the letters I had and he still wanted more letters." Will mimics the counselor. " 'Well you have to get a letter stating that to get going in this field you have got to have a degree.' He ought to know!" Will's voice is raised.

"How many times did you phone him before you got an appointment?" I ask.

"I'd try and catch him in his office. I could never get ahold of him on the phone. And I'd give him my address and he'd say he didn't have it and he'd never send me a letter." Will shakes his head. "You know he should have sent me a letter stating that he was closing my case. I don't see where he is doing any good. I think he's giving a lot of people a lot more discouragement than they are already getting from unemployment and from welfare."

Will says he is going to phone the counselor's supervisor. "I'm sure he's got the paperwork all figured out. I didn't show up for my last appointment but why should I go through more tests on my lungs. You've seen the paperwork I've gotten. I've got letters from schools, from drug rehabs. I've got a lot of letters saying I should continue in this field. But to him that don't matter. He's gotta come up with another letter and that's bullshit."

"How long have you been working with him?"

"I signed up back in April of last year. My tests were in March. I can understand a year but to keep putting obstacles in the way is like—you know—I went down to welfare and wrote a statement about trying to get into school and I had to fill out a work form for them so I'll probably have to go through the work thing." City welfare recipients who can work arrive at seven in the morning and they are sent out in work groups. In the past Will has worked as a member of cleanup crews in the cemeteries and he has also worked cutting brush.

Will changes the subject. "State welfare has just changed the rules on Laurie. So that's a lot of bullshit. And Ricky is still not covered on the medical cards. If he gets hurt, we're screwed."

It seems inconsistent to me that Laurie's two older children have Medicaid but her youngest son doesn't. "I still don't understand why he isn't covered."

" 'Cause I'm here," Will tells me.

"If you're not here?"

"If I go, then Laurie will get coverage for him. And she'll get money for him too."

"Has anyone actually told you that?"

"Laurie, they told you if I'm not here that he can get covered?"

"Yes," Laurie says.

I am persistent. "They said that to you?"

Laurie nods her head. "If the father is not living in the home then the child can be covered, but if the father is living in the home the child can't be covered by anything, except food stamps if they're eligible," Laurie pulls a face, "whatever that means."

"When did they tell you that?"

"They told me a long time ago. She just told me that again when I went for an appointment the twenty-seventh."

"So if Will isn't living with you?"

"They will increase my check because Will isn't included in the check and the only thing that Ricky gets is food stamps."

"I'm tired of trying and I'm tired of busting my ass." Will's voice is strained. "I'm tired of being out there looking for a job and not getting anywhere. I was so upset today when I was in welfare I couldn't write my age down. I put my birth date but I couldn't put down thirty or thirty-one. I didn't have a clue." Will is slumped forward, his elbows on his knees, his hands together. "I guess you could say I'm a person of low self-esteem. They're supposed to help you, not pawn you off. You go to state welfare, you're looking at close to two months before you can get anything from them." Will sits back, his arms are wide. His voice is raised. "So what are you supposed to do until then? You go to the city. The city says check here, check there. All right? Well, you are already feeling down-and-out and you've gotta go around running to all these places and they're all treating you like assholes." Will shakes his head. "I've got lost in the shuffle of life. It's not easy. It's easier to pick up a bottle or pick up a joint and let everything blow over."

The conversation is back to oil—or the lack of it. Will and Laurie are once again trying to find a way to fill their tank. Will says that before Christmas they ended up with no heat. He talks about Laurie's trying to find a way to pay for a shipment of oil. "Laurie got the runaround. The worst one was the Santa Fund. They were quite obnoxious to her, and we know that other families have got oil from them."

"They don't do that," Laurie says. "They told me they don't do that. It really made me mad because she looked at me like," Laurie assumes the role of Santa's helper, " 'Well, there's nothing I can do about it. Go to the city.' " Laurie shakes her head. "She wouldn't even talk to me about it. She walked off. I'm standing there and this lady just walked off!"

SO WHAT WAS THIS DOING TO THE REST OF MY BODY?

In the spring of 1991 I helped Laurie study for a GED. She was often sick—sometimes too sick to work with me. During this time we often talked about what had happened to her when she was diagnosed with cervical cancer.

On January 20, 1990, Laurie was examined by a physician because she was experiencing intense abdominal pain and uncontrollable vaginal bleeding. On January 27, the physician wrote in a report that "the entire post half of the cervix" had been "replaced by a large cauliflower-like lesion, chunks of which" had been "removed for path. exam."

It was February when Laurie found out she had cancer. She was twenty-five years old. Will was in a drug rehabilitation center.

Will remembers. "When you're first getting clean and sober, dealing with life on life's terms is hard, never mind a major thing like cancer. I think Laurie being sick was a lot of incentive not to drink and drug because there would be no way I could help her if I was drunk. The doctors never told her about cancer support groups or anything, we got the big runaround going from doctor to doctor. The doctor she was seeing could have done the hysterectomy right there instead of sending her to other hospitals."

Will is correct. Laurie could have been treated for cancer in the city. Instead she was passed from one doctor to another in different cities around the state. The physician who diagnosed that she was suffering from uterine cancer referred her to the physician who delivered her third child. This doctor told Laurie that she had cancer and referred her to another physician at a large teaching hospital approximately two hours from her home by car.

"I told him I had no way of getting there," Laurie tells me. "All he said was, 'You'll find a way.' "

At first the physician that Laurie saw at the teaching hospital told her that she would need a radical hysterectomy. She filled in the necessary paperwork in preparation for surgery. However, Laurie says that the physician changed his mind and recommended radiation treatment after Laurie developed bronchitis.

"They said it was severe," Will says, "but it wasn't as severe as I have seen it."

"I've had it worse," Laurie agrees. "When I went and saw the doctor again, he checked the cancer out and he said, 'Well, it's getting pretty active and you've got to go down and see this breathing specialist.' So I went down and I saw the breathing specialist and then they sent me to this other doctor and I don't know what he was exactly for, I can't remember, it had something to do with the breathing. Then I had to go back and see the first doctor who was going to do the surgery and he says, 'Well at this point I don't really want to wait to,' you know, 'because this could take time to clear up'—the bronchitis. He said, 'With you it might take one week on the medication that you're on and then you'll be okay to have the surgery but I don't think you should wait.' "

"He said you shouldn't wait one week?" I ask.

"Yeh," Laurie says, "because he said it might drag on longer than a week.

But it never had before with me. I've had bronchitis a lot and once I get the medication a week later it's gone, you know, it's all cleared up. He said he didn't want to take that chance and that I should consider radiation therapy."

"Yeh, he ended up not wanting to operate," Will says. "He said she would be better off getting radiation, and he said it would take care of it and so we said yes not knowing what we were getting into. He made it sound good. He really did. He didn't make it sound like the long-term effects would be that bad."

Laurie picks up the story. "And he explained to me about radiation, you know, that it would kill the cancer and everything but to get into detail I would have to talk to this other doctor in—." Laurie names another city in the state.

"They had you running all over the state!" I say.

She nods and presses her lips together. "And he said he was going to send me to this other doctor, so he sent all my records to him and then—"

"But Laurie," I interrupt, "how long did it take for the records to get there? I mean how long was the wait between him saying that—"

"It was at least three weeks, three to four weeks before I heard anything." She tries to continue. "And they sent me—"

"So how was your bronchitis at that point?" I interrupt a second time.

"It was gone." Laurie smiles. "It had been gone for about two weeks, at least two and a half weeks."

"They discovered the cancer in January," Will says, "but it was May when they did anything about it."

Again Laurie moves on. "And so this other hospital sent me the paperwork through the mail telling me when my appointment was and what the name of the doctor was that I would be seeing and to come in and talk to them. So I went in on the appointment day and I registered and everything and then I went to see this doctor and he's talking to me again telling me how radiation will take care of the problem but he thought I was kind of young for radiation."

"He never said that she'd be sick two years later," Will interjects.

"You know," Laurie continues, "he explained stuff to me, but it was so confusing at that point from seeing all these other doctors that I'm going, you know. 'Okay okay okay.' "

Laurie tries to smile. Her face is flushed—anxiety brings her color up. "You know half the words they were using I didn't really understand and I'd say well, you know, 'What's that? What's gonna happen?' And he explained to me that I'd be put on this little table and they would put," Laurie hesitates as if searching for a medical explanation, "I don't know, it was like," again she hesitates, then in a rush she continues, "I was laying on this table and there was this almost like a square thing, a vent kind of. . . ."

Laurie explains the procedure and her physical reactions to the treatment, which included extreme discomfort and the infection triggered by the effects of the radiation on her bladder.

For one month, five days a week, Laurie managed to find rides for the one-hour car trip to and from the hospital. At the end of this time, she was hospitalized and a radiation implant was inserted into her uterus and left there for three days.

In a report written on December 20, 1990, one of the doctors treating Laurie with radiation summarized the events that had taken place:

> [Laurie] was evaluated by Drs. D., W., and B. for a micro-invasive carcinoma of the cervix, squamous cell type, with lymphatic invasion. She was not felt to be a surgical candidate given her apparent severe bronchitis.
>
> For this reason, she was treated with external beam irradiation and intracavitary cesium insertion.

Laurie explains intracavitary cesium insertion. "They told me the nurses would be standing behind a shield and stuff and I wouldn't be able to have visitors for very long at a time because there would be radiation all through the room."

"Why did they decide to take you into hospital?" I ask, "Did they say they hadn't gotten rid of the cancer?"

"They just wanted to make sure," Laurie explains, "this was just an extra blast of more direct radiation to make sure that it wasn't going to come back." She looks worried, as if what she is about to say is nagging at her. "The thing that really got me was they were telling me that, you know, it wasn't really going to hurt me that badly, but if they wouldn't let other people into the room for very long then what was it doing to me being right in there all the time? That didn't really make much sense to me, saying that the nurses had to stand behind this shield and so what was this doing to the rest of my body?" Laurie raises her voice. "And this guy came in and took a radiation lev—," she hesitates, "you know, he had one of those. . . ?"

"Geiger counters?"

"Yeh, he came in with it. This really made me feel wonderful. He came in with it when I first got into the room and checked the radiation level." Laurie reruns the conversation.

"'Is it all right? Is it dangerous or anything?' 'Oh no. The levels are fine.' But then when I left three days after, before I could leave he had to come in again and do it again to make sure I guess that I wasn't"—she laughs— "glowin' or something, I don't know." Laurie's voice fades, as if she is speaking to herself. "As if he was trying to work out if it was safe for me to leave."

She becomes more animated. " 'Well, why have you got to do it again?' 'Oh just to check the levels,' " she responds in a man's deep voice. Then speaking for herself, "So he didn't really give me an explanation of why he would have to do it before I left."

"Did anyone at any time give you some information on why this procedure instead of a hysterectomy?" I ask.

"All they ever really said to me was that they didn't want to wait."

"But when the cancer specialist sent the stuff to the radiology department in another hospital it took three weeks before you got an appointment."

"Huh-huh."

"So it was probably a month before you started radiation?"

"Yeh. It had to have been. Easy. It was a while."

"Do you think it was longer?"

"I'm not exactly sure how long I waited," Laurie says, trying to remember. "I was so nervous and upset at the time—"

"It was the middle of June when she came home." Will remembers he took care of the kids and used a month's food stamps in one week.

"We won't talk about that!" Laurie frowns at Will as if she is still scolding him.

"Do you think there was another reason why they decided to go for radiation?" I ask.

"Personally I think it was cheaper," Laurie says. "I've been sick ever since the radiation. It was real intensive. In the beginning I was constantly sick, then it mellowed out and I wasn't sick all the time. Still that was two and a half years ago and I am still getting sick. I get infections constantly, bladder infections, and after they take care of that, after so many months I get another one. The last one I got was really bad. They had to cauterize my bladder to stop all the bleeding. One of the doctors I saw said, 'Oh, it can't be that bad.'" Laurie looks angry. "'Well, I'm the one feeling it. You can't tell me it's not that bad!'" She tells him off now, although I think she is too shy to have done so to his face.

She looks at me. Her skin is blotchy with hives. "After the radiation it's been one thing after another. I mean I get these pains that go from the lower part of my stomach all the way across my back, and I tell them about it and

184 · TOXIC LITERACIES

they just give me pills and they don't ever really tell me why it's happening." She pretends to be the doctor. " 'Okay, you take these and you'll be fine.' 'But what if—' Again she's the doctor. 'Well, we don't know.' "

Will joins in the conversation. "I want to find out the overall damage of what radiation does, that's what I want to know. We've never been told. In my opinion we've never been told the long-term effects of radiation."

"No," Laurie agrees, "it was mostly the short-term stuff."

Will again brings up the length of time Laurie had to wait. "When somebody has cancer I thought it was serious and they're supposed to do something immediately. What Laurie got was the big runaround from doctor to doctor. Why? Because she's on Medicaid. You know that if she had Blue Cross/Blue Shield she'd get it done right on the spot, but she doesn't so she is shuffled around from doctor to doctor till one finally decided to do something about it."

I ask a number of lawyers whether Laurie could sue for malpractice, but the answer is always the same. There were so many doctors involved it would be difficult to establish liability, and without a settlement guarantee lawyers do not want to represent her.

"As you can imagine," a lawyer explains with suitable concern, "obtaining expert testimony is very expensive. It would cost two hundred and fifty to four hundred dollars an hour for an expert to look at the records."

"That's a month's rent," I tell the lawyer. "She takes care of her family on less than $250 a week."

"She had a duty under the law to attempt to mitigate the damage," the lawyer continues as if she didn't hear me. "I'm afraid the outcome would be she had a duty to follow up. It wasn't reasonable for her to sit back and wait." Then, unbelievably, "She also has to prove that she would have had a better result with another procedure." The clock is ticking. "Part of the reality is that anytime you sue a doctor you sue an insurance company and they have lawyers working full time to make sure that doctors don't lose." A slight pause. "Good luck." Click.

"To me they're like politicians," Will says when we talk about the possibility of a lawsuit. "They all cover up for each other."

"You can't get the records from one doctor to another," Laurie adds, nodding her head in agreement. "They say they don't have this doctor's records or they can't give them to you by mail. God, there are so many doctors."

In January 1992 Laurie develops a severe bladder infection. When I visit, I find her sitting in an armchair, her legs bent in front of her and arms are wrapped tightly around them. She appears swollen, as if she's suddenly gained twenty-five pounds. When she gets up she remains bent over and she walks holding on to furniture with one hand while she holds her stomach with the other.

Laurie says that the doctor in the walk-in clinic at the local hospital prescribed antibiotics but they are not working. For several weeks Laurie's condition does not improve. She is bleeding every time she urinates, and the pain of urination is almost more than she can stand.

When the infection does not respond to antibiotics, Laurie is referred to the department of urology at the city hospital. There are at least three urology reports written by three different physicians about Laurie's bladder infections and the procedures that were performed.

In one of the reports, dated February 2, 1992, a physician describes the "pathologic diagnosis" as "ulcerative and hemorrhagic cystitis."

A report written on February 10 describes the procedures that were performed, and the physician states his "impression" that

> bleeding and bladder changes are secondary to resolving hemorrhagic cystitis, which appears to have spared a significant part of the bladder; to radiation cystitis from the combination of external beam and especially intracavitary radiation; or to malignancy.

In a third report written on February 11, the physician states that "no evidence of malignancy was identified." He also states, "Patient has history of cervical cancer with radiation treatment. Cytology favors cellular changes due to radiation."

Laurie says they've told her there is no reoccurrence of the cancer. However, given the mention of malignancy in the second report, I encourage her to ask for further clarification.

Eight months later Laurie is still sick. When I visit her on November 1, 1992, she has a stomach virus. She is covered by a pink blanket and is sitting in a chair by the window. She says that the day before she felt nauseated but that she no longer feels sick. "I just have cramps," she says with a grimace. The doctor she is seeing in the city has sent her to a doctor in a hospital in another state. "I had three pap smears and there was something wrong with all of them." She smiles. "The doctor I went to see was real nice. He did some tests and several biopsies and he said the results were okay." Laurie continues, "I gave him my Medicaid card, but I've just got a bill from him for five hundred dollars."

"What happened?"

"Welfare returned the bill. They said they had no record on me. They couldn't find my identification number and said that there was no such person on Medicaid."

OURS IS NOT TO REASON WHY

As Laurie struggles to overcome the effects of radiation and keep her family together, the conservative city council continues to reduce essential services and the governor of the state works hard to minimize assistance to the poor. Service providers are scrambling to maintain their funding.

In an interview a mental health worker states, "There are a lot of little groups out there and a lot of it is that they don't want to give up their turf." Another agency worker talks about "lots of separate services." She bemoans "the lack of collaboration" and emphasizes "the need for coordination."

At a meeting on child abuse a caregiver says, "In this community we have a little of this kind of service and a little of that kind of service." She goes on to suggest, "It may be necessary for the service providers to take a step back and look at the needs [of families] from the view of the parents and consider the kind of system that will best enable and empower families in the most positive sense." It is a radical idea. I admire the caregiver for being so outspoken, for most caseworkers and the families they serve—including Laurie and Will—know that the purpose of public agencies is *not* to empower families in any positive sense.

Every three months Laurie has to go to state welfare to verify her eligibility. The purpose of her visit is to *investigate* her, to make sure that she is not *cheating*, to *humiliate* her, to remind her that she is a welfare mother who lives off the state. Laurie is not asked about her health, how she is coping with the aftermath of radiation, if her house is warm, or if her children have enough to eat.

In the eyes of society Laurie is a *menial*, a *worthless human being* who is denigrated by politicians and vilified by political talk-show hosts. She is a welfare queen—the witch in our midst. The woman we publicly loathe. In the official documentation we deny her existence. If we could we'd exterminate her.

You're exaggerating again.

I am not exaggerating. If she had a burial plot we'd use it against her!

When Laurie goes to verify her eligibility for welfare at the end of 1992 I go with her. Laurie takes her rent receipts and heating bills, and an envelope which she says is filled with additional documentation that might be needed. In my car Laurie jokes with me about her last welfare verification. "Last time I went he reminded me about the lump-sum policy!" she says.

"What's that?"

"If I win on a scratch ticket I have to report it."

"Do you buy scratch tickets?"

"No."

We go to the same welfare office to which I accompanied Sam. While we wait I read the posters on the wall. One of the food stamp posters makes it clear that the government considers welfare fraud criminal behavior. "Cheating can now be a felony in this state. Up to 15 years and $2,000 are the penalty for people guilty of cheating in this program." I am reminded that in nineteenth-century England starving people were deported for stealing a loaf of bread.

The poster pronounces that the information food stamp recipients provide will be compared with the records of the Department of Employment Security, the Veterans Administration, and the Social Security Administration. I try to imagine how many bureaucrats it takes to determine whether or not Laurie is cheating. I wonder how much money we would save if we just gave her the money. Probably a lot.

After a short while a small middle-aged man takes Laurie and me back to one of the cubicles. He sits on one side of the table. Laurie and I sit on the other. In front of the caseworker is a stack of forms. He takes one of the forms and begins asking Laurie questions.

Does Laurie have a bank account?

"Yes," Laurie says, as she searches for it in the envelope that she brought with her. She gives the caseworker her bankbook. "There was three dollars in it but that was about two years ago."

"Is there any money in it now?"

"I don't know if the three dollars is still in there." Laurie looks quizzical.

The thought of the three dollars in Laurie's bank account makes me nervous. I'm caught up in the pathology of the questions, the way they are asked, the assumption that she is cheating, that she's a fraud.

"It's probably gone in bank charges," I interject and laugh.

Laurie smiles. The caseworker does not seem to think it's funny.

"Do you have a burial plot or an agreement with a funeral home?"

Laurie grimaces. "No."

"What if she did?" I ask.

"Assets." The caseworker gives me a sideways glance. "A burial plot is counted as an asset." He looks straight at Laurie. "You would have to declare it."

"I don't have one," Laurie's voice is barely audible.

The caseworker picks up another form, which appears to be identical to the first. "Some of these questions I might have already asked you, but ours is not to reason why." He stumbles over a question. "It gets old after a while," he says, "and your eyes go buggy."

The meeting lasts an hour. In that time Laurie signs six sets of forms, four of which include declarations that she is telling the truth. As she signs one of the forms, the caseworker makes it clear that her signature gives them the right to investigate her, to check with the IRS, with banks, and other agencies. She is told that a representative of the agency might also investigate her home.

Laurie looks pale and tired. She says that an investigator has already been to her home three times. Slowly she gets up. As she leaves she says, "I don't know what they thought they'd find."

I AM NOTIFYING YOUR TECHNICIAN AND THIS COULD AFFECT YOUR BENEFITS

Several weeks after Laurie goes to the state welfare office for recertification she is told that in order to receive financial assistance she must attend GED classes at the local high school.

In January 1993, Laurie enrolls in school and starts attending classes. Her ulcerative and hemorrhagic cystitis makes it difficult to sit through the three-hour classes. "It's embarrassing. I have to keep getting up to go to the bathroom."

Sometimes Laurie is in too much pain to walk to the high school. She misses several classes. The instructor reports her to state welfare. Laurie asks her doctor for a note to explain that she is sick. She receives a letter stating that she is mandated to attend the GED classes.

On February 10, Laurie gets a memo. "The attendance record has just arrived from the high school and you have been absent repeatedly. As you know, you are mandatory [sic] to attend these classes." The memo writer snitches. "I am notifying your case technician and this could affect your benefits." Laurie gathers together her medical records and takes them to the state welfare office. She shows them to her caseworker. Her caseworker says she could be lying. Laurie gives the caseworker the note that was written by her doctor on February 7. The caseworker tells Laurie that the note does not indicate that she is still sick. Laurie is exhausted. It takes her almost an hour to walk to the welfare office to show them her documentation and an equal amount of time to walk to the hospital to get notes from her doctor.

When the caseworker does not accept the note from her doctor Laurie decides to go back to the hospital to ask her doctor for a letter stating that she is unable to sit for long periods. She takes this letter back to the social welfare agency, and she is temporarily released from her "obligation" to attend GED classes. By this time Laurie is really sick. For the next few weeks she rarely leaves the house. Most of the time she lies on the couch. The pain is unbearable. Her lower back is aching, her stomach cramping. She is rushing to the toilet, burning, bleeding. She is constantly sick.

LEARNING FROM LAURIE AND WILL

Patterns emerge in the ways in which official texts are used in the lives of Laurie and Will—literacy configurations of institutional abuse that I often observe when working with families who are marginalized by American society.

Will can find seasonal employment—there is usually a restaurant that will give him a job in the kitchen preparing food for hungry tourists. When factories have a high volume of orders, Will works on the assembly line. He takes up the slack. He is hired and instantly expendable.

When Will works, Laurie loses her benefits. When he is laid off, she has to reapply to get them back. Laurie and Will scramble to feed their children and pay their bills. They get behind with their rent. In the past they have been evicted.

The forms that Laurie fills out state that there are only three people living in her house. If Will didn't live with her, she would get more benefits. Ricky would be eligible for Medicaid, he could go to the doctor and visit the dentist—if there was a dentist in the city who accepted Medicaid.

Will and Laurie have known each other since they were in high school. Will helps Laurie parent her two oldest children. He takes an interest in their schooling and talks with their teachers. Ricky—the little boy that Laurie and Will made together—often goes places with his Dad. When Laurie is sick, Will takes care of her. But if he were out of the house? Welfare insists Laurie would be better off.

When Will is out of work he loses his identity. Officially he doesn't count, in the official documentation he is denied his existence, he becomes a figment of Laurie's imagination, a fictitious husband, a make-believe dad, all rights and obligations officially suspended, he is belittled and rejected.

"Your benefits would go up if Will left you."

Will cops an attitude. Look at me. I'm in your face. This is *my* family. I am a part of *your* reality.

Sometimes, Will helps me with Sam. "It's 4:30 A.M.," he writes in his journal. "This is my usual bedtime but today it's the time I woke up. I am happy today because Sam is getting out of the hospital. I'm dressed. Don't have time for coffee. Maybe Luke made some. I drive down my street to Luke's house. This is the only time I get to drive. It's only a football field in length but I enjoy this drive. The lights are on at Luke's. I walk in. He's in the bathroom combing his hair. It's long but looks good. He's also dressed up. Just give us ties and suit coats and we would look like upstanding citizens. Luke feels good this morning. We share a common bond and that is helping people get and stay clean and sober."

Another entry. "My aunt wants me to rake her yard and my grand-mother wants me to rake her yard. Ernie at the recycle shop wants me to paint a new store. You know if I wasn't sober and clean nobody would want me except the cops. I feel wanted today. I love it."

Will wants a chance to participate in society. He is bright, articulate, all he wants is the opportunity. He applies for vocational rehabilitation. He goes back and forth for over a year. His telephone calls go unanswered. He receives no letters. He makes off-chance visits. He hangs around, tries to get the counselor's attention, takes tests, asks for letters of recommendation, makes telephone calls, waits for a letter, gets fed up with the demand of yet another physical. Then he misses an appointment.

Case closed.

You're good for manual labor. That's all. Work in a kitchen during the tourist season. On the assembly line when the orders come in. Out of work. Food stamps stopped. Oil tank empty. Help us, we're poor.

Laurie has cancer. Oh God, won't somebody help us! She's irradiated.

"He made radiation sound good," Will says of the doctor who changed his mind about performing a radical hysterectomy. "He said she'd be better off getting radiation." The official documentation looks authentic. The medical reports are authoritative. There are descriptions of procedures. But after radiation there are reports of *CYSTOSCOPY, BLADDER BIOPSIES, THE FULGURATION OF BLEEDING POINTS.*

Then comes the realization. However authoritative, the reports are questionable. QUESTION THEM! We have got to question.

Was the determination to use radiation instead of surgery to eradicate the cancer from Laurie's body a medical decision?

Laurie doesn't think so. She is convinced that because Medicaid pays only a fraction of the cost of private surgery the doctor changed his mind about performing a big-bucks operation.

I agree with Laurie. Two opinions in two weeks and I have a hysterectomy. In the hospital my doctor sits with me. He shows me his coin collection. He telephones me when I get home. "How are you feeling?" He follows up. "I'm prescribing a little medication." He cares for me—and Travelers pays his bills.

Of course Laurie's financial status was a factor.

Remember the doctor quoted in the city paper? In America caring for the sick is a business, a commercial enterprise that requires a financial transaction. So when the patient has no money, certain kinds of information are required to legitimize the inappropriate procedures determined to be necessary by doctors who tacitly decree that Laurie is not a suitable candidate for a hysterectomy.

Bronchitis is the ploy. A lung infection the unsuspecting decoy. Laurie waits three, four, almost five months for her cancer to be treated. Then, ZAP, HER OVARIES ARE FRIED. She is irradiated. Menopausal at twenty-five.

Left to her own devices, without a cancer support group, Laurie struggles to survive.

The doctors who "treat" her protect themselves with official documentation that legitimizes their cheap procedures and validates their unethical behavior. On December 20, 1990—four months after her radiation treatment for cervical cancer—a doctor writes that Laurie is in good health. "She has been feeling in her usual good health, with no new problems at all."

Bullshit.

Laurie is sick. She is experiencing difficulties adjusting to her hormone replacement therapy. In addition to stomach cramping she is experiencing hot flashes and she is nauseated. She suffers from lower back pain and rectal bleeding. She has ulcerative and hemorrhagic cystitis. Medical interventions alleviate some of her symptoms and discomfort but she rarely appears to be "healthy."

Worse, the pain she suffers makes her suspect. Official agencies that are supposed to provide her with a "safety net" are suspicious and the documentation is manipulated to make it appear that she is cheating the system. Forget about entitlement. There is none. *In the middle of winter Laurie is in recovery from cancer and she has no heat.*

She is told not to lie, to go to school, get a job. What do you mean you are too sick to go to school? Get documentation. No, your hospital records won't do.

Laurie says her caseworker does not believe she is sick. When state welfare wants a doctor's note Will cracks. "I got mad and I said, 'Human resources, yeh, like you really care about people.' I said, 'You just want to make her run around and there she is sick.' You know, she can't do anything and they go, 'What about her doctor's appointment?' and I told them 'I've already made her one.' " Will's voice is tight. His body is tense. "I just walked out because I was really losing it. I can't deal with it. I don't have the patience. They don't care about people, you know. I don't know what they care about, but they don't care about people."

"Forms," Laurie says, without any prompting from me. We laugh. "I swear," Laurie continues, "that's all they care about is forms."

"Yeh," Will agrees. "Paperwork, that's all they want."

" 'Fill this out, fill that out!' " Laurie almost shouts as she imitates her caseworker. " 'No. You've gotta get this. You've gotta get that!' What really irritates me is that when I have a recertification appointment, they tell me to bring all this stuff with me and then they don't even ask for half of it." She raises her hands in exasperation. "So why do I have to bring all this stuff if they don't want it? Then they always ask for something that is not even on the paperwork. 'You've gotta have it.' And when I ask them why I didn't know that I had to have it, they say, 'We don't know!' " Laurie pretends to tell off her caseworker. " 'Well, *you're* the ones who sent the paperwork! How could you not know?' "

"One time they asked us for laundromat receipts," Will laughs. But he knows it's not funny. State welfare is threatening to stop Laurie's benefits. She has to go to school or go to work. "How can she work?" Will asks. "She spends most of her time on the couch or in bed. Now if it's going to be like this all the time, how can they expect her to work if she couldn't sit in class for a few hours? So now she is supposed to work eight hours a day?"

"I'm really confused," Laurie says. "I've gotta go in and see them and if I don't have another doctor's note they're either going to delay what I get or cancel it altogether. They might shut me off and I'll have to reapply."

"I wonder why you weren't told about this at the recertification meeting?"

"They never said anything and they haven't sent me anything like, well you've gotta do a job search or you've gotta do this or you've gotta do that or you've gotta bring a doctor's note saying you can't. But all of a sudden they've gotta have this doctor's note or they're going to shut me off without even asking me if I can go to work."

"These people think they can play God over you and pick and choose what you're gonna do," Will says, "and that's not right. It's not Laurie's fault that she is sick, it's just not right."

In Washington conservative members of the House of Representatives denigrate what they refer to as the C word. They are derisive of liberal members of the House who "play the compassion card."

Forget it. It's all rhetoric. There is no compassion. Just pathology. We don't care what happens to Laurie.

A LIFE AIRTIGHT

In my writing so far I have been relentless—I know, excruciatingly so—in presenting the details of the configurations of bureaucratic abuse and neglect that are a part of the lives of Cindy, Sam, and Laurie and Will. But I am concerned that I have not been quite as relentless in sharing with you the possibilities of the lives of the men and women with whom I work.

We are enculturated into believing that those who live in the margins of society are illiterate, that they have no skills, that they are lazy, indolent, and insolent, that they are criminals, that they have nothing to offer to society. This is not my experience, and it is for this reason that I want you to meet Kathryn.

Kathryn is the victim of bureaucratically sanctioned human rights violations that re-create and perpetuate the abusive circumstances of her early life and critically affect her ability to take care of herself and her children. But this time I am not going to spend much time on the official documentation that shapes her life. Instead, I want to focus on the ways in which Kathryn *resists* the official encoding of her life as a "delinquent," a "drug addict," and a human being of marginal worth.

Kathryn is a poet. She writes poems about the events that take place in her life. Some of her poems she writes for friends, but many she writes for herself. Some of the poems Kathryn signs, and some of the poems are signed by "Chrissy," one of Kathryn's other selves. I want you to listen to Kathryn's personal accounts of her struggle to stay alive. I want you to read her poetry. I want you to understand why she rails against society.

But first you must meet her. December 28, 1990. Kathryn is sitting in the literacy project office smoking a cigarette. The tape recorder is on, and she is telling what has just taken place in her life and the response of the city's mental health institution.

"They told me I was a manic depressive." Kathryn's voice is strong. She drags on her cigarette. "They said that I was going on medication and that I wasn't allowed to go home by myself." Another drag. She inhales slowly, exhales, and speaks quickly. "I had to be under protective custody for the weekend and if I couldn't find anybody to take me they were going to put me in the hospital." Kathryn is angry.

"So I said, 'We'll see about that.' I yelled at them. I told them to fuck off." She laughs as she often does when she is nervous. Then her countenance changes. "It was Christmas and I wanted to be with my kids." She looks at me. "I didn't think that they had a right to do that." Kathryn looks down at the table, and her voice trails off.

"Me and my baby were not getting on and my doctor told me to go down and talk to them." "Them" is mental health. Kathryn talks about her new baby. "Because I just lose it. I told the counselor that my baby didn't like me and I didn't like him either. I was honest with him. And my doctor said going to mental health was to prevent abuse. To prevent it going too far."

Kathryn stubs out her cigarette and takes another one out of the packet. "And so I called him up yesterday to yell at him and I told him, 'I don't want to live with mental health and the visiting nurse keeping track of me.'" I said, 'I am not an abusive ma. I have never hit any of my kids.' And the doctor said, 'Well the nurse is just a measure to prevent that.' I said, 'Well I have never hit my kids, I've punched a wall but I've never abused my kids in any shape, manner, or form.' You know." Rhythmically, she taps her packet of cigarettes on the table. "Now I have a nurse coming out to see me twice a week, which is a real pain in the ass because I don't think I need her. She just comes out and she talks to me and she plays with the baby."

"Why don't you like her?"

"The visiting nurse is a threat to me." Kathryn knows what could happen to her baby. "*You* don't walk in and say let's put him in a foster home. *They* do."

"Do you think that might happen?"

"Of course it might happen." She sits smoking her cigarette. For a moment she is quiet. "You know if you are asking for help that's one thing, but if you are asking for help and they come in and say put him in a foster home that's telling me that they think I am incompetent and they are threatening me." Kathryn's voice deepens. She sounds angry. "You know and that's just not right!"

She rushes on. "That lady knows nothing about me excepting the fact that I am having a hard time and I think a lot of mothers go through a hard time and you know if you threaten them when somebody is having a hard time that you're going to put their kid in a foster home that is only going to increase their problems and the kid is not going to have a place to go and nobody to love him."

Kathryn says that more than anything she wants to love her baby. "I don't trust the lady," she looks fierce. "I don't like her. I don't like her insinuating that he needs to be in a foster home." Kathryn speaks in a sweet voice when quoting the visiting nurse. "She said, 'Why don't you put him in a foster home?' And I said, *'No!'* And she said, 'Well it is an option.' And I said, *'No. It ain't an option!'* "

Kathryn comes across as a tough woman but there are tears in her eyes. "And she talked about adoption too, and I said, 'I ain't giving up my kid for adoption.' And she stuck with the foster home idea and she pries into my life and I don't think she belongs there."

She looks alarmed as she talks of telling her doctor about the drugs prescribed for her by mental health. "And you know, she comes back today and I was talking on the phone to my doctor's office and I told his office the medication that I was on—because they have to know that—and this lady started writing it down." Kathryn plays out the scene. "And I turned around and said, 'What are you writing?' And she said, 'I'm writing down the medication.' And I said, 'Why do you need to know what I am on? I mean you don't need to know that.'"

Kathryn narrows her eyes. "And you know she still wrote it down. And then, she says, 'Does the medication knock you out?' And I am saying, 'No. I get up for him.' And then, she says, 'Well maybe we should make other arrangements.' And I say, 'We don't have to make nothing, because this baby is not neglected. I get up with him in the night if he wakes up.' And she says, 'Well I think we should make arrangements because if it knocks you out. . . .'"

Kathryn's voice is raised. "I say, 'No. You can't ruin me.' " She looks trapped. "You know, and the lady is just a threat. She's not my friend." She talks again of the visiting nurse and mental health wanting to take away her baby. "That seems to be their solution. They just don't do it in a caring way. I don't like her."

I'D SIT ON HIS LAP AND HE'D GIVE ME BEER

In November 1989, Kathryn is attending meetings. She is in recovery from alcohol and drug addiction and she is going to the AA and NA meetings that I attend with members of the community with whom I am working.

Kathryn is friendly, loud, and brash. She chain smokes, lighting one cigarette as she stubs out another. She laughs a lot, making a small high-pitched sound something like a chuckle except that it is fragile and brittle and filled with pain. I learn that Kathryn is married, that she has a two-year-old daughter, and that she works the checkout at a local store. She talks about her daughter a lot, but I know very little about Kathryn's story except that she is working her program and living drug free.

Then she is gone. She disappears. Members of the recovery community say that she is back out but that's all that is said. No one talks about her. They focus on their own recovery as if her drug addiction might be contagious, that they might catch it, get reinfected, and drink and drug themselves.

In May 1990 I meet Kathryn again. She visits the office of the city literacy project and we become friends. Kathryn is sitting at the long table we like to gather around and talk. She is wearing turquoise and silver rings on each of her fingers, and five pairs of silver and turquoise earrings dangle from her ears. Around her neck are three—or is it four?—silver chains. On her left arm is tattooed "Friends Forever," and on her right arm there is a tattoo of a rose.

She talks about her childhood, about being given joints when she was little. "I know they were joints, because I remember they were small and held on a bobby pin."

Her father was an alcoholic. He left her mother when Kathryn was quite young. "I remember him coming around just to hit me," Kathryn recalls.

She talks about the way her father physically abused her brother, throwing him across the room. Kathryn gives her nervous laugh. "He'd just hit me." She lights a cigarette. She says she is trying to cut down. She turns the cigarette packet over and over. She is swaying slightly back and forth.

Kathryn says her brother raped her. He sexually abused her for years. Again she laughs but it is a painful sound. She changes the subject. She talks about her grandfather. "I'd sit on his lap and he'd give me beer." Again the laugh. Kathryn says that her aunt was a dealer and that by the time Kathryn was ten, her aunt was giving her pot.

She remembers one Christmas. "It was really good." She smiles, "I got a watch." Then the laugh. "My dad hid it for me in a carton of cigarettes." Kathryn no longer likes Christmas. Her mother died on Christmas Day when she was fifteen years old.

Later in the conversation Kathryn talks about school. "I learned to read and write before I was in kindergarten," she says. "My brother taught me cursive writing before kindergarten." When she was little she liked school—even though some of the children made fun of her. "I considered myself a smart kid. One of the ones who could get good grades."

By the time she was in fourth and fifth grade, she was experiencing difficulties in school and her home life was becoming more and more complicated. Again the little laugh. "When I was twelve I tried to commit suicide." She was placed in a psychiatric unit at a hospital and she stayed there for nine months. "While I was in hospital, they took me up and showed me a school," Kathryn remembers. "And it was summer so there were no kids there and I agreed to go there."

Kathryn says that she did not know it was a reform school. By the time she realized what was happening, it was too late. She was admitted—committed?—to the school and she had to stay there for three years.

Kathryn often talks about the reform school—once she tells me they put her in restraints to keep her there—but she is always puzzled by what happened to her during that period. She says that if she was only at the school for three years, then there are two years for which she cannot account. "I have no memory of what happened to me." Again the laugh. "I've lost two years!"

When Kathryn was eighteen she went to college. She wanted to major in English. But after two months she dropped out. "The drugs didn't help much," Kathryn says.

For the next two years she lived on the streets. When she was nineteen she gave birth to a baby girl, but after eleven months of trying to take care of her, she gave her daughter up for adoption. "I gave her a life," Kathryn explains, "that's what I did. I gave her a life."

Kathryn first got sober at the end of 1987. For twenty-seven days she attended AA meetings and then she went back out. Eventually she was admitted to the drug and alcohol treatment program at the local hospital. Again the laugh that punctuates Kathryn's accounts of her most painful experiences. "It was the only hospital that would take me," she says. "They wanted me to have extensive treatment."

When Kathryn was discharged from the hospital she tried to move away from the city, back to the town where she had lived when she was drugging and drinking, but her old friends made fun of her. "I was only there for three days, because everyone thought I was a joke being straight." Kathryn moved back to the city. "I lived with a friend from rehab for a while," Kathryn says, "but I went back out."

Kathryn eventually detoxed herself. She was living with a man who was also in recovery, and after a while they got married. When she was twenty-five she gave birth to another child—a little girl whom she often brings to the literacy project office. But Kathryn's marriage did not work. She was beaten by her husband on a regular basis. Eventually he threw her out. She was back on the streets and after twenty-three months of sobriety she began using again. "I did what I had to do to get drugs." She lived in a park and she sold her leather Harley Davidson jacket for cocaine. She was also pregnant. Kathryn used cocaine during the first trimester, but she tried to stop using when she realized she was going to have a baby. Then she went back to AA meetings and tried to stay sober. For the second and third trimesters of her pregnancy Kathryn was clean.

When she was five months pregnant and back in the program, a man whom she met through her sponsor told her she could live with him. "I paid him three hundred and twenty dollars a month for the use of one room." She is living in this man's apartment at the time she visits the office.

Kathryn says she sees her daughter every day, but she explains that she is uncomfortable about bringing her to the apartment of her friend because there are always people drinking. One of the men in the building walks around stoned and naked.

State and city welfare give Kathryn a "hard time" because they say she is living with her boyfriend. Kathryn laughs, not a nervous laugh this time, but a real laugh, loud and contagious. "He's gay," she says, "we're just friends, he's not interested in me."

THEY MAKE YOU FEEL LIKE YOU'RE NOT A VERY GOOD PERSON

In September 1990, Kathryn is still trying to find a place of her own. The man with whom she is staying tells her that she cannot live in his apartment when she has the baby. But welfare won't help her. First they want proof that she is pregnant, even though she is in the third trimester of her pregnancy. Kathryn looks incredulous. Her belly is big. She lifts her shirt. She is swollen and above her sweat pants her skin is pale and pulled tight. We laugh. How could they doubt that she is pregnant? Kathryn shakes her head. "They won't help me get an apartment until a month before the baby is due."

Worse, Kathryn says she visited the WIC clinic (the program for women, infants, and children) in a local church to ask for assistance. "They won't help me," she says. "Not until after the baby is born." And even then WIC will take into consideration the income of the man who has let her rent a room. "I feel I'm standing behind my baby," she says, "and nobody will help me."

In October Kathryn finds a place to live—a little pink trailer on a deserted campground about five miles out of the city. Her ex-husband lets her keep the car—a relic that needs constant attention—and arrangements are made for her daughter to visit her every day from eight in the morning until five at night.

Much of Kathryn's time is taken up with making arrangements for the birth of her baby and with obtaining the assistance she needs. There are several weeks when she is without food because her food stamps do not arrive. Friends help her out while she tries to straighten out the situation with the welfare office. Most of Kathryn's difficulties are with the social agencies that are supposed to help her as she prepares to have her baby.

She can't reach her case manager when her food stamps do not arrive. She telephones the state welfare office. She is exasperated and short-tempered. Angrily she tells the person who answers the phone that she wants to speak to her case manager, that she is pregnant, and that she has no food. Her calls are met with indifference. "They make you feel like you're not a very good person," she says.

"What could the social agencies do to help you?" I ask.

"Be more reliable," she responds without hesitation. "If my check would be on time and I could pay my rent on time, and that would make life easier."

Kathryn says she lives in constant fear that her benefits will be cut. "They inform you of any changes that they've made after they've made them," she says. Like Laurie's, the official version of Kathryn's life is constantly revised. Every three months she goes back to the state welfare office and fills in all the forms again.

One day Kathryn visits the project office with her two-year-old daughter, Cheri, and we go to the soda shop for hamburgers and french fries. Back in the office Kathryn says, "I'm growing up through her eyes." Cheri sits on Kathryn's lap and they talk about the baby. Kathryn lifts up her sweatshirt and shows Cheri her stomach. "What's in here?" she asks, pointing to her stomach. "Baby?"

"Baby," Cheri says.

Kathryn lies down on the floor and Cheri climbs on her. Then she lies down beside her mother and, curled up in her arms, she eventually goes to sleep.

On November 7, Kathryn's baby is born. It's a boy. Kathryn stays in the hospital for several days. Then she is sent home with a two-day supply of baby formula. She says she does not want to breast feed Harley because she is worried that her milk would be contaminated by her use of drugs. She cares for her baby on her own in the isolated pink trailer that becomes her home. Friends bring her baby formula and give her diapers. She receives no assistance from any social agency. She manages for three weeks before her appointment at WIC. At first she is unable to drive, so members of AA drive out to the trailer to pick her up and take her and her new baby to AA meetings. Every day her ex-husband or his girlfriend drops Cheri off at the trailer, and Kathryn takes care of her as well as her new baby. Most of the time she is on her own with both children. Cheri finds it difficult to adjust to her new brother, who is colicky, cries a lot, and finds it difficult to sleep.

Kathryn is exhausted. Isolated. On her own. Without family. Except for her babies, who test her endurance to the limit.

The stores are filled with presents and people talk about Christmas. Kathryn thinks of her mother. Sick. Dying. The baby cries. Cheri wants to play.

Kathryn tries to find inexpensive presents. She is on her own. Lonely. Alone. *A child.* She is the child inside her body. She says she looks at herself and she is too big. She feels as if she is in somebody else's body.

She goes to an AA meeting. The car in front stops abruptly at a changing light. Kathryn does not stop quickly enough. Her face hits the windshield. She is disorientated. She goes to see a doctor. Kathryn tells the doctor she is concerned because she is not bonding with her baby. He tells her to go to the mental health clinic, which is where I began Kathryn's story.

At mental health Kathryn talks about the little girl inside her. The counselor tells her that this is abnormal, and a psychiatrist is called. The psychiatrist wants to hospitalize her but Kathryn refuses. She swears at them. She is out of control. She needs help and they are taking away her children. Her son is given to her AA sponsor and her daughter stays with her father.

Kathryn is placed in protective custody. An AA member becomes responsible for her.

She is heavily medicated. She is given lithium and an antipsychotic drug. She spends her adult life trying to get off drugs and then mental health prescribes them for her, but no counseling. No one asks her Sammy's questions: What's happening? How have you been managing? How can we help you?

Kathryn comes to the literacy project's Christmas party. She is sedated—doped—unable to stand without holding on. She smiles an empty smile, her eyes are drug ridden and vacant, and her voice is passive and flat. They have taken away her intelligence. She grins mindlessly. "They put me in protective custody, but I told them I was coming to the party."

Participants in the project embrace her. More than anything she needs people to care for her, she needs love. She is included in the activities, she ignores her protective custody until her curfew, and then she holds on tight as I hug her before, regretfully, she leaves.

Later, in our office, she talks about mental health. "They told me to stuff everything."

"What does that mean?"

"Put a lid on it. Bottle it."

"Put a lid on what?"

"On my different feelings."

"The little girl?"

"Yeh, them feelings. They told me not to deal with them and I said, 'But I have to deal with it. I can't just keep putting it off.' This morning I got up and got in the shower for an hour an' a half trying to get clean."

Kathryn moves in slow motion. She has no emotion, her affect is leveled out. She is two-dimensional, a monochrome version of herself, colorless, her personality taken away.

I gave birth to my first baby in a city far away from my family. My husband left for work at seven o'clock in the morning and sometimes did not get home until seven o'clock in the evening. I was alone, but he did come home. I don't know what I would have done if I had been on my own. Lose it. Get depressed. Be unable to take care of my baby."

Kathryn struggles on. She decorates her trailer and on Christmas Day she is allowed to have her son and she gets to see her daughter, but she says she is relieved when the day is over. Now all she has to face is the new year.

Mental health continues to supply her with drugs but *there is no therapy*. Kathryn is allowed to have her baby son back, but her ex-husband has custody of Cheri and Kathryn no longer gets to see her. Eventually, the visiting nurse arranges for a counselor, but the woman has difficulty coping with the little girl inside of Kathryn's body. Kathryn believes that the little girl is a manifestation of her pain and she gets upset. "She told me I was abnormal," Kathryn says. "How is that going to help me?" Every day is a struggle.

Since Kathryn was put in protective custody the visiting nurse comes once a week to talk with her about her baby. You've heard Kathryn speak of the nurse. At first when the nurse comes to visit, she tries to persuade Kathryn to give her baby up for adoption. But as the nurse gets to know Kathryn their relationship changes. The nurse arranges for respite care. Each week Kathryn spends four hours on her own while a nurse's aide stays in her trailer and takes care of her baby.

Harley is no longer colicky. Kathryn is more relaxed about taking care of him. For several months in the spring she is without a car. She spends her time filling the walls of her pink trailer with photographs, cuttings from magazines, and pieces of her own writing.

In July 1991, Kathryn reflects in her journal on what happened to her when she gave birth to her baby.

> I was suffering from postpartum depression and I wasn't getting along with my son. Instead of talking about the problem mental health labeled me manic depressive. I remember speaking to them about a little girl who felt like she wanted to come out—she was a child of anger and rage—I was dumbfounded when the response I got was "Where does she come out from?" "Your stomach?" "Your head?" "Where?" They thought I meant literally come out. In a sense she did come out in my behavior.
>
> They lacked the ability to understand. People can go to school and get degrees but that actually means nothing. They have to be able to listen to a person and have compassion.
>
> I needed someone to help me deal with my anger—my hurt. There is still a little girl inside of me. One that sometimes (very often) becomes scared and unsure. Her steps are made with much caution. She is afraid of people. People hurt. At the same time she wants to learn to trust again, to believe she is good, she does have worth.

YOUR LITTLE FACE COMES TO PASS OVER THE PAGES OF MY MIND

Since Kathryn was a small child she has written about what is happening to her. Her writing, poetry and prose, is filled with anger and resentment, she cries out in pain, expresses her love, and writes to herself explanations of her attempts to recover from drug and alcohol addiction.

One day when I visit her in her pink trailer she takes a battered cardboard briefcase out of a cupboard and puts it on the table. It is filled with notebooks and crumpled pieces of paper.

"How long have you been writing?"

"Since I was a little kid."

Among the papers that Kathryn keeps in her briefcase is a play that she wrote in 1982. At the top of the first page is a circled A and beneath it is written, "Well-done." It is a play about Aphrodite and Eros. At the end of the play Eros meets a woman named Chrissy, who several years later a psychiatrist counts as one of Kathryn's other selves.

In the play Eros asks Chrissy her name and she says, "Chrissy. I am a mere mortal. I travel the mountains and write words of wisdom. Poetry is the best. I love it."

One poem Kathryn wrote to her first daughter telling her about her young sister:

> Your little face
> > comes to pass
> over the pages of my mind—
> > the smile of someone young
> seeking knowledge
> trying somehow
> > to ease the pain.
>
> We live in a town apart
> > Yet it feels like miles
> Wanting so much to seek
> > > you out
> Yet afraid
> Maybe I won't maintain control
> > The love I hold
> Never did fade.
>
> Thinking—trying to define "fair"
> Your little sister
> > grows without you—
> Is it fair?
> Fair to her or to you?
>
> Someday—maybe—
> both of you shall understand.

In another poem to her first daughter she asks

> I wonder if you were
> afraid when you woke up
> and I was gone?

When Kathryn was homeless and living in a park, and she knew she was going to use, she wrote a poem that she called "The World Airtight."

I live in the world
          My world—airtight.
Denying myself—Denying others
                    from me.
The outside warm
          green with life
The inside cold
          no relief in sight.
The impending doom.
I run so far
          in just one day.
No! You really don't know
          the real me.
I can't let her out.
Surely you jest.
It's the sinful fate
There's no laughter
                    no tears
Only me—
on the stage—
being what I'm good at.
The actor—the poet—the person
                    running scared.
I glance outside
          feeling sad inside.
I've given in—given up
          on life's race—
People—places—things—
how can I compete.
My world's airtight.

Desperate, Kathryn writes:

I wish to
stretch out my arms
          and seek your love
Daddy where did you go?

Many of the poems Chrissy writes. The following are verses from several poems:

> I sit and think
> Yes think about it all.
> I wonder how it ended up like this
> My soul is shattered
> My heart so scarred
> I feel like I'm lost
> got hit or something
>
> . . .
> Yes I sit and think
> Yet answers never come
> and sleep
> so hard to find.
>
> Keep silent—don't push for answers
> Sometimes she's a child
> and gets lost easily.
> She has dreams
> she can't reach them.
>
> . . .
> Our bruises are deep
> God how they hurt.
> Don't you need to show it
> Take off that mask
> Wake Up!
> Please don't let go.
> I'm losing my ground
> I'm lost for
> words . . .

Sometimes Kathryn writes to Chrissy or to herself about Chrissy. In a letter addressed "Dear Self" Kathryn reflects:

Do you realize that this is the start of a new year. 1988 is on the way or is here. . . . I feel a new person is developing. Yeah Chrissy—the other side of me—is going, is fading into the background. . . .

Sometimes she writes angrily to Chrissy:

Hi

How the hell are you? Feel like running today? Oh yeah. We'll get real far this way. . . .

At the bottom of one poem she writes:

Note: I feel like getting wasted—I'm scared. The feeling is so strong—so weird—I have no control. I'm not me. . . . I need help. I need me.

Kathryn writes in her trailer to her son. "I want him to know about me." She writes letters to friends, notes to herself, poems, prose—an essay about a friend who is a vet, rules for visiting her trailer—

Dear visitors—

This is my world you enter when you walk through the door. We are a happy family and wish to remain so. My request is simple. If you have come here for pleasant conversation or seeking helpful advice that's great—come on in! Friends are welcome.

If on the other hand your tongue is swift and you're looking for someone to argue with or you want to trample on my feelings—

MY ONE SUGGESTION FOR YOU IS TO TURN AND LEAVE. I DON'T NEED YOU IN THIS PLACE I CALL HOME—IT IS MY SPACE. RESPECT IT. Thanks.

Writing provides Kathryn with continuity, her explanations help her make connections, she measures her progress in the pages of her journals, the papers in the cardboard briefcase give her life a sense of permanence. Putting pen to paper is an antidote to the instability of her relationships with the social agencies that are supposed to help her.

Kathryn wrote the following piece, which she entitled "Reinstatement," in 1993 after she left the city.

When you go for reinstatement for AFDC they take about 20–25 of you at a time into one room. Here they explain that you have been given a number. They have a tape recorder which tells you your rights and responsibilities. During this time everyone is busy filling out the application they've been handed as they walked through the door. They do not call you by name. You go by the number they have given you. When that number is called you then go up to the woman who has called it. Rather mechanically they go over the application and then you are dismissed. If you want to ask a question there is no real opportunity to do so—unless, of course, you don't mind asking in the company of 20 some odd other people.

IT'S A WAY FOR THE SYSTEM TO GET AROUND THE SYSTEM

In November 1993, I go with Kathryn to the welfare agency in the city where she is living. She has been told that her welfare payments are going to be stopped. She has two options, go to work or go to school.

Realistically there are no jobs. The state is still in a deep recession, and even if there were jobs, Kathryn is unlikely to get one. Her resistance to those in authority who control her life has become more extreme, and one of the ways she makes this statement is with the tattoos on her body.

The other option is college. I encourage Kathryn to think about the possibility. Over the years we have had many conversations about her writing. She would like to be a journalist but the thought of going back to school overwhelms her.

I offer to pay for her to take a writing course so that she can explore the possibilities. Kathryn is enthusiastic. She talks about what she imagines it would be like to go to college. She worries about the students and the faculty. "What do you think they'd think of someone like me?"

At the state welfare office. There are mothers and babies, a bone-thin young girl who does not look old enough to have a child, old men with broken teeth, young men in jeans frayed by wear and not some high-priced artificial manufacturing process, drab middle-aged women, a lank-haired woman pushing a broken man in a wheelchair.

Behind a screen stand two women who if they stood in the waiting room could be mistaken for clients. They look beat-up and tired, but when Kathryn speaks to one of them the woman manages to smile.

Kathryn gives her name and she says she has an appointment with Melanie. We find two seats. Kathryn is nervous. She calls across the room to a worn-out woman and they joke about being at the welfare office.

Then Kathryn's name is called by a woman standing in the doorway to the back offices. The woman points at the corridor behind her and she tells Kathryn to go all the way down and wait in the area that has blue seats. I go with her.

On each side of the corridor are small rooms in which people sit in chairs on either side of a table. Caseworkers and clients look at the forms they share across the table. Sometimes it is only the lack of a coat that distinguishes the one from the other. I play a game—who is the caseworker and who is the client?

The blue seats are filled so Kathryn and I stand—but only for a minute. Melanie, a plump young woman with long dark hair, comes and greets Kathryn.

Kathryn, in her usual up-front in-your-face-way, thanks the woman for being polite to her. The woman smiles.

We follow her past more small cubicles filled with workers and clients. There are no windows, just diffuse lights and recirculated air. Melanie's cubicle is just big enough for a desk, two chairs, and a filing cabinet. Somehow we fit in another chair.

Melanie talks quickly. She tells Kathryn that she needs to contact colleges and talk to the admissions office about associate degree programs that are marketable. She says hairdressing and cosmetology are bad choices because they pay minimum wage and there are no benefits. She names colleges and talks about SATs.

I ask her how Kathryn is supposed to get to the colleges. She has no car and there is no public transportation. Melanie smiles and says Kathryn would receive twenty-three cents a mile for transportation.

"She still has no means of transportation to any of the colleges that you've mentioned," I persist. The caseworker talks about a technical college near to the city in which Kathryn is living.

"I would still have to find some way of getting there," Kathryn tells her.

Melanie ignores the problem of transportation and moves on. Still smiling and talking rapidly she gives Kathryn a list of associate degree programs at the technical college and she tells her to go through the list and find a program that interests her. Kathryn and I look at the list together. None of the options seem to focus on writing—there is no journalism or technical writing.

I think about my children, both of whom are in college. I think of our discussions about colleges and where they are located, our discussions about different degree programs, what they might each like to study, the possibilities of employment, whether that is their main concern or whether they are more interested in going to college to further their education.

We talk about undergraduate programs that will lead to advanced degrees and open up professional possibilities. We look at brochures, make telephone calls, consider their options. My daughter tries a college, my son a university. They both transfer to other academic institutions. They change their majors, drop and add courses. We talk on the telephone about their classes. We discuss assignments. We send money and pay for extracurricular activities—an institute on peace and justice, Spanish immersion. More money for photography equipment. Everything is in flux, nothing is certain. I wonder what would have happened to my children if someone they didn't know and who knew nothing about them sat them down and told them to "pick a program."

"You've gotta be kidding!"

No, she's not kidding. Melanie tells Kathryn to contact the technical college and talk with admissions about their programs. Without taking a breath she moves on. She asks Kathryn if she has children and starts talking about child care. Wait! I try to backtrack. I tell Melanie that it is really difficult to decide on a career from a list, and I ask her if there is some sort of orientation program that Kathryn can attend that would provide her with some more in-depth information. Melanie says there is a three-week course Kathryn can attend on college preparation. She is in a hurry. She presses buttons and makes several phone calls.

Kathryn whispers to me that she is not sure she wants to do anything on the list. The programs are mostly in the service industry, manual, menial, providing nothing more than low-tech, minimum-wage skills.

Melanie says that she can get Kathryn into an orientation program that starts next Monday and that there is a meeting about the program this Thursday. She opens a file drawer and pulls out more paperwork, fills in a number of forms, and tells Kathryn that the orientation will cost welfare $750 and so she must make sure she completes the program.

Neither Kathryn nor I know what Melanie has written on the forms.

Back to child care. Quick. Melanie says welfare will pay just over a dollar an hour with a maximum of twelve dollars a day. She takes another pile of forms out of a drawer. She skims through the rules and regulations, talking quickly, mechanically. It's a recitation. She continues without hesitation.

Breath!

Take a breath.

Give us time to catch up. To understand what you are saying. I don't understand the rules and regulations.

Ask Kathryn if she knows what you are saying!

Fuck. I give up.

Melanie does not stop. She speeds up. She explains that if the money is given by *Kathryn* to pay the child care provider—who has to sign the forms so she will know how much money is allocated—then the child care provider will not have to pay tax on the money.

I question the legality of this arrangement. "It's a way for the system to get around the system," Melanie says, looking pleased with the arrangement. I wonder if this is a felony, like buying toothpaste with food stamps.

Briskly, Melanie goes on to explain that the money for child care cannot be paid to anyone living in the same house as Kathryn. She does not ask Kathryn about her present child care arrangements. The regulations do not consider the well-being of the child. They are designed to stop mothers from cheating.

Kathryn explains that she is living with the woman who takes care of her baby. "Members of the household can't be paid," Melanie says. Kathryn looks upset.

"You can't pay her," Melanie says, with a smile. "The baby must be taken to a day care or given to someone outside of the home to take care of him."

"He's happy where he is," Kathryn tells Melanie without losing her deferential welfare demeanor. "Why should I take him some place else?"

Melanie ignores the question. She goes through the child care forms, gives them to Kathryn, and tells her to bring them back next week. For the first time Melanie hesitates.

She looks at Kathryn.

Melanie tells Kathryn about her boyfriend's tattoos. She says it is costing him $200 an inch to have them removed. "He couldn't get a job," she says. Melanie stares at the skull tattooed on Kathryn's cheek. "You might have to have that tattoo removed."

"I won't do that," Kathryn tells her. "People have to go beyond the way I look to see what I am worth."

Melanie persists—insists. She tells Kathryn that if she wants a job, the tattoo will have to be removed. Then she focuses on clothes. "The one wearing a suit gets the job. It doesn't matter if the other one is better qualified."

Melanie fills in some more forms and she files them without giving Kathryn the opportunity to read them. She tells Kathryn to be at the orientation on Thursday.

That's it. We leave.

"I feel as if my life has just been taken away from me," Kathryn says. "I've been turned into a set of forms and I don't know what is written on them." We walk down the corridor. "I'm surprised that I don't have to tell them when I pee."

"Come on, let's get some coffee."

"I need a cigarette. Can we stop for me to get some?"

"Sure."

Kathryn walks into Dunkin' Donuts smoking a cigarette. She jokes with the women standing at the counter. She tells them she has just had her life taken away from her. She says that she is going to college. She is filled with bravado, brave and totally afraid.

She turns to me. "Do they put you in restraints in college?" she asks.
The women laugh.
"Why?"
"They did at the reform school."
Again the women laugh, but I can tell by Kathryn's face that it's not funny.
"Were you ever restrained?"
"Sure."
"What for?"
"I didn't want to be there."
I smile at her. We both know that under the present circumstances she doesn't stand a chance of going to college. Melanie was going through the motions, thick piles of forms, do what we tell you, forget about your baby.
Kathryn lights another cigarette. "What if they tell me I can't write?"
"You know you can write," I tell her.
Kathryn says she will try to go to the orientation.
She is out of her depth, as my children would be in a similar situation.
One of her friends who is told to go to school to study for a GED ends up under a suicide watch at the state hospital.
Kathryn skips the orientation. She knows that she is in a double bind. She is criticized for being on welfare but the system has no intention of helping her find a job or go to college. It is all a sham. There is no way out—it was never intended that there should be.

LEARNING FROM KATHRYN

I want to go back for a moment to July 28, 1993. The late afternoon sun is still warm when I meet Kathryn and we have dinner together at an outdoor cafe. Since she moved away from the city I don't see her very often. But next week she is going to read some of her essays at a literacy exchange I have organized, and so we meet to discuss her participation. Kathryn is excited, and she flusters the waiter when she teases him. She is impertinent, a little outrageous—or maybe courageous? Around her sit men and women in business clothes, uptight and polite.

Kathryn has a skull tattooed on her cheek. In the mouth of the skull is a rose. Her hair is short, bleached, and spiked. She is extravagant in her definition of self. She is in the faces of those around her, protected from them by the skull and the rose.

On her hand is a tattoo of a spider in a web, but no jewelry.

"Where are your rings and earrings?"

"I sold them." Kathryn laughs. In a loud voice she says, "I've gotta live and I'm not selling anything else." She gets glances from other tables. We both laugh.

She calls the waiter and orders another soda. Again she teases him. Another waiter comes back with her drink. "What happened to our waiter?" Kathryn asks.

"He's new."

"You frightened him," I tell her. Again we laugh.

When Kathryn left the city she came to live with a family that she has known since she was a child. The mother in the family takes care of Harley, so Kathryn gives her welfare check to the woman. She says it's worth it because the woman takes good care of Harley.

"I owe him that," she says.

"What about you?"

"I manage." She laughs. This time it's the familiar high-pitched sound that she makes when she is nervous. "But I don't have much jewelry left."

We reminisce. I tell Kathryn that I've been listening to the audiotape we made at the end of December 1990. Even though the tape recorder was always on when Kathryn visited the office of the literacy project, she knows immediately which tape I am talking about. The years drop away, and it is clear that Kathryn has painfully vivid memories of what happened to her three years ago when she tried to get help following the birth of her son. Kathryn tells me the story once again, echoing what she said on the tape. It is fresh in her mind and she speaks as if it were yesterday. Then she reflects on the way in which she was treated. "I know now that they could have helped me. They could have helped me bond with my baby. Instead they just doped me up. They never tried to help me deal with the problem."

A week later at the literacy exchange, Kathryn wears new clothes. She has on tight black pants and black boots, a purple half-shirt with no sleeves, and a black crocheted vest. Visible are many of the tattoos that are usually hidden beneath her clothes. Kathryn's tattoos tell the story of her life, each is significant, a part of her identity, from the spider caught in the web on her one hand to the butterfly on her shoulder that flies away free. In reality Kathryn is trapped and she liberates herself symbolically.

At the exchange Kathryn sits close to me. Around us sit twenty men and women—literacy workers—from different parts of the United States and Canada. Kathryn says she's nervous. She has brought three essays with her but she says she isn't ready to read. Instead, she begins by talking about living in the city, about dealing with social agencies, and about the birth of Harley.

Kathryn is the teacher as she talks about her relationships with those in authority. And then she reads.

> Some say I'm an outlaw lady. Tight-jeaned and tattooed and I say truly you have judged for you know nothing of me. . . .
>
> Sad is the fact you do not seek deep enough to see me for all I really am. If you care to sit and talk I'll tell you of the illustrations that are a part of me. The children. The freedom. The death. The life. The faith.
>
> The love of self. . . .
>
> Sad isn't it, I have a lot to give but you call me outlaw. You label me. . . .
>
> I'll tell you it's a hard fact Society—she has no respect. She tells people how they should act. She lines them up in neat little rows then blows them away. And if perchance a mistake is made it's covered up by big words, pretty pictures, and a lot of closed eyes and turned heads.
>
> So I ask you—You decide. Who is truly the outlaw here?

When Kathryn finishes reading she talks to the participants of the literacy exchange about the print that filled the walls of her pink trailer that was her home when she lived in the city.

"Do you still fill your walls with writing?" I ask her at the end of her presentation.

"No," she says, and that's the end of the of conversation.

Afterward while we are at dinner, the young woman who drove Kathryn to the exchange whispers to me. "Kathryn doesn't have any walls."

"What do you mean?"

"She lives in the attic, on a mattress on the bare boards. There are no walls and the roof isn't insulated. She sleeps up there in the winter without heat. Harley sleeps downstairs with the family."

Kathryn picks up on our conversation. "I'm okay," she says. But she's not. How could she be? She lives in a world of sickness and insanity. She has multiple personalities. She shouts at us and we do not hear her. She is in our faces and we do not see her. She is an outcast. An outlaw. We turn our head as she's blown away. And we accept no responsibility. She is nothing but a number. An abstraction. *No one. Nothing.* We don't protest when she is dumbed down by welfare agencies. At a conference with Ph.D.'s she talks articulately. *She is intelligent. She understands the social arrangements.*

Bureaucracies treat her with hostility. In her writings she deals with the mutant behavior of social agencies. "You can be caught up in the negative lane where racism and hatred are alive and you can still maintain your sanity."

More than anything, Kathryn wants her life to be recognized. When I give her an early draft of what I've written about her, she is pleased that I have included excerpts from her poems. She wants people to know that she is a good person, that she is more than a number at a welfare agency, that to survive she constantly has to reassess her relationship with society, that in response to us she has become the outlaw lady, and that defiantly through her symbolic representations she has found a way to resist the corruption of bureaucracies.

We have hurt her. She is crippled by us and we drug her into passivity. But still she shouts, "I believe I have the right to be uniquely me."

SIGN UP FOR THE CITY MANAGER

March 26, 1991. The news is out. The council fired the city manager! It happened last night, at 2 A.M., at an executive session, after the city council passed a tax-freeze budget that will force layoffs of teachers, police officers, and firefighters.

"This community is extremely angry about this whole situation," says the chair of the city's Critical Issues Committee. The committee is meeting tonight to organize a protest.

The local newspaper rouses the community.

The ousted manager has ten days to appeal the decision.

Familiar with the functions and uses of official documentation, the city manager can control the text. By studying the way in which he responds to the mayor and city council we learn how men of power and privilege advantage themselves through the manipulation of paper.

REACTION LINE AVAILABLE

Anyone wishing to express an opinion on the decision to fire the city manager can call the local newspaper. Calls will be answered electronically. After thirty seconds the device will cut off automatically. Reactions from people who fail to state their name will not be considered.

Members of the community call. They give their names. They call the manager "capable" and "competent," and the city council "irresponsible." They state that the council is out of touch with the community.

"I'm truly appalled that a small group of narrow-minded individuals, led by a pompous overinflated dictator, should have the power to totally destroy our city government."

"Maybe we should impeach the council and keep the city manager."

"I have buckets of tar and feathers, if it's needed for the 'wonderful' mayor."

The maximum number of calls possible within the time frame is received.

Another newspaper article quotes a member of the city council who does not support the straight-arrow majority. "They're using nothing short of gestapo tactics. I'm embarrassed by the acts of the majority of this council. I encourage the manager to pursue whatever avenue of appeals he can."

"Can this be the bottom line?" asked the manager's secretary when she heard the news. "I can't believe it. I have no comment. I feel he's tried hard as he could, made every effort to comply. I can't believe it. This is like treason or something. I'm sick."

"SHOCKED" MANAGER PLANS APPEAL

"I'm very surprised," says the manager, whose smiling picture is published in the local paper. "I am terribly disappointed." He says he will follow all procedural steps in the city charter to appeal the council's decision. He says at the present time he is gathering information on which to base his appeal.

In the meantime the Critical Issues Committee is collecting signatures: "Sign Up for the City Manager." They quickly gather over a thousand signatures and continue to collect more. The mayor is asked about the petition. "The petition is invalid," he says in a tape-recorded interview. "They're trying to get people to sign a petition on blind faith."

The manager hires two lawyers and takes the city council to court for violating the city's right-to-know law and engaging in prejudgment. His contract with the city, which was signed on June 25, 1990, was for an indefinite term. The council can fire the manager only in accordance with the City Charter, Article IV, Section 4.03. The termination of his contract requires that the council pass a resolution evidencing their intent to terminate. If requested, there must be a public hearing before the termination is final.

The agenda items for the council meeting on March 25, 1991, did not include the termination. A straight-arrow council member asked for a vote to go into executive session to discuss a "personal matter." Members of the public who were attending the marathon meeting were asked to leave the room. The city clerk who usually recorded the votes was sent home. The resolution was distributed. It was the first time that the manager had seen the resolution. He requested an open meeting, but members of the community had gone home. The resolution was presented, voted on, and passed.

A familiar scenario? Think back to Cindy's court appearances. Remember when she was sentenced at the superior court but there were no witnesses? The psychiatrist there to testify on her behalf left because the court-appointed attorney told her the hearing was canceled. An hour later the judge went ahead with the hearing.

The superior court hearing on the manager's complaint, held at taxpayers' expense, begins on May 15 and ends on May 20. During the three and a half days of testimony, members of the council who are the defendants in the case elucidate—the court documentation states "most for the first time"—their reasons for voting to terminate the manager's contract.

The mayor complains that he is frustrated with the manager for approving an allowance for police officers to purchase the desk of the chief of police and give it to him as a retirement present. This is inane. *Insane.* A straight-arrow councilman complains that he was dissatisfied with the manager's tardiness in responding to councillors' inquiries.

A straight-arrow councilwoman expresses her unhappiness at the manager for telling a regional newspaper reporter the amount of legal fees that the city has incurred as a result of the straight arrows' governance.

On May 23, 1991, after due consideration, the superior court judge determines that the firing is illegal. He rules in favor of the manager. "The Supreme Court has emphasized," the judge writes, with a legal reference at the highest level, "the importance of assuring 'that the public's right to know should not depend upon the ability of individuals to finance litigation.'" The court orders the city to pay the fees for the two private attorneys the manager hired to represent him.

MANAGER'S JOB
ON THE LINE—AGAIN

A notice is posted on a window at the front of city hall. On July 10, 1991, the city council is going to fire the city manager for a second time at a special meeting of the council.

The city newspaper runs an editorial. "A strong manager is not the city's problem. Rather, it is the elected leadership which seems closed-minded and unyielding at times when compromise and dialogue are needed."

On the same page a political cartoonist draws likenesses of the straight arrows on the phone together. "WHAT MEETING?" "I DON'T KNOW." "NOT ME!" "NO COMMENT!" (This from the mayor.) The manager is shown commenting, "THEY'RE B-A-A-CK." In the corner of the cartoon are two tiny citizens: "They didn't raise taxes!" "What about legal fees?" The answer—not given in the cartoon—is that the fees are accumulating rapidly.

The meeting is scheduled to begin at 6 P.M. in the meeting room at the city's public library. Outside a small group of women and men are holding up signs in favor of the manager. "KEEP THE MANAGER/SAVE OUR CITY." "KEEP THE MANAGER/YOU RESIGN." Inside a man in a red T-shirt is setting up a videocamera, center right. A woman in a T-shirt and shorts is standing near the front and to the far left behind another videocamera.

I sit near the front, center left. I see the private lawyer who represented Cindy. He is one of the lawyers representing the city manager. I ask him why people are setting up videocameras. He says at the superior court hearing there was trouble with the audio recording that was made of the March council meeting. "So we decided to video." He smiles as he leaves and walks over to where the manager is standing.

I overhear a man behind me. "I've heard they've brought in people from other towns who support their position." "I heard the same thing," a woman says. People are coming into the room. It is hot and people are dressed for an even hotter debate. I look behind me at a sea of signs. One says "PLEASE ALLOW PUBLIC INPUT TONIGHT." The room is loud with voices. The councillors are taking their seats. It is well known that one of the council members owes the city big bucks in back taxes. I smile at someone's "UNPAID TAXES HURT THE CITY" sign.

The roll is taken. One councilman is absent. The first item of business is a traffic ordinance. The second is a property tax issue. Why haven't some buildings been taken over by the city for nonpayment? Motions. Amendments. Discussion of motion as amended. Vote.

The mayor announces a recess so he can confer with counsel. Mayhem. Someone shouts, "I hope you'll be back before two A.M.!"

In addition to the videocameras set up by friends of the manager at the request of his private lawyers, there is also a camera crew from one of the state's TV stations. The local radio stations are also recording the event. One is going to provide live coverage of the firing.

Wait. The cartoon in the local paper is passed around. People laugh and make straight-arrow jokes about the one councillor's back taxes. They stand and move around. It's hot and humid. The crowd is roused. It wouldn't take much for the laughter to turn into angry shouts and for the meeting to get out of control. Police officers are stationed around the room. They watch the crowd and wait.

I Guess I Need to Know What Just Happened

The council is returning. Most people are back in their seats. Behind me people with signs are standing. "WE WANT TO SPEAK/PLEASE LISTEN." "NO RESOLUTIONS WITHOUT PUBLIC INPUT."

The noise continues. The mayor and council sit and watch the crowd. A councilman looks at his watch. There is a low hum of voices. "I'd like to call this council meeting back into order," the mayor speaks into his microphone.

The room is quiet. Shhh.

"The next item on the agenda is the resolution relating to the manager's termination and at this time, City Manager, do you wish it to be an open meeting or a closed meeting?"

The manager, who is wearing a dark gray suit, starched white shirt, and dark striped tie, leans forward, resting his elbows on the table in front of him. He holds up two pieces of paper, which I presume is the resolution, as he speaks into the microphone. "Mr. Mayor, just to be consistent with my past practices I would specifically ask that the meeting be held open."

"Is that acceptable to the council?" the mayor asks.

The council responds that it is acceptable.

The mayor continues.

"At this time I would like to read the following resolution. 'In the year—' "

Interruption. A councilman who is not a straight arrow asks if the city manager has the attachment to the resolution. The attachment, entitled "Pink Book of Issues Leading to the Removal of City Manager," contains seventy reasons why the manager's contract should be terminated.

"He does not have the attachment." The mayor looks irritated. "I did not want it to become a public document. You were aware of the previous discussion a few minutes ago as to how that came to pass, and I need not elaborate any further. At the end he will be afforded the pink book."

The councilman persists. "Should he not be entitled to all of it?"

The mayor raises his voice. "He is entitled to the—" he hesitates. "I'm going to yield that question to legal counsel. I'm not going to—"

"Boo!" Shouts! More boos! The mayor is shouting into the microphone. "As a matter of fact I am going to ask legal counsel if we should revert back to, uh, recess to confer with legal counsel." The audience is shouting, booing, hissing. The mayor tries to shout down the crowd. "If there are any other questions regarding legal matters we will go into executive session to discuss it."

"*OPEN GOVERNMENT!*" someone shouts.

"*THEY'RE AFRAID!*"

The lawyer who represents the city has refused to take part in the proceedings. The mayor, in a short-sleeved, open-necked shirt, talks with his own private lawyer, who is wearing a light blue suit. The lawyer steps back and an angry-looking mayor leans over and hands his pink book to the manager. The crowd claps.

"In all due fairness," the mayor says, "I think I will declare a recess until the city manager has—has completed reading the document." The manager says he wants the document read aloud. The mayor opens his briefcase and takes out another copy and gives it to the manager.

The crowd claps and cheers.

Story time.

The mayor's voice changes into a print register, rising and falling as he reads without punctuating the text. "I wish to read the following resolution. In the year nine hundred and ninety-one the resolution relative to the position of the city manager resolved by the council of the city as follows."

Get ready. Take a breath.

"Whereas the position of city manager requires and demands close cooperation and communication between a manager and a city council as a body and the individuals thereof and whereas the majority of the city council is of firm opinion that such cooperation and communication does not exist between it and the city manager in a level which is acceptable to the efficient government of the city and whereas the city council is of the opinion that the relationship between it and its individual members and the city manager is incapable of correction at this time and whereas the city council is of the opinion that the city manager is not the kind of leader for the hard economic times in the city it is now therefore being resolved by the city council that it is the intent of the city council to remove the city manager pursuant to Section 4-A of the city manager's employment agreement in pursuant to the procedures specific under the city charter for failure to cooperate and to communicate effectively with the city council and its individual members which failure is not in the best interest of the city or its citizens."

The mayor opens the pink book. He's going to read *all* fifty-odd pages. It's going to be a *long* meeting.

"I compiled, um, as a preface to the pink book I compiled a partial statement of reasons why the council gave notice of intent to remove the city manager. Other councillors contributed to it. The document was assembled from personal files. It does not claim to be an exhaustive file." He drones on. "It is not intended to meet any legal standard approved of proof. It is a representative account of things that happened. It tells why ordinary prudent men and women who happen to be in charge—"

"Who are they!" someone shouts.

"—of governing the city may feel obliged to take this unpleasant action. By stating only a few general reasons and by holding our peace in public we had hoped to minimize dissension."

Member of the public are laughing. Jeers.

"The manager's own actions and rulings of a judge however have compelled me to list reasons. These are only some of a much longer list of reasons."

Members of the audience are talking. The atmosphere is tense.

"Perhaps only a few of the reasons, taken separately and individually, warrant removal. Occasionally our memories may betray us."

Laughter. More jeers.

The mayor reaches the end of this introductory statement. "Unfortunately, what remains after making all these allowances is a pattern, an unmistakable and undeniable pattern of intimidation, hostility, obstruction, and resistance to continuing business as usual. The people of the city deserve better. Much better."

The audience jeers again.

The mayor ups the decibels. "If we are to be called—" Drowned out. The mayor shouts. "If we are to be called to account for our actions, it is that we must explain why we tolerated this unbelievable situation for so long."

Members of the audience scoff. They taunt the mayor. Their comments are derisive. "Boo! Boo!"

"I'll just continue the meeting right through," the mayor shouts. *"If you don't want the manager to hear what I have to say! Keep talking!"*

"Boo! Boo!"

The mayor begins his endless list of grievances. "The manager tried to intimidate the elected council."

"Boo!"

"He approved the fire chief's longevity payments."

Members of the audience scoff at the mayor's monologue—diatribe? They shout at him when he makes a particularly egregious statement.

"The manager does not organize his time well."

Protests.

"If they [the council] don't ask questions at all he probably will not volunteer information."

More derisive jeers.

The mayor reads louder.

"The manager does not consult with the mayor or the council as to the scheduling of his vacation. After he has decided when he will go he tells them. The manager makes no allowance for the possibility that the mayor or council could have reasons why the city's chief executive going on vacation at a particular time might not be a good idea."

Groans. Some sound like genuine stomach cramps. The underlying hum of people talking grows louder and does not subside.

"The school board, through its School Administrative Unit, was declining to provide the information required by the city's public information law. City was letting the law be flouted. Mayor had to tell manager to send a letter to the superintendent of schools, demanding the information under the state's right-to-know law—"

These are the guys that went into executive session at two o'clock in the morning! The audience is hysterical. It's *Saturday Night Live*! Reality is suspended. It's hot. I'm caught up in the madness. It's funny.

But the mayor is serious. He resumes his reading. Issue number ten focuses on faulty planning. "The manager paid fifty-five dollars an hour to a member of the school board when a consultant had offered to work for fifty dollars an hour."

"Oh come on!" someone shouts.

The mayor pauses and looks at the audience. "The manager used the city clerk as a special delivery messenger for all—"

"Boo! Boo! Boo!" *Shouts. Jeers.*

The manager is reading the pink book for himself. His elbow is on the table, his chin cupped in his hand. He shows no visible emotion. He does not respond to the mayor or the crowd. He is unflappable. Dignified.

The mayor is in a relentless power struggle with the community. "Manager inherited a situation where an attorney in private practice advised the city." The mayor glances at the audience. "In its last year this arrangement is believed to have cost the city more that one hundred and thirty thousand dollars in legal fees."

Again a person shouts. "Oh come on!" The audience is in an uproar. The mayor is represented by a private lawyer. The firing of the city manager is costing the city hundreds of thousands of dollars.

The mayor continues.

The crowd gets louder.

"Is the council having difficulty hearing me?"

"Yes."

"A little bit."

"If the council cannot hear me give me a nod. I'll try and continue!"

He reads on.

"The manager became loud, sarcastic, and abusive towards me—"

The audience claps.

"—in the presence of other persons, including a newspaper reporter."

Laughter.

"Manager angrily said, 'I am God-damn tired of your accusations!' "

More clapping.

A councilman asks if he can take over the reading. The mayor tells him to start with the manager's belligerent attitude—number forty-two in "Issues Leading to the Removal of City Manager."

The councilman reads on while the mayor watches the crowd.

"The manager's proposed budget for fiscal year ninety-one–ninety-two called for spending one thousand dollars more for patriotic celebration than the state law allows."

Laughter.

"Failure to inform a response to questions despite being pressed for explanations. Only when the council discussed the topic in a work session was information brought forth."

More laughter. Someone shouts out, *"ENGLISH PLEASE."*

The remark gets a quick response from the councilman. *"I would doubt you would know how to understand it!"*

"Ohhh!"

"Boo!"

"Wasteful capital improvement projects."

The mayor is still. His arms are folded on the table, but his eyes are narrowed—quite literally—and he scans the room.

The councilman is reading issue number fifty-two—"No reply to request for blank budget outline."

A woman at the back of the room shouts something out. The mayor stands. "Officer!"

The councilman is reading. "Excuse me." The mayor raps his knuckles on the table and the councilman stops reading. "The woman in the back corner with long hair," the mayor is pointing, "who just let out an outburst if she does it again—"

"I just wanted to know—"

"Would you escort that woman out of the room."

"Oh, give me a break!"

"Boo!" Claps. Shouts.

The police officer goes to where the mayor is pointing but he does not know which woman. He points at heads of women until the mayor nods. He has the culprit. He leans over and talks to the woman. The councilman is reading. Heads are turned toward the back of the room where the woman sits. The cameras are on her. The councilman reads. Another police officer goes to the back of the room. The woman refuses to leave. One of the councilmen who is not a straight arrow closes his pink book with an elaborate gesture. He sits back in his chair and shakes his head. The woman stands to the loud applause of the audience. The councilman reads. He is on number fifty-six—"Resists revealing full compensation figures. For months, manager ignores the topic. Then, some vague information is provided—"

The audience claps. People shout.

The mayor bangs his gavel. He closes his eyes for a second and bites his bottom lip. He is watching the audience. He sees a friendly face and smiles, then continues scanning the room. The councilman stumbles on through the pink book.

"Council bashing."

"Ohhh!"

"Public works director complained to the press that budget restraints would cause him to order plowing only when four inches had fallen and not three as before. Why not part-time help? Temporaries and seasonals? Able-bodied welfare recipients? Private contractors?"

Groans.

The councilman completes the reading with issues sixty-nine and seventy.

"Thank you councilman." The mayor is moving quickly. "At this time I would request somebody move the resolution as read." A straight arrow moves the motion. Another straight arrow seconds. "Discussion?"

A councilman who does not share the political persuasion of the straight arrows speaks. "As we went through all these pages and the attachments I would like the record to reflect that all the correspondence in there was from individual council members. Namely two—I didn't see any others—"

Cheers! Claps. The clapping becomes rhythmic.

"Were their taxes paid?"

Laughter. The gavel. Boos!

"Excuse me." It's the mayor. "Is there another gentleman right in that corner in the hallway? Can you please. Officer! Watch the hallway. Someone is hollering from the hallway and disrupting the meeting." The policeman signals that they can't police the hallway as well as the meeting. "Okay, since I apparently can't ask you to do that, I would ask—" The noise increases. The mayor shouts. "I would ask that the door be closed."

"Oh come on!"

"Boo!"

"I can't manage the meeting if everyone talks—"

Laughter. Shouts! Boos!

"I had my say. Don't you want your councillors to have their say? *I* would like to hear what the councillor has to say."

A councilman addresses the mayor and quiets the audience. "Nowhere in the supporting documentation do I see where there were any resolutions that were violations of ordinances. I'm going to say that ninety-eight percent of the information here, that's been presented, I would say falls into the realm of interference by individual council members."

Hoots! The audience is standing. Shouting. Applauding. The mayor pulls his microphone toward him and shouts above the noise. *"I'm going to rule that your comments, Councillor, are out of order!"* The mayor shakes his finger at the councillor. *"That kind of abusive comment is not necessary!"*

He is drowned out by the crowd. *"You are out of order!"* "Boo! Boo!" Shouts! Whistles! Claps!

"I am not out of order, Mr. Mayor!"

Hysterical noises from the crowd. The mayor responds. *"You do not have the floor to attack the councillors. YOU STICK TO THE ISSUES NOT THE COUNCILLORS!"*

The councilman is on his feet waving the pink book at the mayor. **"I have a book here of the documents which I assume will be made public tonight. Everything that's in here is from—"** He names the mayor and one of the straight-arrow councillors.

The crowd is wild. A policeman steps forward. His arms are behind his back, his forearm against his gun holster. Two policemen move away from the side walls and watch the crowd more closely. I try to locate the nearest exit.

"What are your comments regarding the resolution? Stick to the resolution!"

"I am not—"

"Do not attack the council!"

"This is part of the resolution. It is—"

"You can discuss it but you cannot attack the councillors with charges!"

"You presented the charges numerous times! I—"

"I'm ruling you out of order for attacking the council!"

"I am not—"

The crowd is deafening. People are standing up waving their signs.

"You came in here—"

"I've made a ruling, Councillor! Do you wish to challenge the chair?"

"I was not—"

"I've made a ruling!"

"I was not—"

"You are not to attack the council!"

"I am not out of order!"

This reminds me of C-Span coverage of the House of Representatives.

"Then challenge the chair!"

"I have the floor!"

"You cannot attack individual Councillors!"

"I have not. That's the Robert's Rules of Order!" The councilman holds up a copy of the rules.

"We are not running under Robert's Rules!"

The noise from the crowd increases by several decibels.

"A point of order has been called!"

"I won't yield to a point of order!"

"You have no choice!" The mayor bangs his gavel on the table and then waves it at the audience. *"I hate to have to do this!"*

Shouts!

"We cannot conduct the meeting. I will have to start clearing the room one at a time until we can begin to conduct the meeting!" The mayor speaks more calmly to the councilman with whom he's been arguing. *"I would request that you not attack councillors on an individual level and that you don't make charges that you cannot support at this time. At this time just address the resolution as it is read."*

"Mr. Mayor, I take exception that I had charged any councillors. I am only going by what's in the document. If you consider it a charge, um, according to the preface to this it says the documentation was assembled from personal files. I saw no supporting correspondence other than from the mayor and—" He names one of the straight-arrow councilwomen.

Hoots!

The councilman continues in tight-lipped restraint. "I don't think that the city manager has to drop all he is doing and answer every question by the individual council members. If it's something before the council then I think it is most deserving that he does go forth in haste. But I do not see where any of the things here"—he holds up the pink book—"warrant this resolution even being presented."

The crowd is euphoric.

The mayor does not respond. He asks for other comments. Another councilman who did not run on the straight-arrow ticket takes the floor. "Mr. Chairman, who drafted the resolution. Not the attachments, but the resolution itself?"

The mayor looks exasperated and raises his voice. *"That's not a relevant question. The resolution is on the table and you can discuss the resolution."*

"Who drafted the resolution?" The councilman moves forward in his seat. **"Who drafted the resolution?"**

"I believe about half an hour ago you were made aware of the primary information necessary."

"No I was not made aware—"

"Do you have a legal question?"

"I'm asking you—"

"Do you have a legal question about the resolution?"

"NO. I thought it was a simple question actually."

There are shrieks from the audience. Applause!

"The question is out of order. The resolution—who writes the resolution has no bearing. I have read the resolution. The resolution is moved. It is on the table. **The resolution is on the table for discussion! If you wish to discuss the resolution you may—"**

Without missing a beat the councilman lowers his voice and interrupts. "May I address the maker of the resolution?"

Checkmate!

The mayor responds politely. "You may. That is I."

"Thank you. No further questions."

Screams! Hoots! It's better than a rock concert. The audience is delirious.

The straight-arrow councillors profess their independent assessments of the manager. Then the councilman who tried to invoke Robert's Rules has the floor. "I would ask the council to consider that nowhere in the resolution do I see where the city manager ever failed to carry out either a resolution or an ordinance or adhere to the charter. And I guess I would ask these questions. Is there anywhere that the manager has shown malfeasance, dishonesty, or disloyalty? Those three terms came out of the paper tonight. I ask the council to consider has he shown malfeasance, dishonesty, or disloyalty in his day-to-day affairs of the management of the city?"

Applause!

A straight-arrow councilwoman speaks. "As the mayor and the councilman read off the various topics, obviously there were—was a lot of snickers. But I would urge anybody in the privacy of their own homes with no neighbors or friends or relatives egging them on just to sit down and *really* read them and *really* think about them. *Really, really think about them!*"

The crowd scoffs.

One person claps.

The discussion continues. Council members shout down each other and the audience shouts down the council. Eventually a vote is taken and the resolution carries.

For the second time the city council has fired the city manager.

Wait! The crowd is sobering up but it's not over!

The mayor asks if there is any other business to come before the council, and the straight-arrow councilman who took over the reading of the pink book from the mayor starts reading from a prepared script.

"In the year of our lord one thousand nine hundred and ninety one—" The crowd is not prepared for what happens next. "Whereas the city council has voted to terminate the city manager and whereas Section 4.03 of the city charter permits the city council to suspend the city manager after passage of a resolution of intent to terminate, now be it resolved by the city council of the city that the city manager be suspended."

The manager is listening intently. His lawyer, lost in the front seats amidst the crowd, is writing.

"Said suspension to continue until the city manager's removal. The city manager shall continue to receive his pay until removal. This resolution shall take effect upon its passage."

"Do I have a second?"

Another straight arrow moves in and seconds the motion.

"Any point of order?"

The first of the councilmen who argued with the mayor jumps in. He is thinking on his feet, working out how to counter, playing for time. "Going by the rules and orders of the council, can you tell me what the end result will be of the resolution that just passed and the one that's on the floor and where they are related? Does the manager walk in tomorrow into city hall? I would like that answered."

"I will put that in the context of a legal question," the mayor responds. "I will ask again that we take a recess and all confer with legal counsel."

The crowd turns ugly. Their shouts sound more threatening.

The mayor backs down. "*My* answer to the question if *you* do *not* wish a legal answer is that it is in direct accordance with the city charter." The mayor shouts above the noise of the crowd. "He is not to be in command in city hall during his suspension!"

A middle-aged woman in the front of the audience is on her feet. She is waving her arm and shouting. *"Mr. Mayor! Mr. Mayor!"* Looking defeated she sits down.

The crowd is quiet. Subdued. They listen intently.

The mayor continues to shout. "He will be paid according to the charter!"

The councilman has collected his thoughts and he comes back fighting. "Point of order. Whereas we are going by the rules," he reads rapidly from his book of rules, " 'No resolution that is opposed to monetary penalty or authorizes the expenditure of money shall receive two readings at the same meeting.' So I would say the same rule applies to this as applies to the first rule." The mayor tries to take the floor but the councilman continues. "I would say that he should be there tomorrow morning since there is no action."

The tension breaks and the crowd goes wild.

The mayor. "I would rule that the resolution is in order because there is no monetary penalty."

The councilman. "It deals with money. Compensation."

The mayor. "There is *no loss* of compensation."

The councilman. "It authorizes the expenditure of money which will continue to be paid if you're suspending the city manager based on the first resolution."

It's tennis. The heads of the crowd move with the ball.

The mayor steps into a sliced backhand. *"He is being compensated! Do you wish to challenge the chair?"*

The councilman misses the return. **"Mr. Mayor! By your own rules of order the first reading is not—"**

"I have given you a ruling, Councillor! Do you wish to challenge the chair?"

"I'M TELLING YOU—"

A topspin forehand. *"DO YOU WISH TO CHALLENGE THE CHAIR OR SEEK ADVICE FROM LEGAL COUNSEL?"*

"You've got it." The councilman concedes. "Yes I'd like to recess for legal counsel."

The mayor acknowledges his grand slam. *"THERE!"*

The audience talks of resolutions and first readings as the council leaves the room. People explain the rules to each other, move around. They are wound up, and when the council comes back it takes a while before they sit down again.

The mayor. "There has been a challenge to the chair. I have overruled the challenge. All in favor of upholding the chair?" A vote is taken and carried by the straight arrows.

The second dissenting councilman is back in the game. "Point of order. I

believe the charter is explicit that when any individual or any councillors request a legal opinion that legal opinion is to be addressed by the appointed
city solicitor and not by any special counsel that may be present. Whereas the
city solicitor—as I look around the room—I have not seen him this evening. I
believe that any legal questions that have been brought up before this council
tonight that have been answered in any way are not appropriate." The councilman moves forward and speaks directly into the microphone. "It is not an appropriate answer and therefore I would deem that an illegal response."

Claps. Shouts.

The straight-arrow councilman who read the pink book responds. "The
city attorney has already distanced himself from this issue. So what do we do?"

The second dissenting councilman. "If that is in fact the case and he feels
in his opinion that he is unable for whatever reason to answer the question—"

The lawyer in the light blue suit steps forward. He laughs. "Your Honor,
I never give illegal opinions!" No one laughs with him.

The mayor to the dissenting councilman. "Do you wish to discuss the
resolution? Have you done with your point of order?"

"No, I still want to continue."

The crowd is exhausted, their energies spent. Finally the vote. The
straight arrows *for* the resolution, the two dissenting councilmen *against*.
"The resolution carries." The mayor moves on. "Any other business?"

The city manager has his hand up. The mayor grants him permission to
speak. "I guess I need to know what just happened."

Shrieks! Claps! Cheers!

The manager continues. "For the record we are taking the position that
there are procedural errors and that the rules of order of the council were not
followed."

"Were not followed?" The mayor responds, his buttons pressed. "*They
were* followed."

The manager remains calm. "Then we disagree."

The pink book reader proposes that the council go into executive session to discuss a temporary replacement for the manager.

The crowd is yelling.

A man stands up and shouts. *"NO! WE'VE GOT A VOICE HERE!
WE'VE GOT A VOICE HERE!"*

"Officer. Escort that man out of the meeting!"

"NO! THIS IS A PUBLIC MEETING AND I AM PUBLIC!"

"ESCORT THAT MAN IMMEDIATELY OUT OF THE ROOM!"

*"LISTEN THERE IS A FIFTY-MILLION-DOLLAR LAWSUIT GOING
DOWN ON YOU AND THIS CITY IF THIS CONTINUES!"*

Two policemen move in. One takes the man's right arm, the other his left. The man struggles. His right arm is up and his fist is clenched. The policeman tries to hold on.

"NO! NO! NO! NO! NO!"

The crowd is out of control but still the mayor doesn't get it. He calls each council member by name. *"WE'RE GOING INTO EXECUTIVE SESSION AND WE ARE NOT MOVING." He points at the audience. "THEY ARE!"*

The chief of police looks at the mayor in disbelief. His officers wait for orders.

THE CROWD SCREAMS!

People are stamping their feet.

"We won't go!"

"We won't go!"

"We won't go!"

"We won't go!"

The mayor shouts. "CHIEF! CHIEF! CHIEF! **CHIEF!** I rescind that order. That was foolish."

"WE WON'T GO!"

"WE WON'T GO!"

"WE WON'T GO!"

A gray-haired woman who had her hand up for most of the meeting tells off the council. She calls them names, scolds them, and shakes her finger at them.

The man who threatened the lawsuit is escorted out of the room. The mayor and the council leave. The manager sits and watches. A policeman stands beside him surveying the crowd.

There are two ex-mayors in the audience and they walk to the front of the room. They plead with the crowd not to lose control. The cameraman is filming the TV reporter as he interviews a member of the community. A policeman is talking into his radio receiver. The woman sitting next to me says he is calling for backup.

When the councillors return the meeting ends. Not with a bang but a whimper. A vote has been taken in executive session and the minutes have been sealed.

The manager requests permission to speak. "I need some clarification. Am I or am I not to show up for work tomorrow?"

"No."

"Based on the action—"

"You are suspended with pay."

"Based on the action that was taken tonight?"

The mayor nods. The city manager looks away. Outside the room the man who was escorted out by two policemen can be heard shouting something about the city council. The crowd claps when they hear his voice. It is their last act of rebellion before the meeting is adjourned.

The TV reporter interviews the lawyer who is representing the city manager. The lights are in the lawyer's face and he squints into the camera as he is asked questions. There are three microphones in front of him.

The TV crew goes over to speak with the mayor. "Do you feel good about the meeting?"

"I'm disappointed."

The police watch as people leave the room. Outside they stand around, not wanting to go home. The manager comes out and they cheer. Someone says, "It's sad."

I walk back to my car with two women—doctors' wives—who helped to organize the petition on behalf of the city manager. They are preoccupied with the meeting. A friend is going to transcribe the audio portion of the videotape for the lawyers who are representing the manager. They talk intently about making sure there is enough documentation for another superior court hearing.

We stop at an intersection. A mother is waiting to cross the road with her two small children. The doctors' wives do not seem to notice her. Her name is Genny. I know her from the outreach program run by a Roman Catholic church. She is thought to be developmentally disabled and we offered to help her read and write. Genny and her young children have no shoes. There is glass on the sidewalk and their feet are bare.

I say hello to Genny and ask her how's she doing. She is warm and friendly. "What happened to your shoes?" I ask.

"I'm saving them," she says.

"What for?"

She puts her hand on the shoulder of her five-year-old daughter. "So she'll have some when it's time for school."

I talk with Genny for a while and I try to persuade her to let her daughter wear the shoes that she is saving.

"She's only got one pair," she tells me as I leave. "If she wears them now they'll be worn out when she gets to school."

The doctors' wives are waiting for me on the other side of the road. I run to catch up and we walk to our cars together. They are still talking about the manager. I join in the conversation.

Driving home I think about Genny. I got caught up in the hysteria of the meeting. Genny reminded me why I was there. She helped me remember to question, to say to myself, *I guess I need to know what just happened.* I need to ask myself why we protest when the city manager loses his job but we don't even notice when we pass a mother and her children on our streets with bare feet. In the car I wonder if I put Genny on the spot when I asked her why her children were walking along city streets without shoes. With all due respect to the manager, how could we get so riled up over the asinine behavior of the city council when there are kids walking around without shoes? I got riled up too! *What happened to me? To us? Why don't we question?*

I tell myself, *don't be too tired to question.*

By juxtaposing the events in the life of the city manager with the events in the lives of Kathryn, Will and Laurie, Sam, and Cindy we can see whose lives we value and on whom we are willing to spend our tax dollars. Ask. Why are we willing to pay the legal expenses of the manager in addition to the legal expenses of the city while we choose to cripple Laurie with radiation because it is cheaper than surgery? Why do we sign petitions, hold rallies, and go to meetings when the city manager is fired, yet do nothing to help the men, women, and children who in one way or another live their lives without shoes?

HELLO! YOU'RE ON THE AIR. GOOD MORNING!

"I would just like to say that the straight arrows are a disgrace to the city," a caller tells the radio talk-show host. "The manager has been doing his job. Firing him because he disagrees with the philosophy of the council is just not right."

"Hello! You're on the air. Good morning."

"Great day, Max! Great day! First, I want to thank you for broadcasting that meeting last night. I listened in and all I've got to say, Max, is what a hell of a mess!"

"This place is going straight into the dumpster," Max agrees.

The caller continues. "I guess the manager's crowd was there. I don't know how many. Sounded like a pack of raving Indians, you know, stamping their feet and hollering." The caller seems unaware of his racist comment. He continues energetically. "If I ever interrupted a meeting like that they'd take me out in handcuffs."

"Hello. You're on the air. Good morning!"

"I don't know how the mayor can stand up and take that. I wouldn't take the baloney that he's taking for a thousand dollars a minute. I think it's terrible. I've never heard anything like it. We moved here in thirty-nine. I've never seen this city in such a hell of a mess. It looks like more court hearings and more expense to the taxpayers. Around and around we go and where we stop nobody knows! It is terrible them people last night didn't act like educated grown-up people."

The talk-show host picks up on the direction of the caller's comments. "During one of the executive sessions two of our former mayors got up in front of the group and pleaded with them to calm down and restore order, and when the mayor came back he was furious. He was questioning the chief of police why someone else was conducting the meeting!"

Caller. "Oh yeah. That hollering and stamping their feet. Doesn't that sound like kids on the playground? Or fighting over a candy bar? Or something. It's so ridiculous. I'm ashamed. Whatever the outcome is I hope it is good!"

"Hello! You're on the air. Good morning!" Just before a commercial the talk-show host reminds his listeners that the manager and his two private lawyers will hold a press conference in about an hour at city hall. "We're going to take a break. Be right back!"

THEY'VE FORGONE THE TRIAL AND GONE STRAIGHT TO THE HANGING

At ten-thirty on the morning after the meeting, the city manager holds a press conference at city hall. With him are the two private lawyers who represent him. In attendance are members of the press, department heads from city government, and members of the community.

One of the lawyers addresses the gathering. Speaking as a citizen and taxpayer, he says that the council members were acting like dictators, creating the appearance of government without listening to members of the community. He talks of the mayor's "blatant manipulation of the chair" and he calls the meeting an "exercise in power politics at its worst." Then, as the manager's attorney, he talks of state laws, the city charter, and rules of procedure. "At this point," he says, "the manager is insisting on rules of procedure. He wants to do his job. We believe in the rules of proper procedure. The first reading of the resolution is an expression of intent. The reading last night was preliminary. It is not sufficient to fire the manager. There need to be further readings. If there is only a first reading there can't be an action to suspend the manager. The council was so intent on hanging the city manager that they've forgone the trial and gone straight to the hanging. The manager is going to stay on until proper procedures are followed. He can answer every claim in the pink book

234 · TOXIC LITERACIES

and he is going to respond to this list of petty allegations." He stands up. "The manager is going to go downstairs and go to work. He is going to take our advice that their action was defective and he is going to stay on the job."

The meeting ends without the manager's making any public statement. He speaks briefly with a few of the people gathered and then leaves. Without ceremony, he goes downstairs. He walks along the corridor and goes into his office and closes the door.

The following evening—July 12—there is a second reading of the resolution. People arrive early and organize on the lawn outside the library. There are new signs. The new signs are more threatening. "STRAIGHT ARROWS SUPPORT YOUR CITY SERVICES." "PAY YOUR TAXES/KEEP THE MANAGER." "THE COST OF YOUR LIFE IS PRICELESS/KEEP THE MANAGER." "DON'T PUT DOLLARS OVER SAFETY/KEEP THE MANAGER." "ARE YOU SAFE?/KEEP THE MANAGER." You get the idea.

The meeting is a repeat performance except that at the end the mayor announces the new city manager.

Another meeting takes place on the morning of August 17 in the auditorium of the city high school. The news media are present—newspapers and radio and television stations. The meeting drags on all day. The mayor looks tired. The fire has gone out of his voice and when he gets the chance to talk he speaks slowly in a monotone.

The city manager's two private lawyers hold court. Although this is supposed to be a meeting at which the public can speak, one of the manager's lawyers does most of the talking. Slowly, with nit-picking precision, he responds to each of the seventy issues in the pink book. Witnesses are sworn in.

I stop taking notes. I'm tired. If the judge who sentenced Cindy were here, the mayor would get three and a half to seven years. But there isn't a judge and there isn't a jury and everyone attending the meeting knows that the firing of the city manager will end up in a genuine courtroom and his lawyers' legal fees will be reimbursed out of the taxpayers' pockets.

Finally, at the end of the day, some members of the community get to talk. They submit their names on cards and a few of them are given a minute or two to respond to the events that are taking place. After the more than six hours the manager's lawyers have held court, there is little time left for members of the public.

In the weeks, no months, that follow, the firing of the city manager continues to be front-page news. The local paper reports that the legal costs of the firing exceed the city budget for legal representation by three hundred percent. There are bomb threats against the mayor, but the allegations that he and his straight-arrow councillors "technically violated" the city charter are thrown out of court. No criminal charges are brought against them. If they are to be ousted, the electorate will have to do it in November.

Meanwhile the city manager gets to keep his job. The courts rule in his favor, and the taxpayers pay his legal expenses. The exact amount is never published. Several years later, I interview the manager in his office and I ask him how much money was spent. He is vague and does not answer me directly. "I don't think we ever spent the time to add it all up. Maybe we didn't really want to know the cost. It's over a hundred thousand dollars, between a hundred and a hundred and fifty thousand dollars." I say that it is my understanding that the combined legal fees for the manager and the city were around two hundred thousand dollars. He smiles but does not correct me.

LEARNING FROM THE CITY MANAGER

The headlines in the local paper are two inches tall. "Manager Fired (Again)." There is a picture of the man who shouted "I am public!" with a policeman on either side of him, holding his arms.

The manager had access to the media and made his firing by the city council public. When a meeting was held at two o'clock in the morning he challenged the resolution in court, contending that it violated the right-to-know law.

When the pink book was presented at the public meeting, the manager requested that the mayor read it aloud. Then in a presentation that lasted more that six hours, his lawyers responded to each "issue" raised in the document.

The manager. "My challenge to that text was to present factual information that overrode the allegations in the pink book and won out in the end. There are procedures for everything. Procedures for the people you work with. Medical procedures. Legal procedures. I guess I was fortunate. One of those rare opportunities. I had the documentation. I think that the folks that you work with are placed in a very unfortunate position because they see these agencies for a host of reasons, social, educational, economic. These are considered strikes against them. So when they perceive a flaw or weakness or procedural error they're usually written off. It's more difficult for them. In my position I had some credibility of being right and the opportunity to express that."

Cindy had no such opportunity. The probation reports that were written about her were officially kept closed. Access was withheld. Her diaries were taken and never returned. The report written by the psychiatrist was never entered into evidence. Unauthorized. Prohibited. The official text closes in on itself. Cindy is socially isolated. She has no public access. The newspapers report her arrest. Her sentence is published. No questions. No story.

Sam is similarly isolated. There is no public interest in a homeless man crying on the street. He has pneumonia. "Mental health won't see me and the hospital won't treat me." Who cares?

The manager teaches us that to challenge an official text you first have to have access to the documentation. Then you have to bring the matter to the public's attention. Media coverage is essential. Image making becomes important.

Laurie is a welfare recipient. She is also a woman crippled by inappropriate medical procedures. No one knows. Laurie is unable to obtain all her hospital records. There is no one to pay the legal fees for her to have adequate representation.

Cindy, Sam, and Laurie have no avenue of resistance. The city manager has many. That's the difference between poverty and privilege. The women and men with whom I work are controlled by official documentation. The city manager controls the documentation. He has the power to present alternative explanations that maintain the status quo and do not entail any redistribution of power. His position is secure. But at what cost? Who lives and who dies? Do we care?

Do we care enough to advocate for Cindy when official documentation distorts the circumstances of her life and is used to jail her? Do we care enough to stand up for Sam when there is no place on the forms for him to write that he is homeless? Do we care enough to express our outrage when Laurie's body is violated through the manipulation of medical reports? Do we care enough to write to members of congress when the sheer volume of paper, the plethora of bureaucratic rules and regulations, ensures that Kathryn remains destitute, unable to care for her baby or obtain an education?

When did we stop caring? Why don't we stand up? Shout back? Write? The silence is deafening. . . .

4

STAYING ALIVE

CHALLENGING THE DEAD
LANGUAGE OF OFFICIAL TEXTS

Washington. The House of Representatives. The gentleman is still speaking about welfare.

"The welfare system defines corruption. Study after study has shown it is fraught with waste, fraud, and abuse. Studies of the food stamp program have shown up to 20 percent of the money ends up in waste, fraud, and abuse. Why do we want to expand that system?"

He doesn't get it. No one wants to *expand* the system.

He is indignant. "We have got to stop the immorality! We have got to stop the corruption!"

I am tired. I think again of Jerry and Iesha, and of the other families with whom I worked at the beginning of the eighties. I think of Cindy, of Sam, of Laurie and Will, of Kathryn, and of many others like them. I am old. Ancient and without hope. And although not wise, I am a writer. I hold language in my hands and I am traumatized by how destructively it can be used.

In Toni Morrison's Nobel acceptance address, she tells a story about language that has died. *"Like statist language, censored and censoring. Ruthless in its policing duties, it has no desire or purpose other than to maintain the free range of its own narcotic narcissism, its own exclusivity and dominance."* The language of official texts is dead. Censored and censoring. Maintained by those with power and privilege. Their ethnocentricism unquestioned as they preserve their own exclusivity and dominance. "*Unreceptive to interrogation, it cannot form or tolerate new ideas, shape other thoughts, tell another story, fill baffling silences.*"

Officially we are enculturated to believe that many able-bodied people—the very rich gentleman from Florida's alligators—prefer to stay home rather than look for a job. Alternate explanations are not considered. The official text cannot tolerate new ideas. It represents truth—or so we are led to believe. We are enculturated into the dominant ideology.

As the gentleman said, "It is immoral to take money away from hardworking middle-class Americans and give it to people who refuse to work." Who could argue with that?

Question. But we don't question. We acquiesce. We are insignificant. We believe that official texts are "factual." When in "fact" such texts are political constructions that do not represent reality. They are no one's actuality.

Toni Morrison. "*Official language smitheried to sanction ignorance and preserve privilege is a suit of armor, polished to shocking glitter, a husk from which the knight departed long ago.*" She calls official language "*dumb,*" "*predatory,*" and "*sentimental.*"

Dumb because it is ideological. In real terms—in the reality of people's everyday lives—it is *il*-logical. *Predatory* because it preys on people. Official texts are self-perpetuating, self-originating, pathological in construction, people-violating, bureaucrat-generating, and open to corruption. *Sentimental* because we believe that the worn-out texts that control our lives represent the core values of society—all (wo)men are created equal, with liberty and justice for all.

In the House of Representatives, the very rich gentleman uses the Declaration of Independence and Thomas Jefferson to legitimize his well-fed-alligator analogy. *Oppressive. Repressive.* This is the language of political trickery and chicanery.

Toni Morrison. "*Oppressive language does more than represent violence; it is violence; does more than represent the limits of knowledge; it limits knowledge.*" We are duped. Dittoed by those in authority. But—"*Whether it is obscuring state language or the faux language of mindless media; whether it is the proud but calcified language of the academy or the commodity-driven language of science; whether it is the malign language of law-without-ethics, or language designed for the estrangement of minorities, hiding its racist plunder in its literary cheek—it must be rejected, altered and exposed.*"

THE MEASURE OF OUR LIVES

There are times when I am working with Cindy, Sam, Laurie and Will, and Kathryn that I lose myself in the hopelessness of their political situation. When I go with them to the superior court I am caged in inferiority, at the hospital I am ascribed pariah status, and at the prison I am searched and questioned.

I lose my identity.

For months, no years—from November 1989 to September 1991—I rarely see anyone except these men and women and members of my family. Occasionally I talk at conferences but seldom about my work in the city. On those few occasions when I speak about the study, I have difficulty getting through the presentation. I am concerned about voyeurism, ventriloquy, my representations of another's reality.

I carry a copy of Toni Morrison's Nobel lecture with me. I read what she says about oppressive language. *"It is the language that drinks blood, laps vulnerabilities, tucks its fascist boots under crinolines of respectability and patriotism as it moves relentlessly towards the bottom line and the bottomed-out mind."*

But I also read what she says about the power of language. *"The vitality of language lies in its ability to limn the actual, imagined and possible lives of its speakers, readers and writers. Although its poise is sometimes in displacing experience, it is not a substitute for it. It arcs toward the place where meaning may lie."*

This is what I have tried to do. To limn the actual, imagined, and possible lives of the men and women with whom I work. To arc toward the place where meaning may lie.

Toni Morrison is in the pocket of my winter coat. I go into a diner for a cup of coffee and pull her out. *"We die. That may be the meaning of life. But we do language. That may be the measure of our lives."* I revive. Through the juxtaposition of people's lives with official texts we can begin to understand how we *do* language.

Cindy, by sharing her life, provides us with that opportunity. In the details of the official documentation that controls her life we learn which texts are used in the decision-making process and which texts are discarded. She helps us understand that within bureaucratic governmental agencies, social disorder, violence, and human degradation are commonplace, that "systems" are closed and unknown, that lives are invented to maintain the status quo. Sam provides us with the opportunity to expand on these propositions, to modify our findings, to view the possible explanations of official uses of written language from an alternative perspective. By the time we get to Laurie and Will we are aware of the collusive interconnections between official agencies. Laurie and Will provide us with the opportunity to deepen our understanding of the ways in which official documentation is used to distort the realities of family life, to exclude the father from active participation, and to cripple the "welfare" mother. And Kathryn, who is also Chrissy, helps us reflect on the destructiveness of interagency collusion. She helps us understand resistance.

When I read *Phenomenal Woman*, a book of poems by Maya Angelou, I think of Kathryn.

> *However I am perceived and deceived,*
> *however my ignorance and conceits,*
> *lay aside your fears that I will be undone,*
>
> *for I shall not be moved.*

Kathryn will not be moved. Knowing Kathryn sends us back to revisit Cindy and Sam. She makes us think about Laurie and Will, and of how they have stayed together as a family in spite of official rules and regulations that would make Will a deadbeat dad.

Moving back and forth between these men and women who stay alive despite the system, we begin to understand how they have framed their social identities in resistance to the official invention of their public personas. They are antagonistic, defiant, and rebellious. They are dissidents. Political outcasts. *Politicals*. The possibilities of their lives officially denied.

But, *in reality*, what happens to them is a true measure of *our* lives, *our* disregard for human life, and *our* reluctance to acknowledge that the rules and regulations set forth in bureaucratic texts are interpreted differently by those *with* power and privilege *for* those who live in poverty.

We learn this from the city manager. The opportunities he has to interact with the official text are not available to many other members of the community. He has lawyers to represent him—paid for by the city. He has access to the media. He can sway public opinion, go to court, challenge the violation of the right-to-know law, *interrupt the official text*. And we are with him every step of the way. "*I am public!*" We organize. Rally. Sign petitions. Go to meetings.

But not for Cindy, Laurie, or Will. Not for Sam or Kathryn. In this counterpoint of privilege and poverty we find the measure of our lives. We become aware of our vulnerabilities, our false virtues, the *immorality* of our morality. Clearly, we are the fat alligators who are overfed.

MIGHT ALL THESE THINGS HAVE BEEN DIFFERENT IF ONLY WE HAD DONE OTHERWISE?

In Washington there is talk of downsizing government, of block grants to states—literally passing the buck—but there is no critical analysis to discover whether the most vulnerable in our society actually find the support they need from official agencies.

Highly paid consultants crunch numbers, count dollars, count people, estimate the amount of fraud and abuse, stay in their offices at their computers, write reports, and make recommendations.

Politicians are blindfolded. Ignorant of what is really happening, they recite their ideologies for the congressional record and the hosts of money-grubbing radio and TV talk shows. Take sides. Pontificate. Polarize. Pass resolutions into law. And change the regulations.

The result? More paperwork. A recent change in the regulations determines that men and women who suffer from drug addiction or alcoholism and who receive social security disability allowances will no longer be allowed to handle the money that is allotted to them. Sam has to find an agent to pay his bills. Agencies charge money for this service. The fee is fifty dollars. Sam will have to pay the agency out of his monthly check. Fifty dollars a client, one hundred clients, and we have created a new bureaucracy. I arrange to handle Sam's money without the fee. A letter arrives threatening me. I am to provide information about Sam or his benefits will be stopped. The letter is from a private agency that has a contract with the federal government to monitor the agencies that are monitoring the spending of recipients of social security disabilities.

How could we have done this differently? We could begin by considering some of the flaws in the present system. Based on my research for this book, I offer the following observations about the functioning of bureaucratic institutions.

One:
The needs of social institutions are in direct conflict with the needs of the members of society whom they are supposed to serve.

Two:
Social agencies reflect dominant ideologies. Their main purpose is social containment of people suffering from politically defined pathologies.

Three:
Social agencies share dominant ideologies and work collusively. Hospitals and prisons are used interchangeably. The criminal justice system is supported by the social welfare system.

Four:
Waste, fraud, and abuse are inherent to the system. Official texts are used to support il-legal activity.

Five:
Administrators are highly paid—often receiving exorbitant salaries—but do not work directly with the people who are serviced by social agencies.

Six:
Professionals working directly with vulnerable populations are often paid subsistence-level salaries. Their difficulties are compounded as they learn that the realities of their clients' everyday lives do not "fit" with the dominant ideologies that they have been enculturated to believe. Often they find that they have no alternative but to find other employment.

Based on my research with members of the community who are marginalized by society—represented here by Cindy, Sam, Laurie and Will, and Kathryn—I offer the following observations about the lives of the most vulnerable people within our society.

One:
The notion of entitlement is a myth of the dominant political ideologies.

Two:
Lives are reconstructed, fabricated to fit the dominant ideologies of society. The realities of lives that are lived are not represented in official texts.

Three:
Each time a person or a family comes into the arena of a social institution their situation is likely to deteriorate.

Four:
Their difficulties are compounded when assistance is sought from multiple agencies. People are sent back and forth from one agency to another as each institution tries to deny responsibility—from state welfare to city welfare, mental health to the pharmacy, hospital to prison.

Five:

People who are vulnerable to institutional abuse are denied access to the documentation that controls their lives. Documents are kept under wraps officially and unofficially. Very often when such documents are available, copies are too costly for people to obtain.

Once again, might all these things have been different if only we had done otherwise? *Without exception*, there were times in the lives of these men and women with whom I worked when they could have reconstructed their lives. *Without exception* all genuine opportunities were denied them. Invariably, denial occurred through the use of official texts. Through the language of domination. The language of humiliation.

The culture of poverty is ascribed by those in authority.

How can we do it differently?

Make bureaucratic institutions accountable.

Publish administrative costs.

Limit paper-pushing spending.

Publish the numbers of administrators producing paper.

Limit the numbers of administrators.

Increase the numbers of caseworkers working in communities.

Establish storefront centers that are democratic not bureaucratic.

Consider the *ambiguity of alternative explanations*. Of *real* situations.

Look for examples in the private sector. Boston's City Year. The Peace Corps.

Stop using bureaucracies as our shield.

Create systems of reciprocity. Opportunities.

People don't want handouts. They want a chance to participate. Without exploitation. *Real* jobs. Not cutting brush in the cemetery.

Sam explains what we need to do. "I'd get the basics, social security, stuff like that. I'd ask, What's going on? What seems to be your problem? I wouldn't ask them anything else. Just how they've been surviving. I'd find out what they want for help, and go from there. I mean you don't need tons of paperwork just to find out someone is homeless. I don't think that's necessary."

"But it's an impossible task," Will says, commenting on the present situation. "I went to city welfare and then to state welfare. They just ask for copies of whatever and it takes them a while to figure it out. By then it's Tuesday and I've spent two days running around and nothing has happened."

"It gets old," a caseworker tells us, "and after a while your eyes go buggy."

"Forms!" Laurie says, "I swear that's all they care about is forms. 'Fill this out, fill that out!' 'No. You've gotta get this. You've gotta get that!' What really irritates me is that when I have a recertification appointment, they tell me to bring all this stuff with me and then they don't even ask for half of it. So why do I have to bring all this stuff if they don't want it? Then they always ask for something that is not even on the paperwork. 'You've gotta have it.' And when I ask them why I didn't know that I had to have it, they say, 'We don't know!' 'Well *you're* the ones with the paperwork! How could you not know?' "

"I know now that they could have helped me," Kathryn says, reflecting on what happened when she gave birth to her son. "They could have helped me bond with my baby. Instead they doped me up. They never tried to help me deal with the problem."

Remember what Cindy said before she left prison? "It will only work if I have a reason to live." She is living in the same city where she was sent to the prison halfway house. She is not allowed to return to the city in which lived before. She is under intensive parole. Officers arrive announced. They search her apartment. Empty her purse. Examine her telephone bill. Read her letters. Confiscate some of them. She has a chair and a table and a mattress. She works in a factory. A manual laborer. "I can't pay my rent on minimum wage." She laughs. "It's good for me. When I leave work I'm so tired all I want to do is go to bed." It's her birthday. No one remembers. It's Easter. She's on her own. At AA meetings no one speaks to her. "I'm a convict," she says. "The locals don't speak to ex-cons. All I want is a reason to live."

Question.

How do we help Cindy find a reason to live?

Memorial

In Loving Memory

of Laurie

Who Died

May, 1996